Eternal Mysteries Beyond the Grave

Eternal Mysteries Beyond the Grave

Orthodox Teachings on the Existence of God, the Immortality of the Soul, and Life Beyond the Grave

Archimandrite Panteleimon

Holy Trinity Publications
The Printshop of St Job of Pochaev
Holy Trinity Monastery
Jordanville, New York

Printed with the blessing of His Eminence,
Metropolitan Hilarion First Hierarch
of the Russian Orthodox Church Outside of Russia

Eternal Mysteries Beyond the Grave
© 1968, 2012 Holy Trinity Monastery
Second edition 2012

HOLY TRINITY PUBLICATIONS
The Printshop of St Job of Pochaev
Holy Trinity Monastery
Jordanville, New York 13361-0036
www.holytrinitypublications.com

Cover Design: James Bozeman
Original Imagery: copyright Mother Elisabeth Czwikla
http://motherelisabeth.smugmug.com/

ISBN: 978-0-88465-212-0 (paperback)
ISBN: 978-0-88465-224-3 (ePub)
ISBN: 978-0-88465-258-8 (Mobipocket)

Library of Congress Control Number 2011945049

Scripture passages taken from the New King James Version.
Copyright © 1982 by Thomas Nelson, Inc. Used by permission.
Psalms taken from *A Psalter for Prayer*, trans. David James
(Jordanville, N.Y.: Holy Trinity Publications, 2011).
Apocryphal passages taken from the Orthodox Study Bible.
Copyright © 2008 by Thomas Nelson, Inc. Used by permission.

CONTENTS

PREFACE

In our time, full of unbelief and doubt, when a man's "holy of holies," his soul, is intruded upon in order to be totally disrupted and made to lose faith in an unlimited rational Being—faith in Whom which makes sorrowful earthly life tolerable—it should be most useful and salubrious for us to share with others well-attested facts from our own life or that of our relatives and acquaintances; facts which have to do with miracles, wonderful cures, and extraordinary appearances of souls from another world. Unfortunately, however, unusual events which do not issue from this world, instead of being widely proclaimed, remain hidden by tens, hundreds, and thousands of people—partly because of a false sense of shame felt toward unbelievers, and partly because of a jealous protectiveness, a desire to keep the miraculous occurrences from outsiders. Still, truthful accounts about miraculous cures and other unusual occurrences might partly, if not entirely, widen a Christian's moral and religious horizon and strengthen him in his faith in God's ever-watchful Providence. With deep attention and the liveliest interest, five or six years ago I read several weighty volumes written by the Hieromonk Mitrophanes, dealing with the life of our departed beyond death; but I must admit to having found in this work little of the material that I expected there. Indeed, there was a great deal of detailed scholarly work and many proofs of the existence of God. These began almost with the day of creation and continued to our day. In an orderly way, step by step, there was discussed the religious and cultural development of mankind, along with the proof that there have almost never existed people, no matter what their stage of development, who did not have any concept of the Highest Omnipotent Being, God, and of life continued beyond death. There were a number of theological and philosophical discourses, but very few attested historical facts dealing with the appearance of souls from the other world. A few scattered cases of such appearances in France, Italy, and some other places . . . and this is the end of the events recounted. Can this vividly real material be exhausted by five to ten facts?! Of course not! There are thousands of such facts in the Holy Gospel, the Acts of the Apostles, the Prologues, the lives of the saints, in history, in the press, in traditions and legends, throughout cities and villages alike; but they are either forgotten or remain hidden. The first few centuries of Christianity prove, by a series of astounding facts, the existence of God in all its brilliance and greatness; and they prove the immortality of the human soul. The Middle Ages take a step backward: Christianity is mixed with paganism, instead of the true faith people are inspired with superstition, magic is widely practiced, various demonic sciences flourish. In our time there is a fashion for hypnotism—tables that lift into the air, and spiritualism. Mediums, who are specialists in their own way, call at request the souls of the departed, but somehow only when the light is dim and there is absolute quiet. But our theologians teach us that, under the guise of souls of the dead, there are called up not human souls at all, which can appear only by a particular act of God's will; the mediums succeed in attracting only the evil spirits, which assume the appearance of this or that person. There is at present an interest in Buddhism, and the goal of life is seen in the achievement of Nirvana, a senseless sleep in which neither life nor death exists. This is a more opportune time than ever to share instructive tales about the world of the supernatural and also about miracles which until this time have not appeared in a printed account.

In our time people cruelly suffer in their everyday life from a criminal ignorance of the laws and peculiarities of a man's spiritual life. The science of sciences, the education of human beings so that they may become worthy representatives of the human race, cannot be correct and sensible if it is not founded on a broad and true knowledge of man's spiritual life.

But if man will, to the best of his ability, come to know his rational, spiritual, free, immortal soul, he will reverently and joyfully note that this very soul serves as proof not only of his extraordinary nature, immeasurably higher than that of any other creature on earth, but also of the existence of a spiritual moral order, the Head of which is God, that Supreme Being, spiritual, all-wise, all-good, free, personal, and omnipotent, Who has created the whole world, both spiritual and material, and has prepared an existence beyond the grave for the deathless soul of man, preordained to eternal blessedness after physical death.

Archimandrite Panteleimon
January 16, 1968

INTRODUCTION TO THE SECOND EDITION

Eternal Mysteries Beyond the Grave was this monastery's first foray into English-language publishing. Since its first publication in 1968 it has been reprinted twice, and thousands of copies have been sold and distributed around the world. The demand for it continues unabated, showing that Archimandrite Panteleimon was touching a very profound human need when he first compiled it more than forty years ago.

In this new edition we have slightly reordered the content and lightly edited the text to clarify the meaning of certain passages and remove archaic language. We have also added a brief life of the compiler of the work and founder of our monastery, Archimandrite Panteleimon, whose achievements and labors for God deserve to be more widely known. May his memory be eternal.

The basic purpose of the book remains unchanged: to demonstrate that belief in God and life after death are inseparably connected and that abandonment by society of these beliefs can only be to its detriment and ultimately lead to the loss of humanity. The Russian people are perhaps more conscious of this truth than any other nation, having seen many millions perish during seventy years of atheistic rule. It also attests forcibly to the fact that all our actions have consequences, some of which may be immediately apparent and others that will never be known to us in this present life. Accordingly, it behooves us to amend our lives now, so as to fully embrace the salvation that God offers us in His son Jesus Christ.

It is no longer fashionable to speak of a day of judgment or to contemplate what the reality of such a judgment might be. This book thus takes an approach that would be considered out of step with our times and yet clearly speaks to many human hearts as it seeks to inculcate in us the fear of God. Such a fear, according to Holy Scripture, is an essential weapon in our spiritual arsenal as "by the fear of the Lord everyone turns aside from evil" (Prov

15:30 OSB). It is also a very positive thing as "in the fear of the Lord there is hope of strength ⋯ the command of the Lord is a fountain of life" (Prov 14:27–28 OSB).

It is our hope that this book will continue to inspire you, the reader, with the fear of God, and that by so doing you will desire to choose life and not death.

PART I

BELIEF IN GOD AND THE EXISTENCE OF AN AFTERLIFE

CHAPTER I

⁓ ⁓

Orthodox Teachings on the Existence of God

The entire human race has always possessed a belief in the existence of a Supreme Being. He has endowed the universe with a motion which proceeds according to a strict order, a wise goal, and a plan. Every creature and every single object in the world He has destined to its particular purpose. The smallest insect testifies to the wisdom of its Creator; every flower petal is witness to His omnipotence.

According to the words of Holy Scripture, creation is but another witness to the existence of the Creator of the world: "The heavens have declared His righteousness" (Ps 96:6); "For since the creation of the world His invisible attributes are clearly seen, being understood by the things that are made" (Rom 1:20). The examination of the visible world must bring every man still closer to faith in God.

Finally, there is another witness to the existence of an omnipotent, all-wise, and infinitely good Creator. This reliable witness is our soul, which has an inborn necessity to long for the highest good.

Faith in God gives a man a firm, morally sound direction. It gives him a desire to live virtuously; it ennobles human nature, pointing to its divine origin and its moral likeness to God. It makes a man calm and comforts him in misfortunes by this thought, at least, that it is God who has allowed these misfortunes to come about because of His purposes, which are wise but not intelligible to us (e.g., in the cases of the patriarch Job and Joseph). Finally, faith in God endows each of us with the assurance that a man's life is not limited by the confines of this life but will continue beyond death into infinity.

Thus the truth of God's existence has equally firm proof in the history of mankind, in the data of experience, and in the testimony of our own soul. The more man penetrates into recognition of God in nature, the more he observes his own personal experience and is careful to preserve kindness in his heart and purity in his conscience, the clearer does the truth of God's existence become for him.

God's Being is beyond the comprehension, not only of men, but also of the angels. He is the "unapproachable Light." If our eye tires of the created light of the visible sun, how can the eye of our reason help weakening before the light of the eternal Spiritual Sun, before Whom even the highest of the angels cover their faces? The limited reason of man is too weak to comprehend God, as his hand is too weak to scoop out the sea; or, rather, his reason is weaker even than his hand. Can his hand scoop out the sea? Even if this were possible, since the sea has its limits and a measurable depth, it still would be impossible for the very limited vessel of man's mind to suffice for the comprehension of the abyss of God's wisdom, whose breadth is limitless and whose depth is immeasurable.

In recognizing God, we are hindered not only by the natural limitations of our reason but also because our reason has been darkened by sin. "I am surprised at those numerous people," says Symeon the New Theologian, "who do not tremble at occupying themselves with theology while they are full of sin…. We, who do not know either ourselves or that which is before our very eyes, are fearless enough to dare to philosophize about that which is incomprehensible to us; and especially when we are empty of the grace of the Holy Spirit, Who enlightens and teaches all."

There will come a time when many mysteries will be fully revealed to us, but to achieve this state we must cover a long and very demanding journey of correct spiritual development.

The entire Gospel, this great foundation of Christianity, is a disproof of the monstrous idea that the meaning of man's life lies only in science and reason.

The divinely revealed teachings which are expressed in the Bible have endured centuries, although numerous enemies have struggled against them. The Bible was not composed by one author; it came into being gradually, over a period of approximately 1,400 years. It consists of 76 separate books. A great number of various authors have contributed to its growth: learned and unlearned, kings and workers, clergy and simple farmers, statesmen and shepherds.

For entrance into the kingdom of God and into the Church which has been founded by the Lord on earth, for the fulfillment of Christ's commandments, and for a recognition of the mysteries of His teaching—for all this, it is necessary to be blessedly reborn of the Holy Spirit. It is absolutely impossible to actuate Christ's law in our life with the help of nothing but our weak strength, which is prone to sin. Only with the assistance of the Holy Spirit, when our being has been renovated by the force of a new life, full of grace, does the law of Christ become comprehensible.

Christianity has not yet been understood and properly valued by the world. But Christianity is precisely that "unperishing treasure" for which people search so avidly. This treasure is a real, inner communion with Christ, which develops into the limitless joy of eternity.

Spiritual experience testifies to the closeness of our spirit to God's Spirit, to the influence of God on our soul when it comes into a vivid closeness with Him. In this feeling of God's presence or proximity lies the very essence of religious feeling or faith.

For us, faithful and believing sons of the Church, there can exist no doubt whatsoever about the divinity of Jesus Christ, our Savior. But let us talk to a skeptic, and he will declare that Christ was merely a man. This thought is not new. Many centuries ago, Arius, who was later punished by a revolting death, declared the same thing. Now, however, people have gone beyond his position. This heresy is not enough for Satan. He is intent on manifesting his evil power. Now his servants preach that Christ never existed at all, that He is merely a legend, a myth! We are pained, and fear for those who express thoughts of this kind; but let us speak calmly. The appearance of great men in history was by no means prepared for so that they should be known about in advance and expected. The coming of Christ, on the other hand, was predestined thousands of years before it happened, and with such clarity and in such detail that even the place, the time, almost the year of His appearance were pointed out. By the Savior's time, the entire Orient knew about and expected someone infinitely great Who would come from Judea and to Whom all the nations would subject themselves. Apart from Jesus Christ, there has been no person on earth in whom the entire sum of all these signs and prophecies proved itself.

The life of Jesus Christ was accompanied by events so great as have never occurred in the life of any great man; and actions so great as none of the founders of other religions accomplished, nor did other great men achieve so much. The Roman centurion, a pagan who stood at the cross and saw the signs that took place during the Lord's sufferings and death, recognized Him as the Son of God.

How many souls appear to strive diligently toward Christ and yet do not find full faith in Him? Unremittingly they are troubled by doubts; they cannot admit or recognize many things.

In vain do we think that our doubts are something new that never happened before. Such doubts existed even during our Lord's own time and then repeated themselves and still repeat themselves all the time, since the enemy of the human race never rests and perpetually works for our destruction. Alone, without Christ, we cannot overcome Satan's evil power. But if we are reborn in grace into a communion with our Savior, we receive the ability to struggle and to overcome our enemies.

From *The Christian Orthodox Teachings on the True Faith and Its Application to Life*, edited in Russian by Archimandrite Panteleimon (Holy Trinity Monastery: Jordanville, N.Y., 1954).

CHAPTER 2

The Mystery of the Holy Trinity

The concept of God's oneness and of His immense greatness does not represent fully the Christian teachings about God. Christian faith reveals to us the deepest mystery of the Divinity's inner life. It represents God as One in Essence but existing in Three Persons.

The truth that God is One and yet Three distinguishes Christianity from other religions. Not only do the natural religions not know this truth, but also a clear, straightforward revelation of it is absent even in the divinely revealed teaching of the Old Testament. There we have some beginnings, some symbolic, veiled hints, which can be understood in their entire fullness only in the light of the New Testament, which reveals the teaching on the triune God with absolute clarity.

Thus, for instance, in the Old Testament there are some statements which testify to the plurality of Persons in the Divinity: "Let us make man in Our image, according to Our likeness" (Gen 1:26). "Behold, the man has become like one of Us" (Gen 3:22). "Come, let Us go down and there confuse their language" (Gen 11:7).

There are also some events which hint at the Trinity of Persons in God. Among them are the appearance of God to Abraham in the guise of three wayfarers (Gen 18) and the song of the seraphim, heard by the Prophet Isaiah (Isa 6:3). Finally, we can see how the separate Persons are pointed to in the statements about the Angel of the Lord or the Angel of the Covenant, about the Word and the Wisdom of God, the Spirit of the Lord, and so on.

The dogma of the Trinity, while it is the distinguishing mark of Christianity, serves at the same time as the foundation on which the entire content of Christ's teachings rests. All the joyful, redeeming truths of Christianity—dealing with the redemption, sanctification, and beatitude of man—can be accepted only when we have come to believe in God as Three Persons, for all these great benefits have been granted to us by the common, combined action of the divine Persons.

"The totality of our teaching is simple and brief," states St Gregory the Theologian. "It is like the inscription on a column, obvious to everyone. These people are wholehearted worshippers of the Trinity!"

It is because of the great importance and the meaning, central to everything else, of the dogma of the Holy Trinity that the Church has always exhibited a pious zeal, a far-seeing watchfulness, a never-wearying care, and an intense effort of thought in keeping this dogma safe and defending it from various heretics. The Church has given the most precise definition of this dogma, based on John 15:26: "God, Single in Essence, is Triple in Persons: Father, Son, and the Holy Spirit, Trinity single and indivisible." In these few words is expressed the essence of the Christian teaching on the Holy Trinity. But despite this obvious brevity and lack of complexity, the dogma of the Trinity is, nonetheless, one of the very deepest, unfathomable, and inexhaustible mysteries of divine revelation. No matter how much we may strain our reason, we are completely incapable of clarifying to ourselves how three independent divine Persons (not three powers, qualities, or manifestations) of a totally equal Divinity can together form a single, indivisible Being.

The great fathers and teachers of the Church have on many occasions approached this immeasurably deep and elevated truth with their divinely illumined thought. In their attempts to clarify it, to bring it closer to the understanding of our limited reason, they took recourse to different comparisons, taking these now from the phenomena of nature that surround us, now from the spiritual life of man. Some of the comparisons employed are sun, light, warmth (hence the expression "Light of Light," in the Creed); spring, fountain, stream; root, stem, branch; and reason, heart, will.

The teacher of the Slavs, St Cyril, the Equal of the Apostles, in a conversation with Muslim Saracens, talked about the Holy Trinity as follows. He pointed to the sun and said, "Do you see the shining orb in the sky, and the light born of it and the warmth that proceeds from it? God the Father is like the orb of the sun; He has no beginning and is endless. From Him, outside of time, the Son is born, like the light that comes from the sun; and also from Him, the Father, there proceeds the Holy Spirit, as warmth issues from the sun, together with its light. Everyone distinguishes the disc of the sun, its light, and its warmth; but there is still only one sun in the sky. Such is the Holy Trinity: in It there are Three Persons, but God is One and indivisible."

All these and other comparisons facilitate, to some extent, grasping the mystery of the Trinity. Still, they are only very feeble indications of the

Supreme Being's nature. They leave in us a sense of insufficiency, a lack of correspondence with the elevated subject, for the clarification of which they are employed. They are unable to remove from the teaching on the Trinity that veil of unattainability, of mystery, which envelops it and hides it from man's reason.

In connection with this, there is a very instructive tale about the great Western teacher of the Church, the blessed Augustine. When he was once deep in thought on the mystery of the Trinity and was considering a plan for a written discussion of this dogma, he went to the seashore. There he saw a boy playing in the sand and digging a hole in it. When Augustine asked him what he was doing, the boy replied, "I wish to pour the sea into this little hole." Then Augustine said to himself, "Am I not doing the same as this child when I attempt to exhaust with my thoughts the sea of God's infinity and to gather it into the finite limits of my spirit?"

Augustine—that great teacher to the whole world who, for his ability to penetrate with his thought the deepest mysteries of the faith, was honored by the Church with the name of the Theologian, and who wrote about himself that he used to speak about the Trinity more often than he used to breathe— also admitted the insufficiency of all comparisons that are directed toward understanding the dogma of the Trinity. "No matter what I contemplated with my reason, no matter what I was eager to know," he says, "no matter what I used for the enrichment of my mind, or where I searched for a like-ness, I did not find anything on earth that could be used for a comparison with the essence of God."

Consequently, the dogma on the Holy Trinity is the deepest, the most unattainable mystery of the faith. Vain are all efforts to render it completely understandable by our limited reason, to bring it within the boundaries of our thought. "Here is the boundary," remarks St Athanasius the Great, "of that which the cherubim cover and shield with their wings."

Nonetheless, despite its remoteness and unattainability, despite its seem-ing dryness and abstractness, this dogma

1. gives the fullest satisfaction to the thought of the faithful;
2. brings peace and comfort to the heart; and
3. has great importance for our lives, for it can become a force which renews a man and makes him reborn.

The teachings on the Holy Trinity elevate and purify the very idea of monotheism, put it on a firm foundation, and remove those important yet insurmountable difficulties which of necessity arose in man's thoughts in earlier times.

Some thinkers of pre-Christian antiquity, while they rose to the concept of a single Supreme Being, still were unable to solve a question: in what ways are the life and activity of this Being manifested when He is considered by Himself, apart from His relation to the world? Consequently, the Deity was regarded by them as either the same as the world (pantheism); or appeared to be lifeless, locked in itself, a motionless, self-centered principle (deism); or, again, turned into a terrifying, inscrutable fate that ruled over all (fatalism). Christianity, through the dogma of the Trinity, revealed that in the tri-personal Being of God, apart from His relation to the world, there continues a timeless and endless fullness of internal, mysterious life. As an ancient teacher of the Church, Peter Chrysologos, puts it, God is "alone but not lonely." In Him there are several Persons that ceaselessly are in unbroken communion with one another: "God the Father is not born and does not proceed from another Person; the Son of God is eternally born from the Father; the Holy Spirit eternally proceeds from the Father." The inner, concealed life of the Divinity has ever consisted in this interrelationship of the divine Persons, but before the coming of Christ it was hidden by an impenetrable veil.

Through the mystery of the Trinity, Christianity has taught man not only to revere God and to be full of awe before Him, but also to love Him. Through nothing other than this mystery, it has brought into the world the elevated and meaningful idea, joyful to every soul, that God is the limitless and most perfect Love.

For this very reason, the severe, dry monotheism of other religious teachings, because it does not rise to the revealed idea of the divine Trinity, cannot give rise to a true concept of love as the predominant quality of the Divinity.

Love by its nature is inconceivable without an attendant concept of a union, a communion. If God exists in one person, in relation to whom could His love be revealed? To the world? But the world is not eternal like God. The world did not exist always; it appeared in time.

In what way, then, could divine love manifest itself in the eternity before the creation of the world? Moreover, the world is limited, and God's love could not, in reference to it, be revealed in its infinity. The highest degree of love, in order to manifest itself completely, needs the highest possible object. But where is it? Only the mystery of the triune God solves all these difficulties.

It reveals that God's Love was never inactive and unmanifested: the Persons of the Holy Trinity have always been in a ceaseless state of communion and love with one another. "The Father loves the Son" (John 5:20), and the Father calls Him "beloved" (Matt 3:17). The Son says about Himself, "I love the Father."

There is great truth in the brief but expressive words of the blessed Augustine: "The mystery of the Christian Trinity is the mystery of the Divine Love. If you see love, you see the Trinity."

Founded on the dogma of the Holy Trinity is the teaching about God as Love. On this dogma there rests also the entire moral teaching of Christianity, for its essence also consists of the commandment of love.

If we did not confess to a belief in the Holy Trinity, we would have neither the Church, which educates us for heaven, nor the sacraments, by means of which the Church sanctifies, strengthens, and leads us into the land of eternal life. The last judgment, the resurrection of the dead, the recompense in the future life to each man for his deeds—all these would be but empty words for us, were it not for the teaching on the Holy Trinity. All these ideas must be admitted only if we believe in God the Father, Who is eternal love and truth; in God the Son, the Redeemer of men; and in God the Holy Spirit, the Sanctifier and Comforter of the faithful. So very important is this teaching.

At the same time, it is also most incomprehensible. Only because of His compassion for our weakness did God vouchsafe to reveal the mystery of the Holy Trinity to us, under the names of Father, Son, and Holy Spirit. Therefore, we must not understand these names (that is, those of Father and Son) in the same sense as we understand them when they refer to people. Thus the Son of God is also called the Word of God and His Wisdom; but we cannot say this of people. As for understanding how it can be that there are Three Persons in One God, how it can be that the Father is God, and the Son is God, and the Holy Spirit is God—this is beyond any comprehension.

The Trinity of the Persons is the greatest mystery, hidden even from the many-eyed cherubim, who ceaselessly penetrate the unattainable light of the Deity and draw thence for themselves knowledge and blessedness of every kind. "But where there is a mystery, the reason calls on faith" (Chrysostom, *Hom*, 54). Thus, brethren, our reason must of necessity humble itself and be silent before the mystery of God's Three Persons and, feeling its own inability to comprehend it, must call faith to its aid.

With the assistance of divine revelation, our reason is indeed able to dwell on several truths: that there is a God, the Creator and Supporter of heaven and earth; and that God is One; and our reason can attain to the idea of the necessity of God's existence and the necessity of His oneness, since God is completely perfect and limitless; for our reason cannot imagine two completely perfect, limitless, or unlimited beings. But even in the light of divine teachings, our reason cannot entirely comprehend the thought that God, single in Essence, is yet triple in Persons. This teaching we must accept on faith, and in that faith reverently worship the Holy Trinity, the One God in Three Persons, Father, Son, and the Holy Spirit.

The Holy Orthodox Church teaches thus: "God is One in Essence but Three in Persons; Father, Son, and Holy Spirit, Trinity One and indivisible." The divine Essence is not divided, the divine Persons do not merge. The divinity of the Father, the Son, and the Holy Spirit is One; therefore all divine perfections equally belong to the Father, the Son, and the Holy Spirit. The Father is true God, and the Son is true God, and the Holy Spirit is true God; and in the three Hypostases or Persons, there is only One Three-Personed God.

The Hypostases or Persons of the Holy Trinity are distinguished as follows: God the Father is not born and does not proceed from another Person; God the Son is eternally born from the Father; the Holy Spirit eternally proceeds from the Father.

The teaching about the Holy Trinity emerges from the Holy Scriptures, both those of the Old Testament and those of the New. If we look for an indication of it in the New Testament, we find that the Savior Himself, the Second Person of the Holy Trinity, the only-begotten Son of God, when He sent His disciples and apostles to preach His word, bade them, "Go therefore and make disciples of all the nations, baptizing them in the name of the Father and of the Son and of the Holy Spirit" (Matt 28:19). In the words "baptizing them in the name of the Father and of the Son and of the Holy Spirit," the Lord gave to His Church the briefest symbol of faith, the briefest creed, which contains a condensed teaching about the Holy Trinity.

This teaching is the basis of Christian theology. The entire body of teachings about our salvation through Jesus Christ is at the same time a teaching on the Holy Trinity: God the Father sent His only-begotten Son for the salvation of mankind; God the Son, sojourning on earth, announced the will of His Father, fulfilled the will of His Father, promised to send from the Father the all-holy Spirit, the Comforter, and then ascended to heaven, to His Father; God the Holy Spirit, according to the promise of the Son of God, descended upon the apostles, gave them a perfect knowledge of the mysteries of salvation, strengthened them for their apostolic service, and now ceaselessly remains in Christ's Church, acting through God's word and the saving sacraments, acting for the salvation of those who believe in Jesus Christ.

In humble recognition of the strengthlessness of our limited reason, we must accept the mystery of the Holy Trinity with a full infinite faith, but accept it in such a way that this truth should not remain something external, having no relation to us. Instead, it ought to penetrate to the deepest recesses of our spirit, become the best possession of our entire soul, become an active principle which should give direction to our life. Such should be our acquisition of all Christian dogmas, and principally our acquisition of the unattainable mystery of the Holy Trinity.

From *The Christian Orthodox Teachings on the True Faith and Its Application to Life*, edited in Russian by Archimandrite Panteleimon (Holy Trinity Monastery: Jordanville, N.Y., 1954).

CHAPTER 3

The Immortality of Our Soul

Intimately and inseparably connected with the truth of the existence of God, there is also another truth: that of the spiritual quality and immortality of the human soul. The proofs of this immortality are based on two things: first, on the existence of God and on His qualities; and, second, on the longings and demands of the human soul itself.

The first proof is as follows. Undoubtedly, there is God. He manifests Himself to man not only in his soul but also in the visible nature and through His immediate revelations. He is a just and all-holy Being. He has put in the human soul a desire of the good and a revulsion from evil. Thus many people do their utmost to accomplish good deeds, and as they do so they willingly undertake difficult acts of self-sacrifice, as did the ancient Christian martyrs. But frequently it so happens that sinners enjoy well-being during their life on earth while those who are upright and good suffer until they die; and the good suffer, for the most part, because of sinners.

If there did not exist another life, in which every man's actions are to find recompense, then God would not be just and holy. He would be unmerciful toward the upright and indulgent toward sinners. This, however, cannot even be imagined. Therefore, since God is holy and just, there must be another life, in which both sinners and good people will receive the recompense that is their due.

The other proof of immortality is this. God has put in man's mind a longing for truth; in his will, a longing for what is good; in his heart, a longing for blessedness. But man's mind is not satisfied with the knowledge which he acquires on earth, for he sees that this knowledge is far from full and complete. His will, too, encounters many obstacles to perfecting itself and aiming at the good. And even if a man toils greatly on earth for the sake of that which is good, his heart does not find here a real happiness. Besides, rooted in man's soul there is the thought of eternity and endlessness. His soul not only possesses the idea of a limitless Highest Being, but also actually longs for Him with all its heart and will. Man attempts by various means to make his name endure on earth; he wishes that he should be remembered as long as possible even after he has died. Such are efforts to achieve eternity. Finally, almost all nations of the earth believe in a future life. If such a life did not exist, how could the universal belief in it originate?

There is no religion that does not include in its system of tenets a belief in the immortality of the soul. There is no tribe, even among the least developed peoples, which does not hold this belief in some form or other. Some aborigines have been said to possess no faith of this kind, but such statements usually are based on nothing except the superficial observations of travelers. Ideas like that of immortality are very vague and unclear even in the souls of these very primitive people, and they are expressed by them in languages with a very poorly developed vocabulary. It is difficult to express abstract concepts in an undeveloped language, even when such concepts can appear simple to us. Furthermore, aborigines for the most part do not like to be asked about their convictions.

There is no need to speak of aborignes even. People who keep up with contemporary science still firmly hold on to the idea of immortality. Why should the Creator have put into the human soul various high aspirations and hopes for the future if the future did not exist; that is, if there were no better, eternal life? This would contradict God's goodness, wisdom, and holiness. Consequently, just as it is doubtless that there exists an eternal, all-wise, and perfect God, it is equally doubtless that there is an eternal life for man, a life in which the longings of his soul will be satisfied.

After man's death, his body, separated from the soul, returns to earth, but the soul remains whole and immortal: "Then the dust shall return to the earth as it was. And the spirit will return to God who gave it" (Eccl 12:7).

Both divine revelation and our common sense assure us that man's soul does not die but lives after the death of his body. Since it is different from material creation, the soul is not destroyed together with the body and is not "dispersed like empty air" (Wis 2:3), but "goes upward" (Eccl 3:21). It is only natural that the forces which kill the body, although they destroy its sensory organs, cannot put an end to the soul and annihilate its thoughts and wishes. The truth of the immortality of the soul is fully revealed in both the Old and the New Testament. In the Old Testament, death is called a "gathering to one's people" (Gen 49:33) or a "rest" (1 Kings 2:10). In the New Testament, man is generally regarded as a denizen of the future rather than of the present life, and all his hopes, all his treasures are to be sought in the future. Jesus

Christ confirms this truth by His statement about God: "God is not the God of the dead, but of the living" (Matt 22:32).

The existence of the soul continues beyond the grave, and with the soul there continues all that to which the soul has become accustomed in its temporal life. The soul takes with it that frame of mind, those principles and tendencies which it used to have on earth. While the soul is connected with the body and forms one man with it, it is where the body is. But as soon as this union is dissolved, the location of the soul in recognizable space becomes impossible; any close connection of it to a place disappears, for location is necessary for the body, but not for the spirit. Holy Scripture and our common sense convince us that the human soul is a spirit, and as such it does not need a body in order to continue existing; therefore, it can endure without the body after the body has been destroyed. Divine revelation assures us that the souls of the departed will unite with their bodies only "at [Christ's] coming" (1 Cor 15:23), in "the resurrection of the dead" (1 Cor 15:42). Consequently, until that time they remain bodiless. However, divine revelation tells us that, even after the death of its body, the soul reasons, thinks, and clearly recognizes both its own condition and the condition of others.

From the words of Jesus Christ about the death of the rich man, we see that when he was tormented after death, he understood the cause of his torment and thought about the future destiny of his brothers, who were still enjoying earthly life. "And being in torments in Hades," says Jesus Christ about the rich man, "he lifted up his eyes and saw Abraham afar off, and Lazarus in his bosom. Then he cried and said, 'Father Abraham, have mercy on me, and send Lazarus, that he may dip the tip of his finger in water, and cool my tongue; for I am tormented in this flame.' But Abraham said, 'Son, remember that in your lifetime you received your good things, and likewise Lazarus evil things; but now he is comforted and your are tormented. And besides all this, between us and you there is a great gulf fixed, so that those who want to pass from here to you cannot, nor can those from there pass to us.' Then he said, 'I beg you therefore, father, that you would send him to my father's house, for I have five brothers, that he may testify to them, lest they also come to this place of torment'" (Luke 16:23–28).

To add one more proof of the soul's immortality, we may also mention unusual manifestations of its powers, such as presentiments of even the remote future; and this is not only in dreams but also in a waking condition.

What do contemporary thinkers and scientists believe about God and about the immortality of the soul? It would be difficult to recount in detail all that they have stated in contradiction to the widely spread opinion that science denies both the existence of God and of eternal life. Let us rather mention the results of a questionnaire on immortality, which R. Thomsen of Chicago addressed at the beginning of the twentieth entury to the scientists and thinkers of all countries, including Russia.

Of forty-seven replies, the great majority (thirty-nine) were positive and well supported. The same cannot be said about the two negative replies and the four that were evasive, while two of the people questioned gave no definite reply at all. Among the thirty-nine scientists who believed in immortality, there were some of outstanding reputation, such as the chemist [William] Crookes, the psychologist [William] James, the physiologist [Charles] Richet, the biologist [Alfred Russell] Wallace, and others.

Faith and reason oppose each other only where faith is weak. If unbelievers find in teachings about God much that they cannot understand, the obvious answer to their problem is that revelation has come to us not from the domain of our knowledge and our life but from those unlimited spheres where the Highest Being lives and manifests Himself. All objections of reason to revelation will fall of their own accord, since for the most part they are founded on the unwillingness of reason to penetrate deeper into the highest revelation.

The divine knower of hearts, Christ the Savior, first showed to the world that the only source of sound social, political, and historical life is the human spirit; and the more perfect this spirit is, the more perfect will be all that it creates. If you wish that your surroundings should change, change yourself, and educate your heart. This is what Christianity teaches.

A life full of fraternal love and a kingdom of God on earth are possible, but they must be sought not in externals, not by looking around; instead, it is necessary to look inside oneself, into one's heart. But the heart is not the domain over which science has influence; it is rather under the influence of religion.

Note that the desire to live, to live always, which exists in every man's heart, has not been given by the Creator without a purpose. It is one of the first indicators of the soul's immortality, one of the first suggestions that man must prepare for a future life. The desire to live is connected with the wish for happiness. This thirst for happiness is not satisfied here; consequently, there must be a future life in which this flaming desire of our heart might be fulfilled.

We see how God not only puts into man's nature certain longings but also gives man means for their satisfaction. If we are tormented by thirst, we can drink; hunger can be stilled by food; when we are tired from work, we feel the need to strengthen and renew our energy by rest, and sleep refreshes and rests us. But as for happiness, we always are waiting for it, and no one can give it to us.

Can it be that this happiness does not exist? Can it be that God has implanted this desire in us without the intention of ever satisfying it? No. Divine providence, which provides our bodies with all earthly blessings, cannot eternally leave our soul with merely a thirst for happiness. Since happiness does not exist here, it must exist beyond the limits of our life, in the future life with God. Then there is still another desire, akin to the desire for happiness. This is the longing for perfection, which also cannot be satisfied here because of the shortness of our life. It seems to us reasonable to think that God, Who has given us this longing, will satisfy it in the future life.

Note that the abilities of our heart and our reason do not develop and become perfect to the highest degree to which they could possibly attain. Yet God does not leave His creatures incomplete and unfinished. Therefore, it is reasonable to think that in His wisdom, He is reserving another life for our spirits, in which man will become that which he is capable of being.

Every day man is capable of acquiring new knowledge. How much success he can achieve in learning from his childhood to his old age! How he can perfect himself in righteousness! Still he dies, and his mental and moral education remains unfinished. He might have perfected himself further in both the mental and the moral aspects of his being; he might have studied even better the marvelous phenomena of God's universe; he might have uprooted completely all his defects and filled their place in his heart with virtues; in short, he might have approached even closer that ideal which has been indicated by God Himself. But death stops man before he finishes the journey which he should have completed. Because this is so, if it were not for eternal life, God would appear to have left His work incomplete; let us add that He would appear to have allowed man to die precisely at the moment when man was most capable of further perfection!

Can it be imagined that a father, who has given his son an excellent elementary training, should lock him up for the remainder of his life and keep him within four walls instead of allowing him to continue his education and gather the fruit of it? Thus, too, it seems impossible that he who loves what is good, he who aims for perfection (the very idea of which has been given to him by God), should be stopped on his way toward that perfection.

Which one of us has no desire to learn more about the miraculous laws of nature, according to which divine providence rules the universe? Who does not desire to recognize the source of all that exists? What child does not wish to see his father, supposing that he knows this father only by the good received from him? Can God have given us the ability to rise to Him in thought, but denied us a clearer contemplation of His nature, of His perfections, of the ultimate goal of creation?

How lovely is the soul that is perfecting itself in truth and virtue! Can God destroy it before this process of perfection has ended? Perfection, like happiness, is not native to this world; it belongs to a different realm. Every plant has a soul and a climate most suitable to it, but there is no native habitat here for perfection. Where is it, then, if not in the future life? Man is the crown of all earthly creation, but this creation is not finished.

We are merely stones, the purpose of which is to construct a magnificent building. We are in an elementary school, where only the rudiments of learning can be acquired. We are only going through the childhood of that long life which bears the name of eternity. Death will only remove us from the crass earthly wrap, which is insufficient for our future existence.

Let us keep in mind that those who had the purest hearts, who ceaselessly struggled with the enemies of their spirits and gained glory for themselves through their many spiritual victories (as, for instance, St Paul), were uncertain, even after unrelenting toils, that they had attained to the perfection for which they were striving. Let us keep in mind that the Lord must have been pleased and still is pleased by the success which His creatures achieve in righteousness, and that He must be pleased to see how they approach an ever closer likeness to Him. If we remember this, we shall be unable to imagine that the Lord could leave these creatures in the middle of their journey to virtue, or that He could give them death and annihilation as a reward for their efforts. This is inconsistent with divine goodness and wisdom.

An expectation of a future life, together with faith in God, forms the foundation of a well-ordered life on earth, to say nothing of a future life. It is known that nations whose faith in a future life weakened were subject to all kinds of disasters: the basis of family and social life was shaken, and they fell prey to internal struggles and enslavement by external enemies. There was a time when the entire human race, with the exception of Noah and his family, was destroyed by the deluge, sent by God's order because the people of that time had lost their faith in God and in the immortality of their souls. Their flesh had dominated their spirits to such an extent that they forgot about their high destiny, and this is the reason why God said about them, "My spirit shall not always strive with man, for that he also is flesh" (Gen 6:3). A similar situation will prevail before the second coming of Jesus Christ to earth and the ensuing end of the world.

Our times are hard and put a heavy responsibility on each of us. Materialism, which denies the existence of man's soul and a right to immortality, preaches some sort of truth, some so-called honesty, some so-called progress toward a better order, and toward noble goals; but it does not see that all these goals become unnecessary and senseless for the kind of human condition in which it believes. According to materialism, men are like little flies in hot weather. They crowd one another in a vast swarm, push one another, fly around in confusion, mate, feed and warm themselves, and then disappear in a disordered process, only to give space to tomorrow's swarm of exactly the same kind.

When he deprives himself of heaven and makes himself an exclusively earthly creature, man, no matter whether he realizes it or not, becomes like a senseless animal. What is the difference? Even now many people are Christian in name only. Many of them even go to church, buy candles, and pray, but they do not believe in the existence of evil spirits and hardly believe in the immortality of their own souls; or else they simply do not think about such things. Then there are others, quite unlike them; these are often, to all appearances, crass and vicious, but their inner self may for a long time have been longing for a higher purpose and meaning to their life, even though they may not realize it.

The question of immortality is the most important question in our life. Our entire life, both personal and social, is based on our attitude toward the immortality of our soul and its future life. Man's immortality is the continuation of his life after death; that is, his soul continues to exist apart from his body, and this existence takes place in another world, in a different form, and in different conditions. Death does not interrupt man's existence but only changes it. Here on earth we call some people alive and others dead. But who is dead? Not human beings, surely, but only parts of them—their bodies. These bodies are buried in the ground, while the most important part of man, namely, his soul, which is the image and likeness of God, continues to live! It passes into another world and lives there.

God is not a God of the dead but a God of the living, and our earthly life is only a beginning, a preparation for the eternal and endless life. There is no people, and never has been, who do not expect a future life. This hope is inherent in the human soul.

The pagan religions offer, for the greater part, only some conjectures about the immortality of the soul. These conjectures possess a varying degree of clarity. Only Christianity has endowed the belief in immortality with complete credibility and has given it a truthful expression;

and this is because Christianity is not a human teaching, but a divinely revealed truth.

Think of the ancient Greek historian Plutarch, who was widely traveled and saw many different countries and nations during his life. He wrote, "Go to the limits of the earth, travel, and you will see differences everywhere: you will see settlements which possess no laws of any kind; you will see people who do not know what money is; you will encounter cities that have no fortifications; there are whole tribes that do not possess dwellings of any sort; but you will nowhere find a country or a nation in whose midst altars and sacrificial tables are not erected, where sacrifices are not burned and prayers do not rise to heaven."

This hope of eternal life, which has always existed in the human spirit and with which man has been created, was fully and completely developed by Christianity. Thus, for instance, St Paul speaks about the resurrection and future life with striking force and conviction in his first epistle to the Corinthians and his epistle to the Thessalonians. For the apostles, future life became the object of a firm and unshakable conviction, since it was given to them to see with their own eyes this life beyond the grave: they saw it in the risen Christ.

This blessed faith inspired the first Christians. It brightly shone in the lives of more recent saints as well: practically before our eyes it strikingly manifested itself in the life of St Seraphim of Sarov; of the fathers (*startsi*) Leo, Macarius, Ambrose, and Joseph of Optina; of Father John of Kronstadt; all of whom even here on earth had stepped, as it were, beyond the mysterious boundary of this world and lived far beyond its confines. They had a divinely granted knowledge of the future life, and the glow of this life was distinctly reflected in their faces, always joyful like the faces of children, and in their words. They were like the Apostle Paul, who had been taken "to the third heaven" and had heard there "inexpressible words" (2 Cor 12:2, 4).

Human beings who approach perfection and have achieved purity of heart, they who have "acquired the Spirit of God" [from St Seraphim's conversation with Motovilov] even while they are still in this world, have the daring to enter the place of the Creator, and to join angels and the spirits of the saints. While they are still in their earthly bodies, they well know that they will reign with Christ; for already here on earth they have come to know the sweetness of divine illumination and the effect of God's power. The supernatural gifts of communion with God, which the soul can receive when it is still in the body, are only an indication of those heavenly rewards which cannot even be told to man, since we possess no images or words fit for their description.

Once they had risen to the heights of spiritual elevation while still in this life, these holy men experienced a blessedness and joy which resemble the eternal heavenly joy of the life to come. Hence these men were already angels and healed all kinds of illnesses, both mental and physical. When they were praying they were transfigured and shone with the light with which the Savior shone on Mt Tabor. The forces of nature obeyed them; men and beasts, plants, water, and air did their will. Their thoughts, their visions and contemplations have been left for us in their works, and these works, illumined from above, contain accounts of the future life, that life which begins beyond the grave. Some of these accounts are included in this book. Their teachings on immortality can briefly be summarized in a single paragraph:

> Man is a being destined to immortality. Thus he cannot help having a concept and an expectation of it. In some individuals, however, this feeling is strong, while in others it is so weak that it hardly shows itself. Why is this so? The reason is that man in his present condition contains two parts. One of these is immortal and will not disappear with death; the other one is mortal and lives only until death. Each of these parts produces in man a disposition related to it. Both are so tightly knit that they form one whole. Therefore, the feeling of immortality together with the feeling of mortality merge into one indefinite and vague feeling. When a man lives relying chiefly on that which in him is truly immortal, that is, his spirit and his conscience, then the feeling of immortality grows stronger. If, on the other hand, he gives himself over to that which in him is temporal and dead, namely, his flesh and blood, the feeling of mortality grows.

Our soul avidly desires heavenly light and cannot therefore be satisfied with earthly goods. This is why many people who apparently possess all that is necessary for earthly happiness still often experience great sorrow of soul. Blessed Augustine, after he had tasted all the joys and beauties that the earth offers, exclaimed to God, "You have created us for Yourself, and our heart is restless until it finds rest in You."

Death is a great and awesome mystery. The most mysterious part of it is the moment when the soul becomes separated from the body, and man passes from his bodily life into a purely spiritual life. His life used to be temporal; now it becomes eternal.

The human spirit gives up temporal life sooner and more easily than the body. While the body still struggles with death, the spirit is already free. Even before the death struggle has ended for the body, the spirit is already outside the body, floating near it, as it were. This is the explanation of those instances, by no means rare, when a man, or rather his spirit in the guise of his earthly body, appears at some distance from the body to people who are dear to him; and this happens before the final moment of death.

A few more moments, and man passes into eternity. How the very form of his being suddenly changes! His spirit sees itself, its own essence. He sees even the most remote objects, but not with his bodily eyes. Instead, he possesses some sort of sense that is incomprehensible to us. He speaks not in distinctly heard words but in thoughts. He feels and touches, but not with hands; rather, it is sense itself which he possesses, but no longer does he use it through his former bodily instruments.

He moves not on his feet but through the mere effort of his will. He now approaches in a moment places and things which formerly he could reach only with great effort and very slowly by covering a great expanse of space and taking a long time. No natural boundaries contain him now. Now he sees the past as clearly as he does the present. The future too is no longer so hidden as it used to be. There no longer exists the division between him and other places and times. There no longer is space, or hours, days, and years; there are no distances, either small or great. Everything flows into one moment—eternity.

What, then, does he see and feel? Eternity, once it has opened itself to him, fills him with inexpressible dread. Its endlessness swallows his limited being. All his thoughts and feelings lose themselves in endlessness! He sees objects for which we have neither images nor names; he hears that which on earth can be expressed neither by any voice nor by any sound; his experiences and feelings cannot be expressed by us in any words whatsoever. He finds there light and darkness, but not as we know them: a light before which a bright sun would give less light than a candle does here before the sun; a darkness compared to which our darkest night would be lighter than day. He meets there beings similar to him and recognizes in them people who also have departed from this world.

But what a change! These are no longer the faces that were known here; no longer are these bodies that used to exist on earth. These are only the souls of the departed. But these souls have now fully revealed their internal qualities, which now clothe them in an appropriate manner. By manifestations of the inner qualities of each soul, other souls recognize it. Through the force of its feelings, each tries to recognize those to whom it was near in this life.

In eternity, our spirit meets beings very close in their nature to his, but their very approach makes him feel their infinitely greater power. Some of them come out of limitless darkness, and their whole being is made up of darkness and evil. They contain in themselves unimaginable suffering. Their every movement and action are sorrow and destruction.

These, however, are in the lower spheres of the spiritual world, the spheres closest to earth. At a greater distance from it, the spirit sees a limitless sea of unintelligible light from which other beings come, even more powerful than the ones mentioned before. Their nature and their life are made up of nothing but limitless good, unfathomable perfection, and inexpressible love. Divine light fills their entire being and accompanies their every motion.

Thus a man's spirit advances through this marvelous world. By the force of his spiritual nature and the irresistible power of attraction toward a world that is akin to him, he flies on and on to that place, or rather to that degree to which he can attain by his spiritual forces. There he is reborn, changed in a fashion marvelous to himself.

Is this the same spirit that used to live in an earthly man, a limited spirit tied to the body, scarcely noticeable under this body's mass, entirely enslaved by the body and apparently so dependent on it that without it the spirit seemed unable to live and to develop? What has happened to it now?

Now everything that it ever contained, both the good and the bad, quickly and forcefully reveals itself. Man's thoughts and feelings, his moral character, his passions and desires—all this now develops to an infinite extent. He cannot stop or change or overcome this development. The endlessness of eternity makes them all unending. His defects and weaknesses become unbounded evil. His evil becomes endless, his sorrows turn into unending suffering.

Do you visualize the horror of such a condition? Your soul, which now is not good but still suppresses and conceals its evil within itself, will there appear absolutely evil. Your evil feelings, to some extent controlled here, there will become ravings, unless you uproot them here. If you have some power over yourself here, there you will be able to do nothing. All that is in you will pass with you there and develop to endlessness. Man's soul, once it has separated itself from the body, continues with great force to develop in itself those qualities which it acquired during its life on earth. Consequently, the righteous are endlessly confirmed in their virtues and their reliance on God's will, while unrepentant sinners become ever more wicked and come to hate God. By the end of the world's history, there will be only two categories of men, both on earth and in heaven: the righteous, full of limitless love for God, and the sinners, full of hatred toward God.

What will become of you there, faithless and sinful man? If you are not good here, there you will be a dark and evil spirit. Oh, you will not recognize yourself there. Or perhaps it will be better to say that there you will recognize yourself, but recognize all too well. Your wickedness will, by its own drive, carry you toward the eternal, limitless evil, to the society of dark and evil forces. You will be unable to stop on this road or to turn back from it. You will suffer forever. What will be the cause of your sufferings? Your own ravings, caused by your own wickedness. They will give you no rest. The evil company into which you will fall will also eternally surround you and torture you endlessly.

And what of the good soul? What will happen to it? Goodness also will become revealed in its entire fullness and strength. It will develop with all the freedom which it did not have here. It will discover its entire inner worth, which here is largely hidden and is not recognized or valued. Its entire inner light, darkened here in every way; its entire blessedness, suppressed here by various sorrows—all these will now be uncovered and shine forth. And this soul, by the force of its morally developed and virtuously elevated desire, will rise to the higher spheres of that world where, in the midst of limitless light, there dwells the cause and the First Image of everything good. There, in the realm of the brightest and purest beings, it too will become an angel; that is, a being as light, pure, and blessed as an angel.

It will now forever become firm in the good. No evil, either internal or external, will be able to shake or change it or to harm its blessed condition. But the soul will not live in idleness and merely enjoy its blessedness. It will act through its illumined mind; it will contemplate and penetrate the mysteries which here it cannot understand: the mysteries of God, the creation, itself, and the eternal life.

Our condition in the future life will not be a condition of idle leisure. Instead, it will be a harmonious, complete satisfaction of all the longings and desires of our soul, which will undergo an unbroken and endless development. Man's reason, heart, and will are destined to find for themselves many worthy objects and adequate material for their development.

Immediate communion with God, the light that illumines all, will inevitably reveal to us the entirety of the laws that govern the universe. So great a horizon will open itself to us that we in our present life cannot even conceive of its vastness. Only then will that spiritual thirst for knowledge be satisfied, that thirst which torments man in the present life. God alone, Who represents the limitless ocean of being, will then serve as the inexhaustible and the most elevated object for our mind in its eternal longing to reach to the Cause of all that exists.

The second object of our spiritual contemplation will be the process of our redemption, achieved by the Son of God. This is that great and marvelous process which even the minds of the angels only wish to understand, for through it our human nature has, in the person of the Man-God, been elevated to the throne of God.

The third object of our contemplation will be the world of the angels, the world of the most perfect and pure spirits. Mankind itself, its past destinies and its present condition, will also be an object of our thought. It will be of greatest interest to us, as it is even now, when our means of cognition are limited.

Finally, the transfigured and renewed world in all its beauty and diversity will attract our spiritual gaze and evoke a feeling of marvel and of veneration for Him Who has created everything by His wisdom. To this must be added the great moral satisfaction which the blessed will experience as a result of mutual proximity. Among them there will be neither envy nor hate, neither enmity nor falseness; nothing of that which now fills and constantly poisons our life on earth.

Brotherly love, a never disturbed peace, most perfect concord, the purest truth—all these will reign among the blessed inhabitants of the New Jerusalem in heaven. What a limitless realm of cognition and action! What an inexhaustible source of blessedness! All of us need the joyous knowledge of this eternal future life. Faithful Christians always have lived and still live by its light and its breath.

From *A Concise Course of Theology*, compiled in Russian, by Father I. Vinogradov; *Wisdom and Mercy of God*, also in Russian, by Golubinsky (Tuzov Press, 1894); and other sources.

CHAPTER 4

The Origin of Death

Why is it that people die? Divine revelation teaches us that "God did not make death" (Wis 1:13), but "created man for immortality" (Wis 2:23); and that "death entered the world by the envy of the devil" (Wis 2:24). Death invaded our immortal nature by default, through our faithlessness to the source of life, God, and through our disobedience to His life-giving commandment. This is the only correct answer to the question about the origin of death.

But where and how did this horrible parting of free creatures, endowed with reason, from the source of life and immortality—that is, God—happen? The word of God tells us (and who else would be able to do as much?) that this horrible change came about not on earth but in heaven, and did so even before the creation of our earth and the human race. The first occurrence of death was not on earth—in Paradise, as we usually think—but in heaven, at the very throne of God; and the first victim of death was not man but an archangel, perhaps the foremost of the archangels. He was the closest spectator of the divine perfections, the first recipient of the uncreated light, and, consequently, the most blessed of the created beings.

What could his perfection lack, that perfection which should have increased and lasted to all eternity? What but grateful obedience and love for his all-good Creator? But this is precisely what was lacking. Why and how? This is a mystery which we cannot comprehend. But we know that this luminous archangel did not endure in his elevated position, did not content himself with his worth and his blessedness. Instead, he rose against his Creator and benefactor and senselessly thought that he could not only do without His good will but even openly struggle against Him.

The great mystery of God's providence in respect to the incarnation of the divine Word, that highest, most noble, and perfect deed of the creative divine wisdom and power, was from the beginning of time ordained and foreseen by the all-knowing divine intelligence. Even before God ordained the creation of the angels or of men or of any other creature, His eternal counsel already had decided upon the incarnation of God the Word. Therefore, Holy Scripture calls the incarnation of the divine Word "the beginning of the ways of the Lord," and the incarnated Word Himself "the firstborn over all creation" (Col 1:15).

Some teachers of the Church hold the opinion that this mystery, preserved in the treasury of the divine counsel like the most precious pearl in all heaven, was at the beginning of ages revealed in order that the angels should see and marvel at the most marvelous deed of divine wisdom. It was this and nothing else that moved Satan to envy the union of God with man. Having grown proud of his excellence, he said in his heart: I, none but I, the first of the seraphim, the heavenly and immaterial, am worthy of such an honor, rather than man, who is bodily and earthly. "I will be like the Most High" (Isa 14:14). And so it was that Satan like lightning fell from heaven.

Then there took place the struggle of a creature with its Creator, but the archangel with his followers (for his madness was shared by other angels) did not endure against the Almighty and was cast down from heaven into the lowest hell. He was the first victim of death. This was the first graveyard in the entire world. The revolted angels had no bodies as we do, because they were spiritual by nature. Therefore, they could not experience our kind of death. But simultaneously with their revolt and their departure through sin from God, they lost their life, their strength and blessedness, and became dead as far as life in God was concerned. As imperishable spirits, they could not entirely lose their being; they could not come apart and be destroyed as our bodies are destroyed. However, they experienced death a hundred times worse: an eternal and irreversible separation from God, Who is the only source of true life.

This first death in the world of angels was the most horrible of all, for it was eternal death, which has no resurrection. But no matter how horrible this death was, it had no influence on us. Our human race, even our earth and our heaven, in all likelihood, did not exist at that time. Meanwhile, in order to reveal His limitless might and goodness, the Creator deigned to bring into being our visible, sensible, material world. At its head was put man, a being that combined in himself spirit and body. Each soul and entire inner being of Adam and of Eve was similar to those of the angels, but these angel-like creatures were clothed in bodies and in this respect resembled all the other bodily creatures of our earth.

Eternal life directly flowed into man's being from God's Being and filled his soul and his body with power and incorruptibility. Although man possessed a material body, he had the ability to live eternally. But he was also able to die. There was only one way to reach this misfortune: to be separated from God, the source of life. In such an event, man would be on his own. Because he did not have a source of life in himself, he would incur weakness and a dissolution of all that in him was destructible; that is, his entire bodily nature. As for separation from God, to arrive at that there was also only one way: deviation from God's will, that is, sin.

Man was furnished fully and abundantly with all that was necessary to keep him from falling into sin, struggling against God's will, and thus losing his immortality. However, he was free. He possessed the sublime gift of freedom which is necessary for a consciously moral being. At the same time, freedom is a most dangerous gift, for it was through this freedom that man, exactly like the heavenly archangel, could do with himself anything he pleased. He could remain in union with the source of life, his Creator; or he could depart from Him, although this would mean his greatest harm and destruction.

In order to help man discover his freedom and his will and the sooner to use them to a good purpose and thus become confirmed in what is good, the fatherly providence of God gave man a test. This was the specific commandment that prohibited him from tasting the fruit of one of the trees of Paradise. Thus all the opportunities for a fall were reduced to one opportunity; all the varied temptations that innocent man might incur were brought down to one, and that not even a serious temptation. It was not difficult to surmount it.

The all-good Creator did more. To protect man even better from misusing his freedom and also from any outside suggestion, God even pointed to the ruinous results of disobedience to His commandment. He directly declared to man that the immediate result of such disobedience would be death. "For in the day that you eat of it (that is, of the fruit that grows on the forbidden tree) you shall surely die" (Gen 2:17). In the language of the author of the Scripture, the expression here means that you will die inevitably, horribly; you will be subject to the greatest disaster.

Indeed, in Paradise man not only faced an issue of life—for he was alive—but also faced the question of immortality and death. Who could expect us, the human race, to be so unreasonable? We might be called hostile toward ourselves, since we rejected both immortality and life and of our own will chose death.

The word of God was fulfilled; man died. After his sacrilegious tasting of the forbidden tree, there followed his spiritual death; his separation from the life of God (Eph 4:18), his separation from Him Who is the life of all that lives and the light of men (John 1:4); then there followed man's exile from Paradise; his remoteness from the tree of life; his condemnation to labors, illnesses, and grief; his death and the dissolution of his body; and the curse on all living beings for his sake. "Just as through one man sin entered the world, and death through sin, and thus death spread to all men, because all sinned" (Rom 5:12).

In His eternal counsel, the Triune God had decided to create man "in Our image, according to Our likeness" (Gen 1:26). The basic characteristic of the divine image in human nature is its individuality and its spirituality. The most important features of spirituality are a consciousness of oneself and freedom.

God is a self-sufficient and infinite Spirit. The human spirit is created and limited. Consequently, there is an infinite distance between the image and Him Whose image it is. God, as a limitless Spirit, has in Himself the entire fullness of all the possible perfections, with no fault and no limitation. As the all-perfect, He is unchangeable, always the same in His entire Being, in His powers and perfections. In the limitless and changeless Spirit there is also a limitless intelligence, the most perfect knowledge and freedom. This freedom is always holy and good, and cannot be anything but holy and good. Therefore God is omnipotent in the moral sense of the word—He can accomplish all that He wills, since He wills only that which is in accord with His most perfect nature. That which is contrary to this nature, He cannot will. God's freedom is all-perfect, changeless, and incapable of either willing or doing evil. No created being, no matter how elevated and perfect and near to God, can have freedom as perfect and changeless. Otherwise, it would not be a creature, for a creature is only an image of God. It would be a being entirely God's equal.

In the words of the prophet, man is "little lower than the angels ... crowned with glory and honor" (Ps 8:6). From the hands of His Creator, Adam received mighty powers and great perfections. The Lord God illumined Adam's intelligence with the light of His bodily appearances and conversations. He did not omit to strengthen Adam's freedom also by the almighty strength of His grace. Before his fall, Adam constantly was under the influence of this grace. "God," writes the blessed Augustine, "gave to man a good will. He who created man created him good. He also gave man His assisting might, without which Adam would not be able to stand firm in the good, even if he should wish to do so. However, the very wish for the good was left to his free will."

The commandment given to Adam concerned itself with only one slight particular. But despite its particular character, this commandment expressed the entire spirit of the moral law and the entire essence of its demands: love and devotion to God. Thus man was shown a definite pattern for his entire behavior. The direction of his whole life was indicated to him: obedience and yielding to God's will were to be his greatest wish. This is how the blessed Augustine understood God's commandment to Adam: "The tree is good; but do not touch it. Why? Because I am your Lord, and you are a slave; this is the whole reason." If not the Lord, then the commandment itself spoke to Adam of devotion and service to God, and these qualities are the essence of the divine law. God protects His commandment by the warning, "For in the day that you eat of it you shall surely die" (Gen 2:17). The moral law did not predict man's death. The conscience of Adam's still innocent soul was light and peaceful. God's warning revealed to Adam that which his conscience could not yet have told him, namely, the bitter results of breaking the law. This is how the law is completed by the commandment. Fear increased man's respect for God. Finally, God foresaw the temptation which man would undergo at the initiative of the devil. Love and devotion to God, Who has given man life and all its happiness in Paradise, were great enough to save man from temptation. But God gave man still another weapon against the tempter. This weapon was fear of death. Following the same good purpose, He gave man the easiest of commandments: from one tree only was man forbidden to eat the fruit. It is impossible to invent a commandment that should be easier, especially for Adam, who had as his possession the whole of Paradise and the whole earth. The forbidden thing had nothing about it that was particularly irresistible. Therefore it was easy for man to keep the commandment and to withstand the tempter. It is in vain that many people complain about the tree of knowledge. It was planted with a wise and good purpose. The commandment, although it was connected with fear of death, led not to death but to life.

To sum up, God gave to Adam a firm and bright mind and a pure soul. He strengthened his heart with love of what is good. He armed him with fear of death; fortified his freedom by a clear, easy, and definite commandment; and clothed him in the might of His grace. He Himself appeared to Adam and was his teacher and preceptor. After all this, how could any tempter be of danger to Adam? What temptation could overcome his will? None but the temptation that came of his own desire, which indeed conceives and brings forth sin (James 1:14–15). God, as the apostle assures us, does not allow man to be tempted beyond his strength (1 Cor 10:13).

Some argue that since God foresaw the destruction of sinners, He, being a good Creator, should not have brought rational beings to life. It can be said, however, that it is just as probable that the blessedness of the saved righteous, also foreseen by God, moved Him to create man. It is true that, although all the necessary opportunities exist for the salvation of the wicked, they still perish in their sins and do this of their own volition. But while they even dare to reproach the goodness of Him Who gave them life, millions of rational beings still are joyful and praise the Creator for the happiness of their blessed existence. Do the critics wish that evil should be dearer to God than good, so that for the sake of evil God should refuse to let good exist? Even according to our human reasoning, it is not good and not just to deprive many of blessedness only because a few perish at the same time. "God knew," writes St John Chrysostom, "that Adam would fall. But he saw his descendants: Abel, Enos, Enoch, Noah, Elijah, the prophets, the marvelous apostles—that ornament of the human race—and the heavenly crowds of martyrs, who radiate holiness."

"But," someone might say, "everyone is dear to himself." Not only to himself but to God also. The Lord Himself assures us that there is joy in heaven when even one sinner repents (Luke 15:7). What has God not done, what is He not doing even now that the sinner should not perish in his sins but repent and return to God? But let us cease to attempt correcting the all-wise. Let us cease to look for something that should be better than what He has actually created. Although the causes of His particular actions are hidden from us, we can still maintain in our souls this one principle: no evil comes from the all-good.

CHAPTER 5

The Actual Existence of the Devil

Not only the Christian teaching on the trials that souls must pass through after death, but almost all the aspects of Christianity have at their very base the assumption that the devil exists. His existence is to be understood not allegorically but quite literally. He is the personal adversary of God and man. The devil is a being personal and rational in nature, and a denial of his existence and activity shakes and even overthrows the whole harmonious system of the teachings concerning God's rule over the universe. Nevertheless, it is common knowledge that many people are scandalized by the necessity of recognizing the existence of an evil spirit as a person. There are many who readily acknowledge the existence of God and even admit that good spirits exist, but they find it inconvenient and impossible to acknowledge the existence of evil spirits, and will do anything in order to have nothing to do with this problem. Their reluctance makes it necessary for us to discuss this vitally important issue.

We shall turn first of all to the divine revelation as it is expressed in God's word. God's word speaks not only of good spirits but also of evil ones (Luke 7:21). It calls them "unclean" (Matt 10:1), refers to them as "spiritual hosts of wickedness in the heavenly places" (Eph 6:12), and names them "demons" (Luke 8:30, 33, 35). The Scriptures distinguish various demons. The chief of them is usually named the "devil" (1 Pet 5:8), the "tempter" (Matt 4:3), or "Satan" (Rev 20:2, 7). Occasionally, he is termed "Beelzebub" (Luke 11:15), "Belial" (2 Cor 6:15), "the prince of this world" (John 12:31), "the prince of the power of the air" (Eph 2:2), "ruler of demons" (Matt 9:34), and the like. The rest of the evil spirits, who are subservient to him, are called his "angels" (Matt 25:41), the "angels" of "the dragon" or "Satan" (Rev 12:7, 9).

Holy Scripture teaches that this devil and his angels are beings endowed with individuality. They exist in reality and are not merely imaginary. Thus the books of the Old Testament relate how on many occasions there would come before the face of God not only God's angels but also the devil. It was the devil whom the Almighty permitted to test the righteous Job by many evils of various kinds (Job 1:6, 2:2, and elsewhere). We also learn from the Old Testament that "the Spirit of the Lord departed from Saul, and a distressing spirit from the Lord troubled him" (1 Sam 16:14), and how "Satan stood up against Israel, and moved David to number Israel" (1 Chr 21:1). The Prophet Zechariah describes a vision in which he saw Joshua the high priest standing before the face of an angel of the Lord, and the devil standing to the right of Joshua as his accuser (Zech 3:1). Finally, the wise King Solomon testifies that "death entered the world by the envy of the devil" (Wis 2:24). In all these instances, and especially in the first and the last cited, the sense of the text does not admit of interpreting the devil as an abstraction rather than a real person.

The books of the New Testament point even more clearly to the actual existence of the devil as an individual, personal being. A few examples will be sufficient to prove the point.

While explaining the parable of the seed and the tares, the Savior says, "He who sows the good seed is the Son of Man. The field is the world, the good seed are the sons of the kingdom, but the tares are the sons of the wicked one. The enemy who sowed them is the devil, the harvest is the end of the age, and the reapers are the angels" (Matt 13:37–39). Here the devil is obviously a being as real and individual as the Son of Man, the angels, the children of the kingdom, and the children of the wicked one.

When the Pharisees accused the Savior, saying that He "does not cast out demons except by Beelzebub, the ruler of the demons" (Matt 12:24), the Savior did not say to them that Beelzebub and his devils do not exist. Instead of rejecting them as creatures of the Pharisees' imagination, He replied in words which clearly testify to the reality of Satan's existence and to the reality of his kingdom: "If Satan casts out Satan, he is divided against himself. How then will his kingdom stand? And if I cast out demons by Beelzebub, by whom do your sons cast them out? Therefore they shall be your judges. But if I cast out demons by the Spirit of God, surely the kingdom of God has come upon you. Or how can one enter a strong man's house and plunder his goods, unless he first binds the strong man? And then he will plunder his house" (Matt 12:26–29).

When the apostles once asked the Savior in private why they had been unable to cast an impure spirit out of a man, the Lord did not tell them that there had been no evil spirit in the man and that impure spirits do not exist at all. Quite to the contrary, He gave them a rule for casting out evil spirits: "This kind can come out by nothing but prayer and fasting" (Mark 9:29).

The just Judge will say to sinners at the last judgment, "Depart from Me, you cursed, into the everlasting fire prepared for the devil and his angels" (Matt 25:41). These terrible words clearly distinguish the devil and his angels as separate individuals, different from wicked people, although both wicked angels and wicked men will share eternal punishment. The Apostle James says, "Even the devils believe—and tremble!" (Jas 2:19). Consequently, devils are endowed with reason and the power of thought.

The Apostle John testifies as follows: "He who sins is of the devil, for the devil has sinned from the beginning. For this purpose the Son of God was manifested, that He might destroy the works of the devil" (1 John 3:8). Can we admit any possibility that what he means here by the devil is not an actual existing being but something merely imagined?

The Son of God came into the world in order to destroy the devil's works. Consequently, He had to struggle with this prince of darkness. He, as a second Adam, had to gain back for mankind all that was lost by the first Adam. Because the first Adam did not withstand the temptation to which he was exposed, the second Adam was to be exposed to it also. The ancient tempter, who had formerly assumed the guise of a serpent, came to Christ in the wilderness but was resisted and put to shame by Him. Those who reject the existence of the devil and regard him as a figment of the imagination thus admit that Christ came into the world only to destroy the works of such a figment. If, then, the devil is nothing but an abstract personification of the evil principle, then Christ, too, must be admitted to have been only an impersonal idea.

Someone might ask how many fallen or evil spirits there are. Holy Scripture does not inform us of their number, but there must be very many of them, as we can gather from numerous passages (Luke 10:17, 20; Eph 6:12; and others). We read how in the country of the Gadarenes the Savior cast many spirits out of one man, their number being a legion (Luke 8:30)—a very great number indeed. The evil spirits form a kingdom of their own. Some of the teachers of the Church interpret the words of Rev 12:4, "[The dragon's] tail drew a third of the stars of heaven," to mean that the devil succeeded in drawing one third of the angels to follow him in rebellion from God. Others, however—and they are in the majority—think that "an infinite multitude of spirits subject to him were first subverted by him and followed him" (St John of Damascus), and do not specify exactly how many there are.

From St John of Damascus, *A Precise Exposition of the Orthodox Faith*, bk. 2, ch. 4; and other sources.

CHAPTER 6

~ ⋆ ~

The Fallen Angels

The evil spirits are fallen angels. God created them along with the other angels, and at first they all were pure, good, and holy, and generously endowed with many gifts, both natural and given by the grace of God. But some of the angelic spirits became darkened by pride and began to attribute their profusion of various gifts, their excellent qualities, and even the gifts of grace to themselves. They no longer considered themselves created beings. Instead, they began to think of themselves as self-sufficient, and forgot that they had been made by God. Such was the disastrous cause of their disregard of their sacred obligations to God their Creator. Among the most eminent angels, there was one whom the holy Prophet Ezekiel calls the "anointed cherub" (Ezek 28:14) and whom all the other sacred authors number among the highest of the angels. He drew his companions toward arrogance and self-deception. He himself also sank so deeply into pride that he thought himself to be God's equal and openly revolted against God (Isa 14:13–14). He became God's adversary and His desperate enemy. He and the other spirits who rejected obedience to God were cast down from heaven. They drag out their existence on earth, fill the space between heaven and earth (and are therefore called the spirits of the air, or the spirits dwelling in the air), and have also descended into hell, down into the earth. All this is attested to by Holy Scripture (Eph 6:12). The apostle calls the highest spirits who fell principalities and powers. The fallen cherub is the chief and the prince of the kingdom of darkness consisting of fallen angels. He is the beginning, the source, and the fullness of evil. He is the superior to all the other fallen angels in his abilities, and superior to them all in evil. It is natural that the spirits that were urged on by him, and of their own accord subjected their wills to him, must still borrow evil from him, and hence be subservient to him. But while God left it to the volition of the fallen angels to persist in the evil that is beloved by them, He, through His absolute might and wisdom, infinitely superior to the intelligence of the most intelligent creatures, still remains the highest and most powerful Lord of them all. They continue to exist within the confines of God's will. They are held in these confines as in chains and can do only that which God lets them.

Instead of the fallen angels, God created new intelligent creatures— men. He put them in Paradise, which was placed in the lowest heaven that was governed previously by the fallen cherub. Paradise was now under the dominion of the new creature, man. It is quite understandable that the new creature thereupon became the object of envy and hatred on the part of the fallen angel and his fallen companions. Led by their leader, the rejected spirits made the attempt to subvert the newly created human creatures and to make them their partners in the fall. The fallen angels sought to make humans share their fallen attitude toward God, and to taint them with the poison of their own enmity toward God. They succeeded in their purpose. Although man sinned because he was beguiled and deceived, he still of his own volition rejected obedience to God. Of his own volition, he consented to the demons' protests against God; of his own volition he entered into communication with the fallen spirits and began to obey them. He fell away from God and from the throng of the holy spirits, to whom he belonged by the nature not only of his soul but also of his spiritual body. After the fall his soul became like that of the fallen spirits, while his body became like that of an unreasoning animal. The crime committed by the fallen angels toward men ultimately decided the fate of the fallen angels. God's grace completely left them, and they became confirmed in their fall. They, being spirits, were now destined to persist in thoughts and feelings exclusively bodily and material! Being spirits, they were unable to rise from the earth! Being spirits, they were unable to rise to anything spiritual! Thus the fathers of the Church explain the verdict uttered by God over the fallen angel after this angel had brought eternal death upon the newly created man. "On your belly you shall go. And you shall eat dust all the days of your life" (Gen 3:14), said God to the devil. Although man had now joined the number of the fallen angels, his fall was of a totally different character and happened quite differently from the fall of the angels. The angels fell in full realization of what they were doing. They brought about evil within themselves. After they had committed one crime, they obstinately and desperately rushed toward another. Therefore they completely lost share in the good, they were quite filled with evil, and evil is now their only quality. Man, on the contrary, fell unconsciously, without premeditation, beguiled, and deceived. Thus his natural good was not destroyed but became mixed with the evil of the fallen angels. But this natural goodness, since it was mixed with evil and poisoned by evil, became useless, insufficient, and unworthy of God, Who is the entire and the purest Good. Man is most prone to doing evil while he thinks that he is doing good, for he does not see evil when it is covered by the mask of good. Man's reason and his conscience are darkened. The fallen spirits, however, do evil for evil's sake, and find a delight and a glory in doing evil.

Through His unspeakable goodness, God gave to the fallen man a Redeemer and redemption. But the redeemed man is still free: free either to make use of the redemption given him and to return to Paradise, or to reject redemption and remain numbered among the fallen angels. His entire life on earth is the time given to man to express his will. Redemption gives man his communion with God, but since man can freely express his will, he is granted the possibility of remaining in this communion or breaking it. Besides, he is not deprived of the possibility of communing with the fallen spirits—a communion into which he entered of his own volition. Thus man's condition is undecided during his entire life on earth, and all during it God's grace does not cease to assist him until the very minute when man goes over into eternity, but God's grace helps him only if he desires it. The fallen angels also do not cease to use all efforts on their part in order to keep man in communion with themselves—to keep him a captive to sin and to themselves, to eternal death and perdition. The rejected spirit has frequently assailed the holy martyrs and the blessed fathers, even while they were engaged in the greatest works of penance and performing the greatest miracles, and even before their very demise, in the very sight of the heavenly crowns that were to be theirs. The holy Church teaches us that every Christian receives from God at his baptism a holy guardian angel, who, invisibly guarding the Christian, inspires him with every kind of good deed during his life, and reminds him of God's commandments. The prince of darkness, who desires to draw the entire human race into destruction allotted to himself, also appoints one of the wicked spirits to attend man, and this spirit follows his man everywhere and tries to draw him into every kind of sin.

Since the fallen angel is destined to existence on earth, he uses all his efforts to make man also confine himself to earth. Self-deception always lurks in man, and he is therefore prone to obey this prompting to attach himself to earth. Man feels that he is eternal, but since this feeling is corrupted by his deceptive reason and by his corrupted and false conscience, he tends to think of his life on earth as something that will go on for ever. On the basis of his beguiling, false, and destructive feelings, man devotes himself exclusively to cares and labors devoted to establishing himself on earth. He forgets that he is but a passing pilgrim here, and that his enduring abode will be either heaven or hell. If he misuses for temporal gains the time given to him for repentance and for gaining a blessed eternity, he will be unable to get another span of time for a second chance. His loss will be irretrievable, and he will weep for it eternally and fruitlessly in hell. If during his earthly pilgrimage man will not dissociate himself from evil spirits, he will continue in his association with them after death and will continue belonging to them in greater or lesser degree, depending on his closeness to them during his life. Failure to dissociate oneself from the fallen spirits subjects man to eternal perdition. If he dissociates himself from them incompletely, he subjects himself to hard trials on his way to heaven.

Look, my brethren, look what the devil has accomplished, accomplishes now, and will yet accomplish while he brings man's mind down from the spiritual heaven to the material earth and chains man's heart to earthly occupations and to the earth itself. Look, and grow afraid with a healthy fear. Look, and beware; cultivate a necessary and soul-saving care! The fallen spirit has captivated some men by the acquisition of various expensive and rare things, and has attached their thoughts to this pursuit and alienated them from God. Others he has occupied with the study of various sciences and arts, all of them fit for earth only. Having attached all their attention to passing knowledge, the devil deprived them of the vitally necessary knowledge of God. Still others he has busied with the acquisition of wealth, lands, and houses; the cultivation of gardens, fields, and meadows; the keeping of cattle; and among these occupations they, too, forget God. Some others he has persuaded to attach an exaggerated importance to the material aspect of church ritual, while the spiritual importance of such ritual becomes obscured. Having thus taken away from these unfortunates the very essence of Christianity, he has left to them only its distorted material envelope. He has drawn them away from the Church into a false and most foolish error, schism.

The fallen spirit finds this kind of warfare so convenient that he uses it everywhere. This kind of warfare is so convenient for the devil's purposes and for man's destruction that in the last days of the world the devil will use it in order to draw the entire world completely away from God. Indeed, the devil will use this kind of warfare with astonishing success. In the last days of the world, men, through the influence of the prince of this world, will be overpowered by their attachment to the earth and to all things material and bodily. They will give themselves to cares of this earth and to material progress. They will busy themselves with improving and taking care of this earth as if it were to be their eternal abode. Having become materialistic and thoughtful of their flesh only, they will forget eternity, as if it did not exist. They will forget God and abandon Him. The Lord has foretold these days: "And as it was in the days of Noah, so it will be also in the days of the Son of Man. They ate, they drank, they married wives, they were given in marriage, until the day that Noah entered the ark, and the flood came and destroyed them all. Likewise as it was also in the days of Lot: They ate, they drank, they bought, they sold, they planted, they built; but on the day that Lot went out of Sodom it rained fire and brimstone from heaven and destroyed them all. Even so will it be in the day when the Son of Man is revealed" (Luke 17:26–30).

He who has a vivid faith in God and gives himself to God while he rejects his own self—such a man endures undisturbed in the midst of all the temptations raised against him by the spirits of evil. He sees in these spirits only the blind instruments of God's providence. He gives them no attention and hands himself over to God when he is assailed by temptations that issue from the evil spirits. Devotion to God's will is the peaceful and restful haven in all temptations and sorrows, while reliance on one's own powers is destructive.

Even the most experienced monk who has spent a hundred years exercising all the virtues of a monk is not sufficiently experienced compared to a fallen angel, whose experience in his struggle against the servants of God has been perfected over thousands of years. How, then, can an inexperienced beginner succeed in his struggle against such an angel? A beginner does not even have knowledge based on experience about the existence of the fallen angels. A struggle against the devil in which one counts on one's own resources will inevitably lead to defeat. Our ancestor Eve, although she was pure and holy, was affected by the serpent's evil and cunning. Immediately after she entered into conversation with him she transgressed God's commandment and fell. All the fathers of the Church agree that a novice must reject all thought of sin and every kind of daydreaming at the very beginning and must neither enter into debate against sinful thoughts nor entertain them for any other reason, however good the reason may seem. All sinful thoughts are to be rejected immediately as they occur. The ancient monks regarded it absolutely necessary to confess all their thoughts to their spiritual father and to abide by his advice. In no other way, they said, is it possible to be saved, for the instructions of his spiritual father constantly lead the novice along the way of the commandments contained in the Gospel, while nothing separates him better from sin and the devil, the originator of sin, than does the constant and intensive confession of sins at their very beginning. Those monks who for some reason had no spiritual father, and were unable to counteract sin by a constant and frequent recourse to confession of their sinful thoughts, still counteracted the devil by constant and intense prayer. Such was St Mary of Egypt, who dwelt alone in the desert.

If you take recourse to prayer, then you must do this decisively, without waiting to entertain a sinful thought for even the shortest while for any reason whatsoever. Much less are you to seek delight in such thoughts. As soon as you feel the approach of your enemy, begin your prayers, kneel, raise your arms to heaven, or else prostrate on the ground. Attack your enemy by casting a lightning bolt in his face, and he will be unable to resist you and will become accustomed to immediate flight as soon as you face him.

True Christianity is martyrdom. A Christian's life is a chain of struggles and sufferings that constantly follow one another. The victor is given life eternal and is wedded to the Holy Spirit. He whom God desires to enrich with spiritual intelligence and with gifts of the spirit is granted great struggles. Scripture says, "He who overcomes shall inherit all things, and I will be his God, and he shall be My son" (Rev 21:7). Thus let us not be disheartened.

From the *Works of Bishop Ignatius Brianchaninov*, in Russian, vol. 5, (St Petersburg, 1905).

CHAPTER 7

St Anthony's Struggles Against Devils

The holy hermit St Anthony the Great was born in Egypt. His parents were of noble descent and well known for their Christian piety. They brought up their son in such a way that he should know no one except them and no place except his own home. While Anthony was growing up, he felt no urgency to get an education or to draw close to other boys. He stayed home, kept his heart pure, and applied himself to perfecting his observance of the demands of Christianity.

St Anthony's parents died when he was about twenty years old. He was left alone with his sister, who was still a child. At first he took care of his property and of his sister's upbringing, but soon something else attracted his attention.

Near Anthony's village there lived an old man who from his youth had devoted himself in solitude to the attainment of the virtues toward which a monk strives. After he had met him and greatly benefited in his spiritual well-being by this meeting, Anthony began to imitate this old man and to seek solitude in various spots near his village. He entrusted his sister to some unmarried women known to him for their faithful service to Christ, and he himself gained a livelihood by selling some products of his handiwork. Even so, most of the bread he bought he gave to the hungry, and he himself ate very little. His soul was in constant prayerful communion with God, for he knew that Scripture teaches us to pray constantly. Although he did not know how to read, he always listened to the Holy Scriptures read in church, and did this with so deep an attention that he never forgot any of them. Thus he also trained himself to keep most diligently all the commandments of the Lord, his memory serving to remind him of the Holy Scriptures he had heard. Such was Anthony's life, for which he was loved by all the brethren to whom he might come; for he frequently visited his neighbors and the monks of that vicinity in order to learn virtue from them. They saw the life Anthony was leading and called him a man devoted to God. Some of them loved him like a son, while others loved him like a brother.

In the midst of Anthony's ever increasing success in the pursuit of the good, the enemy of the very name of Christian, the devil, felt unable to look on so very virtuous a youth. Armed with all his ancient craftiness, he rose against Anthony and began an attempt to make him sway from his good intentions and slip from the straight path. The devil reminded him of his property, which he had sold in order to give away the money; he made him think that he had not provided for his sister, and that he came of a great family; he suggested to him thoughts of the vain glory of this world, of the pleasures that one can get from various kinds of food, and other delights of life in the world. Anthony firmly withstood the devil. The devil sent upon him impure imaginings, but Anthony dispersed them by ceaseless prayer. The devil sought to delight his senses by natural instincts and to irritate him by lust, but the youth guarded his body by faith, vigilance, and fasting. The devil assumed the appearance of a lovely woman, came to Anthony at night, and tried in every way to awaken passion in Anthony's heart, but Anthony put out passion by the thought of the fire of hell which never goes out, and the never-dying worm that dwells in hell. The devil pressed young Anthony to tread the slippery path close to falling, but he reminded himself of the eternal torments that will follow the last judgment and preserved his spiritual purity in the midst of temptation.

The wicked serpent finally became convinced that he was powerless to overcome Anthony by crafty temptations of this sort. Seeing himself constantly rejected, he gnashed his teeth and felt defeated. After some time, he came to Anthony in the guise of a horrible black boy who was weeping and saying in words of human speech: "I have brought many into temptation and have charmed many, but you, like other saints, have now overcome me by your high attainments."

Actually, the crafty tempter was saying this hoping to make the humble youth proud of himself. "Who are you, and why are you saying this?" St Anthony asked.

"I am the tempter who tempts to fornication," the devil replied. "Through many devices of all kinds I try to incline all young men to this sin. Thus I am called the spirit of fornication. How very many are the people who vowed to be chaste, yet were urged by me to sins of this sort! How many are those who embraced continence yet were turned by me back to their former impure life! I am he for whose sake the Prophet Hosea reproaches the fallen when he says, 'the spirit of harlotry has caused them to stray' (Hos 4:12). Indeed, I caused them to stray. I have frequently tempted you, too, but every time you drove me away."

When Anthony heard this, he thanked the Lord and then addressed the fiend with fearlessness even greater than before: "In many of your attempts you have been put to shame, in many you have been disgraced. Your blackness and the boyish form which you have assumed are but signs of your powerlessness. Now I am no longer afraid of you: 'The Lord is my helper, and I shall look down upon mine enemies'" (Ps 117:7).

The apparition disappeared immediately after these words of Anthony's. Such was the first victory won by Anthony over the devil. It was gained with the help of the strength given through the grace of Christ. Anthony remembered the precautions contained in the Scripture concerning the multitude of deceptions exercised by the devil, and thus he relentlessly continued exercising himself in difficult tasks of a monk's life. Every day he fasted until sunset and spent entire nights in prayer. Sometimes he took food only every second day and allowed himself to sleep only every fourth night. Bread and salt formed his food. He drank little, and that little was water. He slept on burlap or on his hair shirt, and occasionally on the bare ground. He never used any oil with his food, not to mention meat or wine, for these are not consumed even by less diligent monks.

He decided that every hermit should follow the great Prophet Elijah as his example, and to form his own life to this example, he studied it like a mirror. In his attempts to imitate Elijah, Anthony went to the tombs situated not far from the village and took his abode there. First, however, he asked a man he knew to bring him food on appointed days. This man locked Anthony in one of the tombs, and there the holy man devoted himself to silence. When the devil saw this, he grew afraid that Anthony might in due time arm himself completely against any temptation. The devil gathered his demonic companions and—for God in His wisdom did not prevent them—they subjected Anthony to so severe a beating that the holy man lay for a long time motionless and mute. He later told about this experience, and said that his suffering transcended anything that man can endure. However, through the mercy of the Lord God, Who never leaves those who trust in Him, Anthony did not die. A few days later, the man who was supposed to bring him food came to Anthony. When he opened the door and saw the hermit lying on the ground as if dead, he lifted him and brought him into the village.

The rumor spread, and his neighbors and relations came to Anthony. Filled with great sorrow, they began the burial service for him, for they thought he was dead. But at midnight, when they all sank into a deep sleep because they were very tired, Anthony began little by little to come to his senses. He sighed, lifted his head, and saw that only one man was awake: the one who had brought him to the village. Anthony asked him to come near and then begged him not to wake anyone but to carry him back to his former place. The man did as he was told, and Anthony continued to live in solitude. Since his wounds left him no strength to stand, he continued praying while he was lying on his face. After his prayer, he exclaimed in a loud voice: "Devils! Here I am, I myself, Anthony. I do not avoid struggles with you. Know that if you do anything else, even if it be more terrible than what you have already done, still nothing can separate me from my love for Christ." And the holy man sang, "Though a legion were laid against me, yet shall not my heart be afraid" (Ps 26:3).

Then the devil, he who hates good, marveled at Anthony's audacity and at his return after so severe a beating. He called together his subservient devils and told them in his rage, "You see how we have been unable to overcome him either by the spirit of fornication or by bodily wounds. Having experienced both these assaults, he even more bravely derides us. Now arm yourselves, each of you, for an even more relentless and forceful struggle with him. He must be made to feel whom he has provoked."

All at once, the whole multitude of devils came into mad commotion. The devil has many ways of struggling against mankind. Suddenly there was a great clap of thunder, so that the place where Anthony was dwelling shook to its very foundation, and the walls fell apart. An enormous crowd of demons burst into Anthony's dwelling and filled it. They bore the appearance of lions, wolves, asps, snakes, scorpions, lynxes, and bears, and each of these apparitions manifested its ferocity in a manner peculiar to the animal which it represented: a lion was roaring, as if about to swallow Anthony; a buffalo terrified him by its bellowing and by shaking its horns, a snake twisted hissing; wolves were bounding toward him; and a lynx was getting ready to jump. All these apparitions were exceedingly horrible in their outer appearance, and the noise produced by their roaring was even more terrifying. Anthony was first astounded by what he saw, and then he was tormented; but he did not become afraid, and his mind stayed alert and clear. Although he suffered pain from his bodily wounds, he endured unmoved in spirit. He appeared to deride his enemies as he said, "If you had any amount of strength, even one of you would be enough to struggle against me. But the Lord has taken away your strength, and therefore you are trying to frighten me by sheer numbers. Even your coming in the shape of senseless beasts is an evident sign of your weakness."

After some time he manfully continued: "If God has permitted you to have strength to attack and swallow me, here I am. Why do you hesitate? But if you do not have such power over me, why do you toil in vain? The sign of the cross and my faith in God are an unpassable wall surrounding me, which you cannot cross."

After many attempts and vain efforts to terrify the saint, the demons were only gnashing their teeth and had accomplished nothing. On the contrary, they themselves were overcome and put to shame by him.

The merciful Lord Jesus, Who protected His servant, did not leave him during this hard struggle against the demons. As Anthony raised his eyes, he saw the roof of the tomb open and a bright beam descend to him through the darkness. At the approach of this beam, not a single demon remained, Anthony's wounds instantly stopped hurting, and the tomb, which had fallen apart at the approach of the demons, once again became intact. The saint understood that the Lord had visited him. He sighed from the depths of his heart and then, turning his face toward the light that was shining on him, he exclaimed, "Where are You, merciful Jesus? Where are You? Why did You not come at the very first to heal my wounds?"

Then he heard a voice: "Anthony! I am here but I waited to see your manliness. Now that you have endured the struggle so firmly, I shall always help you and shall make you famous throughout the world." When Anthony heard this, he got up and felt so strong that he seemed to have gained more strength than he had lost. At that time, St Anthony was thirty-five years old.

After this, Anthony went to the old man whose guidance he had sought at the very beginning of his life as a hermit. He begged the old man to join him in settling at some remote and unvisited spot in the desert. The old man refused, both because he was very aged and because the kind of life which Anthony proposed was not customary among monks of that time. Anthony then fearlessly went alone on a far journey to a mountain in the desert, which was located in a region unknown to monks. There he lived for twenty years, and gradually his reputation began to spread.

Many people wished to see Anthony and came to him in order to derive some spiritual good from him. When they approached the door of his dwelling, they often heard the voices of various impure spirits shouting to Anthony: "Why did you come into our domains? What concern do you have with this desert? Go away from the realms that belong to others! You are not strong enough to live here and endure our attacks!"

Thus St Anthony struggled against the devils for twenty more years
so far from mankind. Eventually the time came for him to toil not only
for his own salvation but also for the good of others. He continued refus-
ing to see visitors, but once there came so many who wished to follow his
life as an example that they broke down his door by force. They then saw
that his face was bright and his body was healthy. They were amazed that
even after such fasting as his and after such hardships and such struggles
against the devils, he had not changed either in face or in body. From
this time on, the holy man became a teacher, a pastor, and a instructor to
others. He told those who came how they should exert themselves in self-
imposed hardships and became their leader to heaven. God helped him so
much that in due time Anthony gained numberless disciples, all of whom
he had convinced to give up the world and reject their own self. Within
the period of only a few years, there were formed all around numerous
monasteries. He lovingly guided both the old and the young monks who
lived there: those who were old in years and in experience, those who were
young in years or had recently come. Once when the monks gathered to
ask him for advice on forming rules for their monasteries, Anthony spoke
as follows:

> Those who seek wisdom cross the sea and question foreign teachers about
> inane knowledge. We need not go abroad or cross the sea in order to learn
> the most important thing that we must know in order to attain to the king-
> dom of heaven, for our Lord Jesus Christ Himself has said in His gospel:
> "The kingdom of God is within you" (Luke 17:21). All we need to reach
> this kingdom is our good will.

Anthony also taught them how to resist the demons: "God Himself has
directed us to pay constant attention to what happens in our souls, for we
have enemies very crafty in their struggle against us. These are the demons
against whom, according to the words of the apostle (Eph 6:11–12), we must
struggle unceasingly. An infinite number of them flit through the air, and
whole armies of the enemy surround us from all sides. I would not be able
to inform you of the distinctions and differences among them, but I shall
tell you briefly about those ways, familiar to me, in which they attempt to
beguile us. First of all, we must apply all our powers to remembering that
God is not the cause of evil, and that the demons became evil not because He
wished them to be so. Their change occurred in no natural way; it depended
on their own volition. Created by the good God, they at first were good

spirits, but because of their insolence and arrogance they were cast down from heaven to earth. There they lay in their own wickedness and also taught people to believe in false imaginings and to worship idols. They harbor a limitless envy for us Christians. Perpetually they set in motion against us all sorts of evil, for they are afraid that we shall inherit their former glory in heaven. They themselves have sunk into evil in different degrees: some of them have fallen to the very bottom of the abyss of wickedness, while others seem less harmful, but they all, each according to their capacity, fight any kind of virtue by any possible means. This is the reason why we need diligent prayers and works of penance, for God gives man in return for such efforts the gift of reasoning and understanding the differences among the evil spirits, so that man will recognize in every particular instance the craftiness and guile exercised against him. But no matter what kind of guile is used against us, the weapon that will overcome it is always the same: the cross of our Lord.

"I have experienced many insidious beguilements on the part of demons. I am now telling you about these as if you were my children. Having been warned, you should be able to keep safe in the midst of temptations similar to mine. The devils are fierce against all Christians, but especially against monks and against virgins who have devoted themselves to Christ. The devils set traps everywhere for such people and try hard to debauch their hearts by impure thoughts, contrary to God's will. Let, however, none of you fear them because of their wickedness, for the devils can be instantly routed by ardent prayers to God and by fasting. Nevertheless, even if they should pause for a while in their attacks, do not think that you have overcome them completely: after a defeat, the devils usually renew their attacks with an even greater force. They cunningly change their method of attack. If they cannot beguile a man by thoughts, they try to beguile or to frighten him by apparitions. They assume the form of a woman or of a scorpion; or else they may turn into some giant as tall as a temple, or into whole armies of warriors or some other kind of ghosts, which all disappear as soon as the man makes the sign of the cross.

"The virtuous life of the righteous also frightens devils. A pure life and an unblemished faith in God have great power against them. Believe my experience: Satan fears the vigilance of those who live according to God's will. He fears their prayers and fasting, their humility, their voluntary poverty, their modesty, meekness, love, continence, and most of all, their wholehearted love of Christ. The serpent, he who is arrogant beyond all others, knows well that he is destined to be trod upon by the feet of the righteous, according to God's word: 'Behold, I give you the authority to trample on serpents and scorpions, and over all the power of the enemy' (Luke 10:19).

"Many a time the devils have attacked me in the guise of armed warriors; or else, looking like scorpions, horses, beasts, and snakes of all sorts, they filled my dwelling and surrounded me. But they ran away when I began singing: 'Some put their trust in chariots, and some in horses, but we will call upon the Name of the Lord our God' (Ps 19:8). God's grace helped me and dispelled them.

"At one time, they came to me looking very bright and began saying, 'Anthony, we have come to shed light on you.' But I kept my eyes closely shut in order not to see this devilish light, while in my soul I prayed to God, and their ungodly light went out. After a short while they came again and began singing before me and arguing among themselves about the Scriptures, but I was like one deaf and did not listen to them. It sometimes happened that they shook the ground under my feet, but I continued unflinchingly to pray to God. Often I heard shouting, ringing, and the noise of dancing around me, but once I would begin singing, their shouts would turn into tearful groans. I then gave praise to the Lord, Who had destroyed their power and put an end to their madness.

"Believe me, my children: I once saw the devil in the shape of an enormous giant who dared to say about himself: 'I am God's power and wisdom,' and addressed me in these words: 'Anthony, ask me for whatever you please. I shall grant your request.'

"Instead of a response, I spat into his mouth, and then, arming myself with the name of Christ, I rushed at him. This seeming giant instantly melted and disappeared in my hands.

"Another time, while I was fasting, he came to me again. He looked like a monk. He had some bread and tried to convince me to eat. 'You are a man,' he said, 'and thus not free from human weakness. Make some allowance for your flesh, or else you may fall ill.' But I understood that this was one of the crafty serpent's insidious beguilements. I fell on my usual weapon, the sign of Christ's cross, and he immediately turned into a wisp of smoke which disappeared through the window.

"Often the devils attempted to beguile me by the phantom of gold that would suddenly appear in the desert. They expected to captivate me either by the sight of gold or else by the touch of it. On many other occasions the devils would fall to beating me. But I patiently endured the blows and would only exclaim: 'No one can separate me from the love of Christ!' These words inspired them to ferocity and they would turn against each other. Finally they always fled, not because of my bidding, but because Christ Himself drove them away, for Christ has said, 'I saw Satan fall like lightning from heaven' (Luke 10:18).

"Once a demon knocked on my door. As I came out I saw before me an enormous giant whose head seemed to reach the skies. When I asked him who he was, he said, 'I am Satan.' I asked him, 'What do you want?' He replied, 'In vain do all the monks accuse me. Why am I cursed by the Christians?'

" 'They do well to curse you,' I replied, 'for they frequently are beguiled by you.'

" 'I never do them harm,' he replied. 'They themselves upset one another. I have been cursed and cast down from heaven. Did you not hear that the Scripture says, O thou enemy, destructions are come to a perpetual end, and thou hast destroyed cities (Ps 9:7)? And indeed, I no longer have any resting place for myself in the world. All the nations in all countries confess the name of Christ, the deserts are filled with monks. Let them look to themselves instead of cursing me.'

"Amazed at God's grace, I replied, 'This is a strange and unheard-of confession for you to make. I ascribe it not to truthfulness, of which you have none, but to God's power alone. You are the father of falsehood, yet you have been forced to confess to what actually is true. Against your will, you have this time told the truth, for Christ by His coming has laid low your power. You have been deprived of your angelic glory and now drag out a miserable and disgraceful life in all your impurity.' And as soon as I said these words, the demon disappeared."

Thus the holy man was persuading his brethren not to be afraid of the power of the devils—for their power has been tamed and defeated by Christ—but to struggle against them and to fortify their hearts with faith in Christ. The brethren listened joyfully and retained the teachings of their father.

From the "Life of St Anthony the Great," in *Lives of the Saints* for January 17.

CHAPTER 8

What Is Death?

Holy Scripture gives us an exact definition of death: "Then the dust will return to the earth as it was. And the spirit will return to God who gave it" (Eccl 12:7). These words mean that death is a separation of the soul from the body. We call a man dead when his soul has left his body. The body alone, without the soul, is not a complete man. It is but a carcass and cannot be considered a man. Similarly, a soul without a body is only a spirit but not a complete man.

Taken by itself, man's body is dead. Without its soul it incurs dissolution, disintegrates and utterly loses its former life and activity. Holy Scripture gives the name "shadow of death" (Ps 22:4) to the interval between the time when the soul and the body have parted and the time of Christ's second coming to the earth.

The death of our bodies is something like a natural sleep which lasts for a while only and facilitates a renewal of our spiritual and bodily strength. Death is like the sowing of seed in the ground. The seed must disintegrate in order to nurture within itself the root of a new life and to produce out of itself a green plant with all its flowers and fruit—and that for all eternity.

Death is man's destiny, an inescapable destiny. The King and Prophet David says, "What man is he that liveth, and shall not see death?" (Ps 88:49) The holy Apostle Paul teaches us the same truth when he says, "And as it is appointed for men to die once, but after this the judgment" (Heb 9:27).

From Holy Scripture we know that our forebears, Adam and Eve, from whom the entire human race has descended, were created immortal: "So God created man in His own image; in the image of God He created him; male and female He created them" (Gen 1:27); and further the book of Genesis states that God "breathed into his nostrils the breath of life; and man became a living being" (Gen 2:7).

Why then and when did death appear? Holy Scripture reveals that it is the result of sin: "through one man sin entered the world, and death through sin" (Rom 5:12), says the Apostle Paul. Death received its name from God Himself before it even appeared; for the Lord God, in His commandment to Adam and Eve not to taste the fruit of the tree of knowledge, said that "in the day that you eat of it you shall surely die" (Gen 2:17).

From the *Trinity Leaflets*, vol. 2, in Russian (reprinted by the Holy Trinity Monastery, Jordanville, N.Y., 1956).

CHAPTER 9

What Is the Soul, and What Is Its Origin?

His Grace, the Bishop Macarius, in his *Orthodox Dogmatic Theology*, sets forth the Orthodox teachings on the origin of every man and, specifically, the origin of every soul in the following way.

"Even though all men are, by way of natural birth, the descendants of their forefathers Adam and Eve, still God Himself is the Creator not only of the original couple but of every man in particular. The only difference is that He created Adam and Eve out of nothing, through no intervening medium; whereas all their descendants are created through the medium of their parents, by the force of God's blessing, which He granted to our forefathers immediately upon creating them when He said, "Be fruitful and multiply; fill the earth and subdue it" (Gen. 1:28). These words, like any of the words of the Almighty, once having been said do not lose their force until the end of all ages.

"The Holy Church, trusting in divine Scripture, teaches that the soul is formed together with the body. However, it does not receive its being together with the seed from which the body is formed. It is God's will that the soul should appear in the body only when this body has come into being, and simultaneously with the body.

"How shall we understand this creation of individual souls? According to the teaching of the Church, although human souls are individually created, this creation takes place in such a way that they take over from their parents the scourge of the original sin; this, however, would be impossible if God created souls from nothing. Consequently, the newly formed souls are derived from the souls of their parents. Someone might object that such a creation of new souls from parent souls is utterly unintelligible to us, since the human soul is a whole and cannot be visualized as multiplying itself. Indeed, unintelligible it is. But, on the other hand, is it not equally unintelligible how God, Who is the purest Spirit, should be able to give birth from

54

His Being to His Son, and also should be able to give forth the Holy Spirit? Still, divine revelation tells us that God, indeed, eternally gives birth to His Son from His very Being, and eternally gives forth the Holy Spirit, although at the same time God is in no way divided. Thus even the ancient teachers of the Church kept repeating that the mystery of the creation of our souls is comprehensible to God alone."

From E. Tihomirov.

CHAPTER 10

How Significant for Our Lives Is Belief in Immortality?

The immortality of the human soul is not only an abstract and theoretical truth, nor is it only a mystical idea with no relevance to practical situations. Quite the contrary. It is most important whether we acknowledge this most vital truth or choose not to. The consequences of our belief or lack of it are very far-reaching. We have the full right and cause to say that man's entire life, both private and public, is basically and most deeply founded on his faith in the immortality of his soul. As a famous author has remarked, "Without a supreme idea, neither an individual nor a nation can exist. And the supreme idea on earth is but one: namely the idea of the immortality of the human soul, for the rest of the so-called supreme ideas by which alone man can live, flow out of this one idea" (F. M. Dostoevsky). Therefore, faith in immortality is the inseparable companion of every man and every nation as long as they live. This idea alone gives direction and goal to man's whole life. According to the statement of another outstanding thinker, "Immortality, while it promises an eternal life, ties man all the more closely to earth. This seems a paradox: if there is so much of life, that is, if there is not only life on earth but also life immortal, why should we much value life on earth? But the contrary is true, for man comprehends his goal on earth only when he acquires faith in his immortality."

Belief in immortality gives expression to the normal, healthy condition of human nature. It forms the foundation of man's consciously moral life, for such a life needs this belief as its first and most important premise. The entire social structure of the human race is upheld by this belief, which unites people for the sake of their common supreme interests, for the sake of their common supreme destiny, a destiny that does not end with this earthly life. The mortal son of earth must become an eternal denizen of heaven. If he always keeps this great purpose in mind and does not swerve from it, he accordingly plans and puts in order the first preparatory stage of his existence—his earthly life.

If, however, he forgets eternity, he walks in the darkness and does not know where he is going (John 12:35), because his road is not illumined by the light of a belief in immortality. He is on a false road which leads him to a false end.

From E. Tihomirov.

Part II

TEACHING ON THE AFTERLIFE, HEAVEN, AND HELL

CHAPTER 11

❦

Proofs of Immortality

Since the question of the immortality of his soul is most interesting and important for man, it is natural to expect that this question will not only attract his heart but also occupy his intelligence; that is, that it will be an object not only of his religious conviction or faith but also of his theoretical, or philosophic, investigation. And so it is. From time immemorial, man has attempted to penetrate the mysterious realm of life beyond the tomb, and in one way or another has tried to solve the great question of his ultimate fate. After all that has been said in various ages both for and against a belief in immortality, it cannot be denied that immortality has so great a "cloud of witnesses" and proofs that only a blindly prejudiced man who holds to a shallow faith in poorly understood science can consider immortality to be still another of human superstitions and unfulfillable dreams.

What is man's soul? The soul is a unity, a simple and immaterial substance, a self-governing and independently acting being that is conscious of its own identity. In short, the soul is an indivisible spiritual unit, a spiritual atom, so to speak. From this concept of the human soul, there necessarily follows the impossibility of its destruction. And if it cannot be destroyed, it is immortal.

Man is a being in whom the infinite has united with a finite body. This being, born in time, must by its very nature continue into eternity. When man enters his new life there, he keeps all the thoughts, longings, and affections gained here on earth. In eternity, he is no longer confined by bodily limitations and enters into most close relationship with that eternal, extrasensory, moral world of which by his nature he is a member; and with that supreme intelligence from which his soul has received its being.

When we read Moses' account of the creation of man, we see in it some very important details. At first God made man from earth, and then he blew the breath of life into man. Thereupon man became a living being (Gen 2:7).

If we think about these details, we see that man consists of two different parts: a material body made from the soil, and an immaterial soul created by God's breath.

Thus we undoubtedly possess immortal souls, and our future life beyond the grave is not to be doubted. However, our immortality has God as its only basis. He alone possesses immortality in and of Himself and dwells in unapproachable light (1 Tim 6:16). All the other creatures endowed with reason—angels, archangels, all the powers of heaven, and all men both righteous and sinful—receive immortality through the will and grace of Jesus Christ, our Savior, Who says, "I am the resurrection and the life. He who believes in Me, though he may die, he shall live. And whoever lives and believes in Me shall never die" (John 11:25–26).

From S. S-ki, *Future Life Beyond the Grave*, in Russian, Moscow, 1892.

CHAPTER 12

The Particular Judgment

The holy Apostle Paul clearly and definitely teaches about the judgment which every man incurs immediately upon his death. He says, "As it is appointed for men to die once, but after this the judgment" (Heb 9:27). The words of the apostle apparently do not admit any lapse of time between death and the judgment; consequently, it is a particular, individual judgment that he has in mind, rather than the general judgment at the second coming of Christ.

This particular judgment of God over the souls that have left their bodies follows upon the trials of these souls. The Orthodox Church teaches that, during such trials, the departed souls rise from earth through the great expanse of the air, or sky, and that, while angels accompany them, the evil spirits detain them and accuse them of all the sins which they have committed during their lives (*Dogmatic Theology* of Bishop Anthony, in Russian, 8th ed., 1862, p. 244, par. 341).

For the purpose of this judgment, divine justice uses angels, both the holy and the evil ones. The good angels note all the good deeds of a man while he is alive; the others note all his sins. When a soul begins to rise to heaven, the holy angels lead it, while the dark spirits accuse it of those sins which have not been atoned for by proper penitence. Through these sins the evil spirits seek to make the soul a victim of Satan, for sins are marks of the soul's communion with evil and of its eternal fate, common to both evil angels and evil human souls.

The powers of darkness have established particular seats of judgment and particular watches, and through these the souls pass and are tried during their rise through the air. Throughout the space between earth and heaven there watchfully stand contingents of the fallen spirits. Each contingent has under its surveillance a particular kind of sins, and tries the soul when it reaches that stage. In the writings of the fathers of the Church, the watches of demons in the air and their seats of judgment are called "trials," and the spirits that serve there are the "triers."

Our Lord Jesus Christ, Who, while remaining unseen, judges human souls through His angels, also allows the "accuser of our brethren" (Rev 12:10) to have access to the souls so that all deeds of each soul should be evaluated without prejudice. St Basil the Great says, "It is right that the judgment of God should not be forcible but should resemble those procedures which men have among themselves: namely, that the accused should be able to defend himself, and that a man who sees his state of affairs made clear should, even when he is found guilty and punished, confirm the unalterable judgment of God and acknowledge the fairness of his own punishment. If, however, he should be forgiven, he should see that he has been granted mercy according to the law, and that due order has been kept" (*Commentary on Isaiah*, ch. 1).

CHAPTER 13

Church Teaching on the
Trials of the Departed

St Athanasius of Alexandria was the first man to teach about the trials incurred by the departed as they rise through the air immediately after their death. This he did in his famous *Life of St Anthony the Great*, a work that was written around A.D. 365, was translated into Latin very soon after (around 365–370), and enjoyed great respect throughout the Christian world, both in the East and in the West.

Another great teacher of the Church, St Cyril the Bishop of Alexandria, also wrote about these trials. His discourse on this subject usually appears in one of the essential books of our Church, the *Graded Psalter*. We draw on it here.

"When our soul will part from our body," writes St Cyril, "the hosts and powers of heaven will appear at one side of it, while from the other side there will approach the forces of darkness, the evil rulers of this world, the toll keepers of the air who torment the soul and make known all our deeds.... At their sight, the soul will be disgusted, will tremble and shake, and in its confusion and terror will look for protection to the angels of God. But when the angels will cover it and take it up, it will meet with various trials during its rise through the expanse of air. These trials are like custom-houses or tollgates, where travelers are stopped and required to pay fees. The soul will likewise be stopped on its journey to the kingdom of heaven. The evil spirits will bar its way and attempt to keep it from further progress.

"At each of these stops, particular kinds of sins will be taken up. The first torment is that of sins committed through the mouth and with the tongue ... the second deals with the sins of vision ... the third, of hearing ... the fourth, of smell ... the fifth, of all the wicked and despicable deeds committed by means of the hands. Among the other stations of trial are those which search the soul for its other transgressions, such as anger, hate, envy, vanity, and pride.... In short, every passion of the soul, every sin, will have its tormentors and reminders. The holy powers will also be present, not only the evil and impure spirits. While the latter will denounce the sins of each soul—including the sins of speech, action, thought, and intention—the good spirits will bring up the virtues of that soul. The soul, meanwhile, during its stay in their midst will be in great fear and trembling, and its thoughts will be confused until it will be condemned and chained for its deeds, words, and thoughts; or, if it is found worthy, will be justified and made free. The chains spoken of here are the chains which the soul has made for itself with its own sins.

"If the soul is found worthy of salvation because it has led a pious and righteous life, the angels will take it and conduct it to the kingdom of heaven. It will no longer fear anything but rise joyfully, accompanied by the holy powers.... On the other hand, if it should be discovered that the soul has spent its life in sloth and incontinence, it will hear the awful voice: '[He] will not behold the majesty of the Lord' (Isa 26:10). The angels of God will leave the soul, and frightening demons will take it ... bound by indissoluble ties, the soul will be thrown into the land of darkness, the abyss, the infernal prisons, the confinement of hell.

"For the soul, this will be the beginning of days of sorrow and close imprisonment, days of annihilation without end, days of murky darkness. After the disappearance of God's angels, the horrible demons will take the soul and, torturing it pitilessly, will draw it down to the earth. The earth will open and the soul, bound by indissoluble bonds, will fall into the land of darkness and murkiness, those infernal abysmal prisons where the souls of all sinners that ever existed are in safekeeping. In the words of Job, this place is 'a land as dark as darkness itself, as the shadow of death, without any order, where even the light is like darkness' (Job 10:22). Indeed, those are the realms of perpetual illness, unending sorrow, ceaseless weeping, uninterrupted gnashing of teeth, and eternal groaning. Evermore will there sound the cry 'Alas!'; always will there be heard 'Woe!' Everyone will shout but no help will come; everyone will call, but there will come no savior.

"It is impossible to set forth the extreme wretchedness of the sinners; impossible in human terms to express all the sicknesses which will be inflicted upon the souls in the infernal regions. No man can give utterance to the fear and trembling that will be there. Human speech is insufficient to describe the misery of the sinners. Forever they will groan ceaselessly but no one will take mercy upon them; they will call from the abyss but no one will hear them.

"Where then will be the glory of this world, its vanity, its food and other enjoyments, its satisfactions and satiety, its dreams and plans, its peace, its rest, its loveliness, its manliness, the beauty of its women (both deceptive and destructive), its brazen shamelessness, its lovely clothes, its impure and base sweetness of sin? Where then will be those who are captivated by the disgusting sodomic passion, those who anoint and perfume themselves and burn incense around themselves, those who feast to the sound of tympani and strings?

"Where will disappear the arrogance of those who used to live without fear? Where will be love of money and of other possessions and the hard-heartedness that comes of this greed? Where will be inhuman pride which despises everyone and demands that it alone be honored? Where will be the empty and vain human glory? Where will be impurity and insatiable lust? Where will be greatness and lordliness? Where will be kings and princes, elders and lords, those who are proud of their great riches, and those who take no pity of beggars, and those who despise God? Where will be theatres, spectacles, and other entertainments? Where will be the blasphemers, those who inanely provoke laughter, those who laugh at others, those who live on without a care? Where will be soft clothes and soft beds? Where will be tall buildings and wide gates? Where will be those who all their lives never feared anything?

"When all these men will see themselves devoid of everything, they will grow afraid; having grown afraid, they will cry out; in their confusion, they will be moved; they will tremble and feel ill like a woman who gives birth; carried away by a great storm, they will wish that they had not sinned. Where then will be the wisdom of the wise, the skill of the speakers, the vain learning of the educated? 'They were tossed to and fro; they staggered like a drunken man, and were at their wits' end' (Ps. 106:27). 'Where is the wise? Where is the scribe? Where is the disputer of this age?' (1 Cor. 1:20).

"Only brethren, think what we ought to be like, seeing that we must give detailed report about our every action, both great and of little importance. We shall answer even for every idle word (Matt 12:36). And think also what we ought to be like in order to find mercy with God and, at the hour of parting, stand at the right side of our heavenly King? How must we prepare for that inexpressible happiness which will come to those who will stand at the right side of the King and will hear the sweetest voice of this King of kings: 'Come, you blessed of My Father, inherit the kingdom prepared for you from the foundation of the world' (Matt 25:34). Then we shall inherit good things such as 'eye has not seen, nor ear heard, nor have entered into the heart of man the things which God has prepared for those who love Him' (1 Cor 2:9). Then no sorrow, no sickness, no fear will trouble us forevermore. Let us think of this more often than we do now.

"But let us also think of the endless torture of the sinners and of the shame which they will feel before the just Judge when they will be brought to the frightful judgment-seat but will be unable to say a single word in their justification. What disgrace they will incur when they will be separated from others and put on the King's left side! What darkness will cover them when the Lord will speak to them in His anger and 'vex them in His sore displeasure' (Ps 2:5) and when He will say to them, 'Depart from me, you cursed, into the everlasting fire prepared for the devil and his angels' (Matt 25:41).

"Woe is me, woe is me! What a sorrow and what sickness, what a close feeling, what a horror and trembling will press on their spirits when they will hear the terrible voice of all the powers of heaven: 'Let the sinners be turned into hell' (Ps 9:18). What grief, what grief! How will they weep and shout and sob when they will be led away to bitter eternal pain! How they will groan, struggle, and suffer!

"Woe is me, woe is me! What is that place which will enclose this weeping and groaning and gnashing of teeth! This is the so-called Tartarus, of which even the devil himself is afraid. What grief, what grief! What is that pit where the unquenchable fire burns and burns but gives no light!

"Woe is me, woe is me! What is that never-sleeping, poisonous worm that torments the sinners! Woe, woe! What is that outermost darkness, never lighted by anything! Woe is me, woe is me! How merciless and cruel are the angels who are charged to torture the sinners! They cruelly disgrace and beat them!

"Those who are so tortured call with all their strength, but there is no one who might save them. They call upon the Lord but He will not hear them. Then they understand that everything of this earth and this life is but emptiness; that all here which they held to be good becomes revolting to them; that which was sweet delight becomes bitterer than gall or any kind of poison.

"Woe to the sinners! The righteous are standing at the King's right side, but the sinners are in sorrow. Now that they are weeping, the righteous are joyous; the righteous are in a balmy place, while the sinners are restless and grieved. Woe to the sinners! They are condemned while the righteous are glorified. Woe to the sinners! While the righteous enjoy all good things, they are wanting and unhappy. Woe to the sinners! While the righteous are exalted, they are humbled. The righteous are in holy places, the sinners are trampled down. The righteous are in the abodes of the saints, the sinners are in eternal evil. The righteous hear the words 'Come, you blessed of My Father, inherit the kingdom prepared for you from the foundation of the world' (Matt 25:34). But the sinners hear different words: 'Depart from me, you cursed, into the everlasting fire prepared for the devil and his angels' (Matt 25:41).

"The righteous are in Paradise, the sinners in unquenchable fire. The righteous are in enjoyment, the sinners suffer evil. The righteous are exultant, the sinners are bound and tortured. The righteous are singing, the sinners are weeping. The righteous proclaim the thrice-holy song, the sinners weep for their dismal condition, thrice more dismal than anyone can imagine. The righteous experience the sweetness of singing, the sinners endure their own miserable destruction. The righteous are in the bosom of Abraham, the sinners are in the boiling waves of Belial....

"The righteous are blessed, the sinners find no rest. The righteous enjoy the contemplation of God, the sinners are oppressed by the fiery flames. The righteous are chosen vessels, the sinners are vessels of hell. The righteous are purified gold, tested silver, precious stones; the sinners are wood, stalks, hay, material for fire....

"The righteous are in halls of light, the sinners are in a bottomless pit. The righteous are shining in the rays of a glorious light, the sinners are in a stormy darkness. The righteous are with the angels, the sinners with the demons. The righteous exult with the angels, the sinners sob with the demons. The righteous are in the midst of light, the sinners in the midst of darkness. The righteous are comforted by the Holy Spirit, the Paraclete, but the sinners are torn apart by their torments with the demons.

"The righteous stand before the throne of the Highest, the sinners stand before impenetrable darkness. The righteous always openly look at the face of Christ, the sinners forever stand before the face of the devil. The righteous learn from the angels the mysteries of God, the sinners are taught their mysteries by the demons. The righteous lift their prayers, the sinners lift their perpetual weeping. The righteous are in the dwellings on high, the sinners creep along in the lowest places of all. The righteous are in heaven, the sinners are in the abyss. The righteous are in life eternal, the sinners are in the destruction of death. The righteous are in the hand of God, the sinners are where the devils are. The righteous are in communion with God, the sinners are in communion with Satan....

"Alas for those who forgot their calling to be the sons of God, and instead have given themselves over to the sweetness of this world! Alas for those who follow the wisdom of this world! Alas for those who walk in the night of sin! ... Alas for drunkards! Blessed is he who humbles and lowers himself in this life for the sake of God: he will be raised by the almighty God, glorified by the angels, and will not stand at the left side of God at the judgment!

"Blessed is the man who persists in prayer, endures fasts, joyfully goes without sleep, struggles against sleep and drives it away, kneels to praise God, beats his breast, raises his hands, raises his eyes toward heaven, toward the Lord, meditates on Him Who searches 'the minds and hearts' (Rev 2:23).

"They who feed their bodies beyond due measure leave their souls hungry.... They despise fasting, which is an important means for salvation. Instead they sink into gluttony and are conquered by sin, particularly by adulterous lust. Those who do not observe God's commandments are vulnerable to the demons and are condemned to fiery hell. Those who remove themselves from the holy Church and the communion of Holy Mysteries are the enemies of God and the friends of demons. However, the heresies of the godless heretics will finally be put to shame, the race of the faithless will perish, and so will all who oppose God, whose mouths, because they have struggled against God, will finally be closed....

"The only real death is that which comes from the devil. The father of death, the devil, is like a well-armed warrior, always watchful and eager to attack us, especially on holy days, and to enslave us to his power. He is eager to be able to say, 'I have overcome the warriors of Christ by showing to them the beauty of women, by enchanting their ears, by overwhelming them with pride and gluttony, by entangling them in lust, by tempting them with drunkenness; thus have I separated them from God and thrown them into the abyss of error.'

"Let us not permit the impure demons to laugh at us. We have our God, Who is our Savior and the destroyer of demons. Our body is mortal, we shall not escape death, but let us not be troubled. Let us manfully move toward victory over impure demons. If we have fear of God within our hearts, if in our souls we shall always keep the thought of death, then all the demons fully armed will do us no harm. They will be like battering rams that hit a wall without success. Our wall will be found unbreakable, for our Lord God will be with us; to Him belongs the glory, honor, and power forever and ever. Amen."

From the "Sermon on the Departure of the Soul" of St Cyril, Archbishop of Alexandria.

CHAPTER 14

The Mystery of Death

Although scientists have been astonishingly successful in their research, they still assert that life is a mystery. What then shall we say about death? It is an even greater mystery. Is death annihilation? But in that case, life is not worth living. Or is death the beginning of a new life? It is supremely important for our well-being to answer this question, and we are reminded in the Holy Scripture that "Eye has not seen, nor ear heard, nor have entered into the heart of man the things which God has prepared for those who love Him" (1 Cor 2:9). Equally, we can see that everywhere and at all times has man expressed the conviction that death is contrary to nature, and that the dead must come to life again. Such beliefs occur in all religions, no matter what the form in which man's religious life is couched. Thus in different cultures we witness phenomena such as worship of the departed, elaborate tombs like the pyramids, embalming of the dead (mummies), and so on.

What moves man to such beliefs? His soul and its longing for the infinite. The greatest things on earth cannot satisfy the soul. Furthermore, the belief in immortality stems also from man's conscience and his innate feeling of justice, which demands that everyone should receive recompense according to his deserts. Man's heart also passionately desires to be reunited with those who are no longer on earth. His intelligence searches for the truth but cannot be satisfied here on earth.

What then can satisfy man and assure him of the future resurrection of the dead? The deeds and the entire life of Jesus Christ, Who has clearly revealed the future life and immortality. He lifts our spirits and reveals to us that we are the children of a Father Who dwells in heaven, our real father-land. Christ enlightens our conscience, transforms our lives, and mediates for us before God. He calms our hearts by eliminating the barrier between us and God. He opens heaven for everyone, for, having risen from the dead, He assures us of our immortality also. Death, my brethren, is not annihilation but the beginning of a new, better, eternal life with Christ.

A man's death is truly a great mystery. Is it not a mystery that a man, an intelligent, sentient being who embraces with his thought both heaven and earth, who breathes and seems immortal and eternal, should live one day but on the very next day lie as a cold, immovable, decomposing corpse that terrifies all the living? In vain has poor human intelligence attempted for thousands of years to penetrate the darkness of the tomb and lay open the mystery of death—the seal is still unbroken, the veil is still impenetrable!

How simply, however, and how deeply does the word of God solve this mystery! Its answer transcends our intelligence and yet satisfies the most demanding reason: we were created for immortality and were granted all means to achieve it; but we did not stand firm in our destiny, tasted the forbidden fruit, poisoned ourselves with sin, and consequently fell prey to death. What can be simpler and more satisfactory than this answer? Why should we then be bewildered when death itself testifies of its origin: even now when anyone eats anything poisonous, he dies.

Our holy faith not only explains to us the beginnings of death but also reveals its end—something about which reason alone cannot even dare to think. According to the teachings of the Church, we are not given over to death like sheep to be sacrificed, as its prey for all times without return; we are rather like prisoners who are handed over to guards for a temporary imprisonment. The hour will come when "all who are in the graves shall hear His voice and come forth—those who have done good, to the resurrection of life, and those who have done evil, to the resurrection of condemnation" (John 5:28–29). We may wish to know from whence comes this joy-giving mystery, and how it is that in the midst of decomposition and death wholeness and life should shine forth. Our faith fully answers these questions also. It states that we will be resurrected because the power of death has been broken. By whom? By the Son of God, our Savior.

How and by what means? The answer to this question is that Christ took upon Himself our flesh; being the source of life, He nonetheless deigned to subject Himself to death, be entombed, and then, through the fullness of His divinity, shine forth in life and resurrection. What can be more satisfying for a sound reason than an explanation of this kind?

Thus, if anyone should ask you, Christian, "How is it that we have incurred corruption? How is it that we have been united with death?" you can reply firmly together with the Church: "By the order of God," a God Who is just and cannot but punish man for transgression of the eternal laws of His truth. He could not but give man-the-sinner over to the consequences of his own sin, the result of which is death. And, Christian, if anyone should ask you, "How shall we be resurrected? By what force will we arise from our tombs?" you can firmly reply with the word of God: "By the order of God," a merciful God, Who sent His Only Son for the sake of our resurrection, and this Son has died and risen for our sake. Yes, my brethren, a Christian can answer these questions which human intelligence with all its earthly wisdom cannot even approach.

Let us then recognize the excellence of our holy faith and learn how to be grateful for the mystery of immortality which this faith teaches us. How shall we be grateful? First, by not mourning disconsolately for the dead. Only those who have no hope mourn in this way, and if we should mourn excessively it would be a sign that we do not in our hearts believe what our lips confess. Second, we must with all exactness and diligence fulfill those sacred conditions under which the word of God promises us an eternal blessed life. These conditions are a living faith in the conqueror of death and hell, our Redeemer, our Lord Jesus, and an effort to make our life follow His commandments. He who is filled with this kind of faith, he who leads a life above all reproach and doubt—such a man already has in himself the beginnings of life eternal, and already here on earth takes part in the strength which will accrue to him in the life to come.

From the sermons of Innocent, the archbishop of the Chersonese and Taurus, as well as from other sources.

CHAPTER 15

Teaching from the Holy Fathers on the Journey After Death

Even the souls of holy men who have pleased God by their righteous life pass through the trials to which all souls are subject upon their death. The saints, however, are covered by God's grace and pass through these trials with great speed and glory. The Holy Spirit raises them to heaven, the same Holy Spirit Who during their sojourn on earth ceaselessly inspired them with the desire to part from their bodies and be with Christ (Phil 1:23).

Thus we learn about St Mark of Thrace that he passed the expanse of air like a bolt of lightning, and did so in the span of one hour. When St Mark of Thrace was about to die, St Serapion came to him. St Mark met Serapion joyfully and cordially said to him: "God has sent you to prepare with your holy hands my humble body for burial." An hour later he said, "Brother Serapion! Stay awake this night for the sake of my departing!" They both stood up to pray. After prayer, Mark said to Serapion, "After I am gone, put my body in Christ's peace down in this cave, obstruct the entrance with rocks, go home and do not remain here." Serapion asked to accompany Mark, but Mark said, "You are to die not here but at your own place." And then he added, "This is a great day, it is better than all the other days of my life, for today my soul departs from bodily suffering and goes to rest in its heavenly habitation. Today my body will find respite from its many labors and illnesses. Today the light of my rest will receive me."

At these words, the cave was filled with light brighter than the sun, and the air was filled with fragrance. St Mark took Serapion by the hand and said to him: "Let my dead body remain until the general resurrection in that same place where it labored during this temporal life: in that place where were housed my illnesses, labors, and wants. Thou, O Lord, separate my soul from my body, for it was for Thy sake that I endured hunger, thirst, nakedness, cold, heat, and all manner of discomfort. Thou Thyself, O Lord, clothe me in the garment of glory on the terrible day of Thy coming. Rest now, my eyes and my feet, you who have toiled when I stood up all night to pray. I am leaving this temporal life, and I wish all who remain behind to be saved also. Save yourselves, all you who remain, for the sake of God!"

After this exhortation St Mark kissed Serapion and said, "And you, too, save your soul, Serapion! And I adjure you by God, take nothing from my humble body." When Serapion began to weep, there was heard a voice from heaven: "Bring me the chosen vessel from the desert; bring me the doer of truth, the perfect Christian, the faithful slave. Come, Mark, come! Rest in the light of joy and spiritual life!" Mark said to Serapion: "Let us kneel, my brother!" And then there was heard the voice of an archangel who addressed Mark: "Stretch out your arms!" Serapion also heard this voice. Serapion immediately stood up and saw the soul of St Mark, already separated from bodily bounds. It was being carried in angels' hands into the heights of heaven, and the angels were covering it with a brilliantly white garment (*Lives of the Saints* for April 5).

The word of God and the teachings of the Church reveal to us only what we should know about the state of our souls after death. The rest is not revealed because there is no need for us to know that which is superfluous for us in this life. In our present condition not everything is intelligible to us; we cannot contain everything. The holy Apostle Paul, who during his earthly life was taken up into Paradise where he was granted knowledge of the future life, said that he heard there words which are not to be uttered here, words which cannot be recounted by man (2 Cor 12:4).

The Orthodox Church states that man's soul, after it has parted with his body, is brought before God to be judged. This judgment is different from the general, or last judgment in that it is individual and particular: it takes place not before the solemn assemblage of the whole world, and the sentence is given not for all eternity (as it will be at the last judgment), but for the time until the general resurrection. Nevertheless, both judgments are real. The Holy Scripture assures us that the particular judgment is the lot of every man. The Apostle Paul says, "It is appointed for men to die once, but after this the judgment" (Heb 9:27). Our Savior's tale about the rich man and Lazarus also clearly reveals that the soul's destiny is made manifest immediately upon death, and that it depends on the deeds of the man to whom this soul belonged; it follows that there is a judgment immediately after death. The doubtless reality of such a judgment, furthermore, follows from the concept of earthly life as a course of trials, and from the concept of God as the Creator, Judge, and Meter of rewards and punishments. Thus the son of Sirach, who reflects the beliefs of the Old Testament Church, also says that it pleases God "to reward a man on the day of his death according to his ways" (Sir 11:26).

Apparently, these torments are nothing but the particular judgment, which the Lord Jesus Himself passes on men's souls through His angels, although He remains unseen. Why then are the devils present? Because He also admits to this judgment the "accuser of our brethren" (Rev 12:10), that is, the evil spirits. In the course of the judgment, the soul is reminded of all its deeds, which are evaluated without prejudice; and then its lot becomes known.

For the purpose of testing the souls as they rise through the expanse of the air, there are appointed by the powers of darkness particular stations of judgment and watches, and these are arranged in a remarkable order. Troops of the fallen spirits keep watch throughout the spheres of space between the earth and heaven. Every contingent is in charge of a particular kind of sin and, when the soul reaches it, torments the soul with that sin. The fathers of the Church give the name *trials* to these watches of the devils in midair and their seats of judgment.

The teachings of the Church on these trials are found in the works of St Cyril of Alexandria, but did not originate with him and have remained until our time. They are founded on Holy Scripture.

The state of righteous souls before the last judgment is shown to us in the Holy Gospel. They are rewarded for the efforts of their lives by blessedness; thus, the righteous Lazarus was immediately after his death carried to Abraham's bosom; also our Lord said to the robber who repented on the cross, "Today you will be with Me in Paradise" (Luke 23:43). Furthermore, the righteous will enjoy peace, that is, freedom from sorrows and suffering (Rev 7:16–17); they will be in the society of other righteous and of angels, and will serve God by their praises and by prayers for those who live on earth. But this is not their final condition. Everyone will receive his full glory and blessedness according to his works only after the general judgment, when the Lord will come on the appointed day and announce the final judgment, the sentences of which will never be changed (Matt 25:46).

CHAPTER 16

The Mysteries of Life Beyond Death

We can be certain of the reality of life beyond death, for at all times and among all nations has there existed faith, not only in the existence of the Divinity, but also in a future life to come. The ancient Greeks and Romans, the Persians and the Arabs, the aborigines of Polynesia, Melanesia, central and southern Africa, the American Aleutians, and others—all these have believed and still believe in one way or another that man's life does not end with his death but continues in some form or other.

This universality of faith in the existence of life beyond death has a great and edifying significance: it persuasively argues that the future life really exists, for faith in it is innate in man's nature and is one of the basic elements of his religious consciousness. It can be remarked here that all that man innately believes and all that forms a necessary, inseparable part of his consciousness, is always quite true.

Our common sense also beyond doubt assures us that our existence does not end with our life on earth, and that there is in addition a future life beyond death. Let us look at the visible nature of this earth. The deceased famous Russian prelate Philaret speaks about it as follows:

In the entire world we can find no example or indication or proof that anything, no matter how insignificant in itself, perishes. There is nothing in the past that has not in some way prepared us for what is to come in the future. There is no end that does not reveal its beginning. Every separate existence, once it has ceased to be in its own manner, leaves aside only its worn-out material garment and ascends the great, invisible domain of life, and appears once more in a new guise, which sometimes is better and more perfect than its former one. The sun sets only in order to rise again; in the morning the stars die to us, their earthly spectators, but in the evening they rise again; times and ages end and then begin; dying sounds rise again in

77

their echoes; rivers are buried in the sea but are reborn in the springs; a whole world of humble earthly creatures dies in the summer but comes to life in the spring; the seed dies in the ground, but grass and trees rise from it; the worm that creeps on the ground dies, but the winged butterfly is born of it; the life of the bird is buried in the insensible egg, and the bird comes alive from the egg.

If the lower animals incur dissolution in order to be created anew, and die in order to live again, can man, the crown of the earth and the mirror of heaven, fall into his grave only in order to fall apart like dust—more hopeless than the worm, worse than a mustard grain?" (from the works of Philaret, metropolitan of Moscow, vol. 2, 1879 edition, p. 210).

Much more important than the proofs of human intelligence is testimony of the Holy Scripture. For a believer, the word of God is the truth, and is and must be the source of all his knowledge on all subjects, including the great mystery of man's future life.

In the sacred books of the Old Testament, we find sufficiently clear indications that the soul continues its existence even after it has become separated from the body. "Then the dust will return to the earth as it was," says Ecclesiastes, "and the spirit shall return to God who gave it" (Eccl 12:7). The people of ancient times frequently forgot this teaching about our life after death. In their forgetfulness they spent their life on earth in a crude, shameful, and despicable way. The Lord, however, frequently renewed this teaching in the times of the Old Testament, and did it through His chosen men, the prophets, in order that the Hebrew people and others who were connected with them or in some way influenced by them should not lose faith in the future life.

The Son of God was then sent to our earth by God the Father, and His purpose, among other things, was to teach what truth is. On many occasions he assured us of the immortality of our soul and of the reality of the future life. Thus He said, "The hour is coming, and now is, when the dead will hear the voice of the Son of God; and those who hear will live ... for the hour is coming in which all who are in the graves will hear His voice and come forth—those who have done good, to the resurrection of life, and those who have done evil, to the resurrection of condemnation" (John 5:25, 28–29). "I am the resurrection and the life. He who believes in Me, though he may die, he shall live. And whoever lives and believes in Me shall never die" (John 11:25–26). And there are other instances of Christ's words about a future life.

The holy apostles taught as had Christ. The holy Apostle Paul wrote to the Thessalonians, "I do not want you to be ignorant, brethren, concerning those who have fallen asleep, lest you sorrow as others who have no hope," that is, the pagans (1 Thess 4:13). In their epistles, the holy apostles built on this faith in the future life all their admonitions and threats, all their comforts and solace to those whom they were addressing. Thus the holy Apostle Paul, who was entirely certain of the existence of the future life, said about himself, "For to me, to live is Christ, and to die is gain.... For I am hard pressed between the two, having a desire to depart and be with Christ" (Phil 1:21, 23). The greatest fact of history, the resurrection of Christ our Savior from the dead, was made by the apostles the starting point of all their teachings about life beyond the grave. This wonder of wonders is the foundation of all of Christianity, for Christianity stands or falls depending on whether Christ rose, or died and remained dead. On the fact of Christ's resurrection all our hopes for eternal life are also founded. We believe that life eternal will follow the general resurrection of the dead and the ultimate destruction of our last enemy, death.

The resurrection of Jesus Christ not only is the object of our most vivid faith; it is also the most authentic historical event, most satisfactorily witnessed and testified about. The metropolitan of Moscow, Philaret, says, "As Christ truly rose from the dead, so truly shall we rise. Christianity is the religion of the Resurrected, of Him Who has put death to death. Death as we know it is only an inevitable transition to immortality: 'What you sow is not made alive unless it dies' (1 Cor 15:36). These words of the great apostle contain a beautiful analogy between a natural phenomenon and the immortality of man; an analogy full of meaning. The seeds sown in the earth decompose there but keep whole their most important part, from which the future plant will germinate—a plant entirely like that which was its parent. This is not simply life transmitted from one plant to another; the germinating part of the seed completely keeps its own life and then manifests it in another form. The seed is quite like man in this present condition: an individual being apart from all others, endowed with particular qualities and possessing its own individual life. This being dies, is put in the earth, is sown like seed. Does it perish without a trace? Does it decompose and turn into its component parts? No! As a seed appears again in the form of a beautiful plant which is not something different from the seed that was thrown into the ground, but is that very seed which decomposed there. So man, having decomposed in the earth, will turn into a beautiful being with a new, spiritual body; but he will not be a being other than the man who died—he will be the same man but will have become imperishable."

Finally, the existence of life beyond the tomb can be recognized from the experience of many to whom the souls of the departed have appeared.

From *The Christian Orthodox Teachings on the True Faith and Its Application to Life*, edited in Russian by Archimandrite Panteleimon (Holy Trinity Monastery: Jordanville, N.Y., 1954).

CHAPTER 17

A General View on the Immortality of the Soul and on Life Beyond the Grave

Are we going to live after death as we live now? That is, are we going to retain our consciousness and our feelings, or will our soul cease being, together with our body? This question has eminently occupied and troubled the minds of all ages and all nations. It has always clamored for an answer. The clarification of this mystery has been the cause of very many philosophic teachings of all kinds. However, despite all efforts of man's thought, the question remained unsolved until there was heard the voice of God the Word, Who announced the good news to mankind: "I am the resurrection, and the life. He who believes in Me, though he may die, he shall live" (John 11:25).

An assurance of immortality serves as a source of good morality while man is waiting for his transition into eternal life. From this assurance man derives for himself strength which helps him endure life's sorrows and disappointments, and hope for a joyous future state. Only faith and hope make us understand that, in the words of the poet, "life by God to us is given, not in vain and not by chance" (A. S. Pushkin). Only if we possess such a faith will we be saved from the tormenting question: why have we been born into God's world? Only faith and hope enable man to understand that death is but the dawn which follows night. If we possess faith and hope, the thought of death will no longer be frightening, and it will appear no longer as the revolting skeleton of destruction but as a bright comforting angel. A believer's soul will, furthermore, not suffer when he loses his next of kin or others who are close to him; his parting from them will be a promise of meeting in a new and better existence, in the dwellings of the heavenly world beyond the grave. His life may continue and be full of deprivation—but he thanks God for it nonetheless; death may reach him when he has completed barely half of his expected life's journey—but he lovingly throws himself into the embrace of the comforting angel, for he understands the meaning of the divinely revealed words, "In My Father's house are many mansions" (John 14:2).

On the other hand, a decline of morality, an indifference toward religion, restlessness and discomfort of the spirit, and, finally, complete disillusionment—all this comes of disbelief in the soul's immortality and lack of hope in the existence of a future life. Adultery, burglary, deceit, murder, suicide, failure to distinguish between right and wrong, failure to understand properly what love toward one's neighbor should entail—all these are children of such a disbelief and lack of hope. "'Let us eat and drink; for tomorrow we die!'" (1 Cor 15:32)—these words resound in the heart of the man who has lost his faith in immortality.

How often in our time do we hear people say that there is no life beyond the grave, and that afterlife is a figment of our imagination; with death everything presumably ends for man. But who says this? Unfortunately, it is many of the so-called educated men who, consciously or unconsciously, assist the propaganda of the militant atheists, the antichrists who, having turned away from Christ the author of Life and have automatically but inevitably put themselves on the side of the devil, who is the author of spiritual death.

These people believe nothing except that which their own reason acknowledges and their insufficient, miserable five senses recognize. These people do not wish to learn about spiritual life, which forms the best and highest part of human nature. They have no wish to read books which deny their one-sided opinions. They repeat what others have told them and malign that which they have never studied. Atheists particularly like to strengthen their insane discourses by the shameless and entirely false assertion that all real scientists do not believe in God. By means of this bait they have caught and continue to catch many of those who are simpleminded. Still, their assertion is an utterly shameless lie!

It is possible to live one's entire life without Christ and His teachings. It is possible not to believe in the teachings of Christianity; it is possible to make one's life easy and pleasant without Christ; but it is impossible without Him to pass the dark valley of death and, what is even worse, the last judgment.

He who, by his doubts and his arguments, revolts against the heavenly teachings, does nothing but shoot arrows into the sky. The sky is not afraid of wounds and injuries of this kind and has no need to defend itself from them; instead, they are dangerous for the archers, since they fall back on their heads. There is only one way in which a man can prove the divine origin of the Holy Scripture: obedience to its teachings, life according to its rules, a good trial of these principles. After such a trial, you will become convinced that these teachings are divine. You will understand how perfect is the law of the Lord and what comfort it gives the soul.

It is good to mention at this point the words of a holy old man. Someone came to him one day and said, "God does not exist!" The hermit replied quietly and humbly: "Well, what then has happened to Him? He used to exist all the time before you came along, but now you say He no longer does!" The simple words of the old man form a profound and clear reply. It is difficult to think of anything quite so clear and fundamental. You must keep thinking, "no one can save me without myself, without my own effort." You must purify your own heart, then your spirit will become dominant over your body. In order that the spirit should be stronger, that which weakens the spirit must be overcome.

Only internal spiritual experience leads to cognition of God. St Basil the Great studied all branches of learning at the celebrated school of Athens, which at that time attracted the best minds and talents. He acquired oratorical art and studied astronomy, philosophy, physics, medicine, and the natural sciences. He was the pride of his teachers, but all the worldly knowledge could not satisfy his mind, which was looking for something better: enlightenment from above. After he finished his studies, he went to those lands where Christian hermits lived. There he hoped to study fully that which forms the science and the body of knowledge of Christianity. He spent time in Egypt, Carthage, Syria, and Palestine. There he found spiritual guidance and a great collection of theological works, which he diligently studied for a long time.

Unbelievers proudly assert that human intelligence does not acknowledge a world beyond the human senses, a life beyond this life. They forget how the wisest of all mortals, Socrates, came to the recognition that all human knowledge and understanding are as nothing when they are compared with all that man does not know or understand. Socrates' thought in this matter is forceful and convincing, since this wise man acquired it through the experience of his entire life, spent in a search for the truth.

Our life on earth is a perpetual struggle with our passions. As such, it is not understood by people of this world, who are given to serving their flesh and their earthly idols. Nonetheless, this inner struggle of a man with himself, with his moral deficiencies and weaknesses, with his evil thoughts, the passionate impulses of his soul, the wickedness of his heart, the lusts of his body, and the like—this struggle is every Christian's duty. It is the law of a Christian's life. In this struggle with passions and in overcoming them lies the meaning of Christian life and Christian teachings. This is where we find promise of man's spiritual happiness on earth and his blessedness in heaven.

Everyone passionately seeks happiness, but no one understands that this happiness lies not outside us but within our own hearts, once these have been purified of passions; within our intelligence, once it has risen to higher things; and within our enlightened soul and our spirit, made free from the lusts of the flesh. This happiness can be reached in one way only: through man's moral struggle with himself and his own passions.

"Everyone always believes in something, but it is not every faith that has a moral significance and can serve as a foundation for God's work. If I believe only in that which gives me pleasure or in that which I want to believe, then this faith has no moral dignity, since it gives no expression to self-denial," says Vladimir Soloviev. "Such a faith does not take us outside of our limitations. On the contrary, it only reveals, and all the more firmly establishes, such limitations. Moral dignity belongs to none but that faith whose subject in no way depends on my own volition, has nothing to do with my own tastes and opinions, and has been given not to me alone but to me together with everyone else."

On occasion, socialism has claimed that it intends to make Christian morality apply to life. But there is a difference between Christianity and socialism: Christianity bids us give that which is ours, while socialism invites us to take that which is not ours. The wondrous Christian teachings thus become misshapen in the mind which relies on its own resources and refuses help from above and the grace given by Christ.

With the assistance of the fortifying strength of the Holy Spirit, our religion puts man on such heights of self-denial, in such closeness to heaven, that the natural man, no matter how richly gifted and how diversely educated, cannot possibly reach this level by his effort alone; but while "with men this is impossible ... with God all things are possible" (Matt 19:26).

Most people with all their strength refuse to think about death. The pronouncements of God's word do not touch their hearts, which are swept away by the passions and the levity of this world. Sometimes, however, some of those who have departed from this world return to us as witnesses and assure us of that which they have actually experienced, namely, the truthfulness of all that divine revelation tells us about our ultimate destiny.

But can there be any communication between the souls that have departed for another world, and us who are still alive on this earth? Are there actual instances of such appearances of the dead to the living? If such appearances were impossible and never happened, how is it that the living through all ages and among all nations have tried and still try to have communication with departed souls? These attempts have never stopped. Some at least wish to see their near and dear in their dreams, while others expect their visits in waking state and wish to ask the dead about their existence in the world beyond.

Many say nothing on the question of such appearances of the departed. Others laugh and say that no one has ever come from the other world and that no one knows what there may be beyond the grave. This kind of opinion about afterlife has no meaning whatsoever. Accounts of visitations by the dead are passed on from one generation to another, and faith in the existence of a spiritual world endures. Consequently, there is no reason to reject such visitations and even less reason simply to laugh at such a faith and to call superstitious those who attach credence to them.

Although many declare that there is not a word of truth in all the tales about the appearances of the departed, such an opinion cannot be considered weighty enough. A man who is accustomed to thoroughly studying various natural phenomena will not be satisfied with such an offhand denial. A fact remains a fact. It is true that medicine, for example, observes how people who suffer from nervous disturbances frequently experience various sensory illusions and hallucinations. But it does not follow from this observation that all those phenomena which heretofore have received no explanation are therefore nothing but hallucinations. It is very far from the teachings of medicine to make such an assertion.

There are many phenomena that we are forced to acknowledge as actually existing, although we cannot explain them. It would, however, be senseless to deny all that which we cannot explain. Did any explanation of our universe exist a thousand years ago? Can we even now fully explain the laws of light or the laws of gravity? Do we already know so fully the nature of our own soul, all its abilities and their relation to one another? No thinker will doubt for a moment that there are many forces in the universe which are not yet known to us.

Divine revelation itself does not deny that the dead can appear to the living and have so appeared to them. The Holy Scripture shows us that the Jews did not doubt the possibility of such appearances. The Jews at the time of the Savior held a universal belief in them. Jesus Christ assumed it and never said anything which might lead us to think that He did not approve of it or criticized it.

The apostles did not doubt the possibility of actual appearances of spirits: when they saw the Savior walking toward them over the waters of the sea of Gennesaret, they at first thought that He was a spirit (Matt 14:26). In the same Gospel, the rich man who was tormented in hell asked Abraham to send Lazarus on earth so that he might warn the rich man's brothers about the danger of falling into the same terrible condition which he himself was experiencing. It is assumed in this tale that the souls of the dead can return into this world and, with God's permission, appear to the living. During the transfiguration of Jesus Christ on Mt Tabor, Moses and Elijah, who a long time before this had gone into another world, appeared and talked with Christ (Matt 17:3). After our Savior's resurrection, many dead rose also and appeared in Jerusalem (Matt 27:52–53).

Blessed Augustine, in his discussion of such appearances, admits that it is very difficult to find an explanation of much that happens within our soul both in its waking state and when we are asleep. But he also admits that the dead have frequently appeared to the living and have even indicated to them those places where their bodies had been interred without due burial. Moreover, he mentions that in the churches where some dead have been buried there can frequently be heard some noise and the sound of singing, and that people have often seen how the dead have entered the houses in which they used to live on earth.

The holy fathers and teachers of the Church did not doubt the appearances of the dead and not only affirmed them as a truth, but also themselves experienced such visions and fulfilled the wishes of the dead who visited them. Thus to St John Chrysostom there appeared in the city of Comana the bishop Basiliscus, who had died a hundred years before, and who said, "Be of good courage, brother John: tomorrow we shall be together." The holy bishop believed this vision and, because he was then being taken into exile, he asked his guards not to take him any farther that day. He put on clean clothes, took holy communion, and, indeed, died as had been foretold.

The pastors of our Orthodox Church have not only themselves always believed that it is possible for the departed to return and that they actually do so, but also taught their charges not to reject this truth. Thus Metropolitan Philaret (of Moscow) says in one of his homilies, "Visitations from the world of the spirits are not explicable but yet not to be denied." He himself, when his departed father appeared to him and revealed to him on what day he should die, not only did not doubt that this appearance was actual but also began to prepare for his departure to the world beyond (*Reading to Benefit the Soul*, in Russian, 1876, pt. 1). It was he also who once saw in a dream some departed souls who asked him to be favorable to a particular priest. On this occasion the metropolitan did not attribute his dream to the association of ideas but followed the plea of the dead who appeared to him (*The Pilgrim*, in Russian, May 1852).

Innocent, the archbishop of Chersonese and Tauris, says, "Ancient accounts tell us that the belief in the soul's immortality was always associated with the belief in the appearances of the dead. Innumerable are the accounts testifying to this matter.... The dead do appear and, beyond doubt, they do affect this our life, although not very frequently" (*The Works of Innocent*, in Russian, vol. 7).

Nicanor, the archbishop of Chersonese and Odessa, in one of his homilies on the afterlife, asserts the following: "It would be possible to number many facts of the kind that find full credence and are believed to be actual by people that deserve the utmost confidence.... These facts are attested, actual, entirely possible, but it cannot be said that they are quite in keeping with the ordinary course of things, as it has been established by God; they lie outside the realms of the ordinary" (*The Pilgrim*, 1887).

Many scientists and writers, both foreign and Russian, not only believe in the appearance of the departed and tell about extraordinary events from their own lives, but also convince others not to doubt such things. Augustin Calmet, a historical writer and author of commentaries on the Holy Scripture, who lived in the second half of the seventeenth century, writes, "A denial of the possibility and actuality of appearances and actions of the departed souls is willful, for it is made on those grounds only that such things are not to be explained according to the laws of this earthly world. It would be just as willful to deny the possibility and actuality of physiological phenomena merely because they are not to be explained by the laws of pure mechanics."

From A. Calmet, *On the Appearance of Spirits*, pt. 1, p. 115.

CHAPTER 18

The Life of Departed Souls Before
the Universal Judgment

About the condition of sinful souls, it is revealed to us that they are remote from the face of God, shut in hell—the prison of the fallen spirits, a dark place of torture—and feel and recognize there their loss of blessedness, as well as suffer pangs of conscience. In vain do they attempt to better their grievous condition (Luke 16:24–25).

But not all the sinful souls will be subject to the same lot. The condition of each will depend on the moral state of his soul. Besides this, their condition will not be decided upon once and for all. It will be only transitory. After the last judgment, some will pass into a hardened state, that is, an eternal remorselessness. They will become irreversibly evil, while others will pass through to hope for God's mercy and to life eternal (Phil 2:10–11).

The latter group are made up of those sinners who did not bear the fruit of their repentance here on earth, but still they died with the seeds of faith and righteousness in their souls. Therefore they do not endure suffering of the kind that is inflicted on the unrepentant sinners, and they can be helped by the Church. The apostle teaches us, "If anyone sees his brother sinning a sin which does not lead to death, he will ask, and He will give him life for those who commit sin not leading to death. There is sin leading to death. I do not say that he should pray about that" (1 John 5:16). These words mean that if a man has not definitely left the Church, which is the body of Christ, he, as a member of the body, can hope for help from the other members and is capable of receiving such help. "And if one member suffers, all the members suffer with it; or if one member is honored, all the members rejoice with it" (1 Cor 12:26).

Because of this close connection of Christians among themselves, they are able to help even those of their friends who are separated from them by immense distances, those who are held captive or imprisoned, and those who are oppressed by illness. The way to help them is to pray to God (Col 1:9).

According to Scripture, prayer can also influence the souls that have parted with us; its power even extends to the sphere of hell. We have quoted above the words of the apostle about deadly sins, and the Savior also said that there is a sin which is forgiven neither in this life nor in the future life (Matt 12:32). It follows that, as there is a deadly sin for which it is useless to pray and which will be forgiven neither in this nor in the future life, so there are also sins not deadly, and it can be very profitable to pray for such.

"Every man who has in himself even a little of the yeast of virtues but has not yet turned it into bread because, despite his good will, he has been prevented either by indolence or by carelessness, or by procrastination—and has been unexpectedly overtaken and mowed down by death—every such man will not be forgotten by the just Judge and Lord. After his death, the Almighty will inspire his relatives, his friends and neighbors to help him. He will turn their thoughts and hearts toward the departed man and will influence their souls to render assistance to the dead. And when God will thus move them, when the Lord will touch their hearts, they will make haste to make up the negligence of the dead" (St John of Damascus, "Sermon on Those Who Have Died in the Orthodox Faith").

Those who after their death fall into hell receive mercy not for the sake of their own repentance (for which it is then too late), but for the sake of the deeds of mercy performed by the still living, and for the sake of the prayers raised for them by the Church in the name of the Lord Jesus Christ, Who has taken upon Himself the sins of the world and has given us the sure promise: "If you ask anything in My name, I will do it" (John 14:14).

We see then that after death there are two places open to departed souls: Paradise with all its blessings, and hell with its dwellers, the evil spirits, and its torments. The first of these places, Paradise, is prepared for those who have spent their lives righteously; the second, for sinners. However, not all people die either as complete sinners or as complete saints. There are very many who, although they die in their sins, did begin here on earth their penance and had in the depths of their souls the seeds of good and did some good deeds. Where will be the souls of these? It can be seen in Holy Scripture, and particularly in the practice of the Orthodox Church as reflected by its prayers and songs, that the souls of such people, although they will be in hell, are not devoid of hope for remittance of their sins and for salvation from the pains of hell.

Lives of the Saints contains detailed accounts of the torments of the departed. Thus the man who was resurrected by the holy Apostle Philip fell to his feet and said, "I thank you, servant of God, for you have saved me in this hour from many evils: two demons were dragging me along, and if you had not prevented it, they would have thrown me into dire hell" (*Lives of the Saints* for November 14).

St Joseph the Writer of Songs, when he was preparing to depart from this life, prayed thus: "Lord my God! Keep my spirit to the end and grant it me to escape without harm the prince of darkness and the monsters of the air" (*Lives of the Saints* for April 4).

We can then see from what has been said here that the souls of the departed, both the righteous and the sinners, are subject to the particular judgment as they ascend toward heaven. Depending on their deeds, there and then they receive a sentence and their destiny until the general resurrection is announced. "For he who sows to his flesh will of the flesh reap corruption, but he who sows to the Spirit will of the Spirit reap everlasting life" (Gal 6:8).

The Orthodox Church teaches the following about the condition of the souls of the departed before the universal judgment: First, they clearly, and in all detail, realize their sins, through which they insulted God in this life; and they also experience pangs of conscience, which after death, awakens to its greatest capacity. Second, the souls are tormented by longing and desire, because all those things of the flesh to which they had been attached on earth can no longer give them satisfaction; yet they never developed a taste for the heavenly and the spiritual, and now it is too late for them to acquire love for such things. Finally, they suffer because they are far removed from God and His saints, and instead associate with other souls that are as unhappy as they, and also with the evil spirits. They experience actual suffering in hell, but this suffering is only the beginning and a foretaste of future perpetual suffering.

From *Dogmatic Theology* of Anthony, 1852, p. 259.

Part III

TALES FROM BEYOND THE GRAVE

CHAPTER 19

The Journey Beyond Death as Revealed to Gregory, a Disciple of St Basil the New

According to the teachings of the Church, the particular judgment of souls by God is preceded by their torments, or rather a series of tests; these take place in the regions of the air, where the evil spirits have their domain (Eph 6:12). They detain the souls and declare and make manifest all the sins which these souls perpetrated during their lives. We know about these torments in great detail because they were revealed to Gregory, the disciple of the holy monk St Basil the New, who lived in the first half of the tenth century. In a vision, Gregory learned about the hour of death and the passing through torments of a woman known as the blessed Theodora.

When Gregory asked her to tell him about her passing away and about the circumstances that attended her death and followed it, she responded him in great detail. "My child Gregory," she said, "you have asked me about a terrible thing, which is frightening even to recollect.

"When the hour of my death came, I saw faces such as I had never seen before, and heard words such as I had never heard. What shall I say? Cruel and hard-to-endure evils, of which I formerly had no idea, encountered me then because of my evil deeds. However, through the prayers and the assistance of our common spiritual father Basil, I was saved from these hardships. But how shall I tell you about that physical pain, that stress and close feeling which the dying experience? Like a man who, entirely naked, falls into a great fire, burns, melts, and turns into ashes; so the dying are destroyed by their deathly illness in the bitter hour when the soul parts from the body.

"When I drew near the end of my life and the time of my departure had come, I saw a great multitude of demons who had surrounded my couch. Their faces were dark like soot and pitch, their eyes were like glowing coals, their entire appearance was as frightening and evil as fiery hell itself. They began to grow indignant and to make noise like dogs; others howled like wolves. As they looked at me, they were full of anger; they threatened me, kept rushing at me and gnashing their teeth, and appeared ready to devour me. Yet they seemed to wait for a Judge who had not yet come but would do so; they were making ready charts and unrolling scrolls on which were written all my evil deeds. My miserable soul was taken by great fear and trembling. Not only the bitterness of death tormented me but even more the terrible appearance and the cruel demeanor of the frightening demons; these were to me like another death, only a worse one. I kept turning away my eyes in all directions so as not to see their terrible faces, and wished not to hear their voices, but I was unable to be rid of them. They turned everywhere and there was no one to help me.

"When I was at the end of my strength I saw two radiant angels of God, who were like youths of inexpressible beauty. They were coming toward me. Their faces were shining, their gaze was full of love; their hair was like snow, white with a golden tinge; their garments glistened like lightning and were girded with gold. When they came near me, they stopped on the right side of my couch and entered into a quiet conversation between themselves. As I saw them I was filled with joy and looked at them with pleasure.

"The black demons shuddered and retreated some distance. One of the radiant youths, angrily addressing the black ones, said, 'O shameless, cursed, dark, and evil enemies of the human race! Why do you always come first to the dying, and frighten and confuse every parting soul by your words? You have no reason to rejoice, for here you will find nothing. God is merciful to this soul, and you have no part and no allotment in her.' When the angel ceased speaking, the demons tottered, began to cry out, and mutter, and point to all my evil deeds, committed from my youth on. They exclaimed, 'We have no part in her, you say! Whose sins then are these? Did she not do such and such?' With such exclamations they kept their position and were waiting for death. When death came, it was roaring like a lion and was very frightening in appearance. It looked like a human being but had no body; instead it consisted of human bones. Death brought various instruments of torture, such as swords, arrows, javelins, sickles, saws, and others unknown to me. When I saw these, my humble soul trembled with fear. The holy angels said to death, 'Do not tarry, free this soul from its bodily ties, and do it fast and quietly, for she has but a small burden of sins.' Death stepped up to me, took a small axe and separated my legs, then my arms; then with its other instruments it weakened all the rest of my limbs, separating them joint by joint. I lost the use of my arms and legs, my whole body grew numb, and I no longer was able to move. Finally death cut off my head, and I no longer could move it, for it felt as if it belonged to someone else. Lastly, death dissolved in a cup some kind of mixture, and putting the cup to my lips, made me drink. The potion was so bitter that my soul was unable to endure it. It shuddered and went out of my body.

"The light-bearing angels immediately took it in their arms. When I looked back I saw my body lying breathless and immovable. I looked at my body like someone who has taken off his clothes and thrown them down; this was a strange feeling. Meanwhile, although the holy angels were holding me, the demons surrounded us and cried: 'This soul has a multitude of sins—let her answer for them!' They kept pointing to my sins, but the holy angels sought out my good deeds; and indeed, with God's help they found all that, by God's grace, I ever did of good. The angels gathered together everything that was good: all those instances when I gave alms to the needy, or fed the hungry, or gave drink to the thirsty, or clothed the naked, or brought into my house and rested there the homeless, or served the servants of God, or brought comfort to the sick or those who were imprisoned; or when I went with diligence to God's house and prayed with all my heart and shed tears, or when I attentively listened to what was read and sung in church, or brought to church incense and candles, or filled with oil the church lamps before the icons, or kissed the icons with awe and reverence; or when I fasted and abstained on Wednesdays, Fridays, or during other fasts, or when I prostrated myself before God and spent nights awake in prayer, or when I sighed to God and wept for my sins, or confessed my sins before my spiritual father with great regret for what I had done, and then tried with all my strength to balance my sins with good deeds; or when I did anything good to my neighbors, when I bore no anger to my enemies, bore no grudges and meekly endured hurts and reproaches, did good in return for evil, humbled myself, felt sorry for those who suffered and commiserated with those to whom anything bad happened, comforted those who were weeping and rendered them assistance, supported any good beginning and tried to turn people away from what was bad; or for myself turned my eyes away from vanity and kept my tongue from oaths, lies, or bearing false witness, or speaking without need—and all my other good deeds, even the least important ones, did the holy angels gather and make ready to put on the scale in order to balance my evil deeds.

"The demons, however, saw this and gnashed their teeth at me. They wanted to tear me instantly from the angels' arms and to carry me down to the bottom of hell. At this time, holy Basil himself appeared unexpectedly and said to the holy angels: 'Holy angels! This soul did great service to ease my old age, and therefore I prayed for her to God, and God has given her to me.' Having said this, he took something out that appeared like a little bag of gold and gave it to the angels with the words, 'Here is the treasure of prayers before the Lord for this soul! As you pass through the torments of the air and the evil spirits begin to torment her, pay her debts with this.'

"He then disappeared, but the evil spirits, when they saw the gift from holy Basil, at first stood dumbfounded. Then they raised plaintive cries and became invisible. Then Basil, the man who had pleased God, came again. He bore many vessels of pure oil and precious myrrh, and all these, one after the other, he poured on me. I was filled with spiritual fragrance and felt that I had changed and become very light. Once more the holy man said to the angels: 'When, holy angels, you will have done for this soul all that is needed, lead her to the dwelling that the Lord has prepared for me, and let her remain there.' Then once more he became invisible. The holy angels took me up, and we went eastward through the air."

THE FIRST TORMENT

"As we were rising from the earth to the heights of heaven, we were first met by the spirits of the first torment. Here the souls are tormented for the sins of idle speech; that is, for speaking without thinking, or speaking what is vile and shameless, or speaking without need or order. We stopped, and many scrolls were brought out on which there were recorded all the words that I had uttered from my youth on, either needlessly or unreasonably, and especially when such words expressed anything unclean or blasphemous, as young people frequently bear on their tongue.

"There I saw recorded all my angry words, foul words, worldly shameless songs, wild cries and laughter. The evil spirits accused me of all this and indicated the time and place, when and where and in whose company I spoke these vain words or evoked the wrath of God by my unseemly words, even though at the time I did not consider such things sinful; and paying no great attention to them did not confess them to my spiritual father, and never repented. Now I kept silent, as if I had lost my voice. I was unable to reply because the evil spirits accused me rightly. But while I was silent in my shame and trembled with fear, the holy angels offered some of my good deeds and, since these were not enough, they added something from the treasure given me by the holy man Basil; and thus they paid my debts at this station."

SECOND TORMENT

"Thence we ascended and drew near the torment of lying. Here is tested every lying word: failure to keep oaths, vain use of God's name, failure to keep vows given to God, insincere or false confession of sins, and the like. The spirits of this station are evil and ruthless. They stopped us and began to question us closely. However, I was accused of two things only: first, that I occasionally lied in matters of small importance—something that I did not even consider sinful; second, that, because of a false sense of shame, I sometimes insincerely confessed my sins to my spiritual father. As for false oaths or false witness, none of these, through Christ's grace, was found in me. Here the holy angels put down for my sins some of my good deeds, but the prayers of my spiritual father did even more to save me. We went on."

THIRD TORMENT

"We reached the station where souls answer for speaking evil of others and spreading rumors about them. When we were stopped here, I understood how heavy is the sin of speaking evil about one's neighbor, and how great an evil it is to spread bad rumors, judge the deeds of others, damage someone's reputation, slander, give bad words to people, or laugh at other's deficiencies. Such sinners are regarded as antichrists, since even before Christ has judged their neighbors they already allow themselves this right of judgment. In me, however, through the grace of Christ, they did not find many of these sins, for all the days of my life I always diligently strove not to condemn anyone, never to spread falsehoods about people, never to laugh at anyone, and never to give anyone bad words. Only occasionally, when I heard how other people condemn, malign, or laugh, did I too happen to agree with them to some extent in thought, or even, in my carelessness, add my word to what they were saying; but even then I instantly caught myself and stopped. But here I was held responsible even for the inclination. Here also the angels freed me by means of the prayers of the holy man Basil, and we continued to ascend."

FOURTH TORMENT

"We reached the station where gluttony is punished, and evil spirits immediately rushed out to meet us, for they hoped to find a victim. Their faces resembled those of sensuous gluttons and despicable drunkards. They walked around us like dogs and immediately showed their count of all the instances when I ate secretly from others, or without need, or when I ate in the morning before I had even prayed and signed myself with the mark of the cross; or when, during the holy fasts, I ate before the church service was over. They also revealed all the instances when I was drunk and even showed us those very cups, goblets, and others vessels from which I became intoxicated at such and such a time, during such and such a feast, with such and such companions. And every other instance of my gluttony was pointed out to me, and the demons already rejoiced, as if they had put their hands on me. I was trembling at the sight of such accusations and did not know how to object. But the holy angels took out enough from what was given to us by the holy man Basil, balanced my sins with this and set me free. When the spirits saw the ransom, they cried out, 'Woe! our labors and hopes have perished!' and threw their records of my gluttony into the air. I, however, rejoiced, and we went on.

"As we were ascending, the holy angels talked among themselves and said words to this effect: 'Truly does this soul have great help from Basil, a man who has pleased God. If it had not been for his prayers, she would have suffered a great deal in those stations of the air.' I took courage and said to them: 'It seems, holy angels, that none of the earth dwellers knows what happens here and what the soul can expect after death.' But the angels replied: 'Does not the divine Scripture testify concerning all of this? It is read in churches and preached by priests. Only those people who are passionately devoted to the vanities of earth take no heed of what they are told, and since they consider daily gluttony and drunkenness to be the greatest pleasure, they eat beyond measure and drink without thinking of the fear of God. Their belly is their God. They have no thought of future life and do not remember what is said in Scripture: "Woe to you who are full, for you shall hunger" (Luke 6:25).

"'Still, even the gluttonous can be saved. Those who are merciful and kindhearted to the needy and beggars and help those who ask for help—such men can easily obtain from God forgiveness of their sins, and because of their kindheartedness toward their neighbors, pass the stations of torment without stopping. It is said in Scripture that alms save us from death and cleanse every kind of sin; those who give alms and do justice will be filled with life (Tob 12:9). But he who does not strive to cleanse his sins by good deeds cannot escape the dark tormentors who lead the sinners down to hell and hold them bound until the terrible judgment at Christ's second coming. You, too, would not have escaped here your evil lot, were it not that you have received the treasure of holy Basil's prayers.'"

FIFTH TORMENT

"During this conversation we reached the station of sloth, where sinners are accused of all those days and hours which they spent in idleness. Here, too, are detained those who did not work themselves but lived by the labor of others; and those who were hired to work, took their wages, but did not fulfill the duties which they had taken upon themselves. And also are stopped here those who do not care to praise God and are too lazy to go to church on holidays and Sundays, either in the morning or to the Divine Liturgy, or to other church services. And here too people are accused of despondency and general carelessness about things that have to do with the salvation of their souls; this happens to both laymen and those who are ordained. Many are thence led into the abyss. I, too, was accused there of much and could not have freed myself if the holy angels had not balanced my deficiencies by the gifts of the holy man Basil."

SIXTH TORMENT

"Thence we came to the torment of stealing, and although we were briefly stopped there, we went on after we had given a small ransom only: for no stealing was found on my record, except some very unimportant occurrences in my childhood, and those stemmed from lack of reason."

SEVENTH TORMENT

"We passed without stopping through the station of avarice and love of money. By God's grace I never loved riches. I was content with what God gave me and never was avaricious; on the contrary, I diligently gave to the needy that which I had."

EIGHTH TORMENT

"When we rose still higher, we came to the station of usury, where those are accused who lend money for illegal interest. Here, too, are stopped those who gain riches by exploiting their neighbors, those who take bribes, or who by some other way steal indirectly, acquiring what really belongs to others. The tormentors, when they did not find me guilty of such sins, gnashed their teeth with annoyance, but we went on, praising God in the meanwhile."

NINTH TORMENT

"Now there lay before us the torment of injustice. Here are punished the unjust judges who acquit the guilty and condemn the innocent, all for the sake of gain; and also those who do not give the appointed wages to those whom they have hired, and the merchants who use false weights and measures, and all the others who are in some way unjust. We, however, by God's grace, passed this station without incurring any grief after we had given only a little bit for my sins in this regard."

TENTH TORMENT

"As for the torment of envy, we passed it without giving anything at all in payment, for I never had been envious. Here also people have to face the accusations of lack of love, hatred toward their brethren, unfriendliness, and other manifestations of hatred. Through the mercy of Christ our God, I was found innocent of all these sins; and although I saw the savagery of the demons, I was no longer afraid of them. Joyfully we went on."

ELEVENTH TORMENT

"Then we passed the station of pride, where arrogant spirits make accusations of vanity, absolute reliance on oneself rather than on God, disdain of others, and bragging; and here too the souls are tormented for their failure to give proper honor to their parents, their government, or their other superiors appointed by God, and for failure to obey them. Here we put down very little for my sins, and I was free."

TWELFTH TORMENT

"As we continued rising toward heaven, we encountered the torment of anger and ruthlessness. Happy is the man who never in his life felt anger. The eldest of the evil spirits was sitting here on a throne, and he was full of anger, ruthlessness, and pride. Ruthlessly and angrily he ordered his servants to torment and accuse me. They licked their chops like dogs and began to point out not only all those occasions when I actually said something angry or unfeeling to anyone, or harmed anyone by my words, but even those instances when I merely looked angrily at my children or punished them severely. All these cases they represented vividly and even indicated the time when everything happened, the persons on whom I poured out my anger, the very words which I then used, and in whose presence I used them. The angels replied to all this by offering part of the treasure, and we went on."

THIRTEENTH TORMENT

"After this, the torment of bearing grudges lay before us. Here merciless accusations await those who nurture in their hearts evil thoughts against their neighbors and return evil for evil. God's mercy saved me here too, for I did not tend to have such wicked designs and did not keep in mind offenses of others toward me; on the contrary, whenever I could, I displayed love and meekness toward those who offended me, and thus overcame their evil by my goodness. Here we paid nothing. Joyful in the Lord, we went on.

"Here I dared to ask my angel leaders: 'Tell me how can these terrible rulers of the air know in such detail all the evil deeds of men, and not only the open ones but even those that are secret?' The angels replied: 'Every Christian, as soon as he is baptized, receives from God an appointed guardian angel who guards him invisibly and inspires him night and day to every kind of good deed; he also records all his good deeds, for which that man later can hope to receive from the Lord grace and eternal recompense in the heavenly kingdom. The prince of darkness, who desires to draw into his own destruction the whole race of men as well, also appoints one of his evil spirits to walk in the man's steps and record all his evil deeds. It is his duty to inspire man to such deeds by any vile trickery in his power; and when he succeeds in his designs, he records all the wickedness of which the man has made himself guilty. Such an evil spirit spreads the report of every man's sins to all the stations of torment, and this is how the sins become known to the princes of the air. When the soul parts from its body and desires to go to its Creator in heaven, the evil spirits prevent the soul and show to it its sins. If the soul has done more good deeds than evil, they cannot keep it; but if the sins outweigh the good deeds, they keep the soul for some time, shut it up in the prison where it cannot know God, and torment it as much as God's power allows them, until that soul, by means of prayers of the Church and good deeds done for its sake by those who are still on earth, should be granted forgiveness.

"'Those who believe in the Holy Trinity and take as frequently as possible the holy communion of the Holy Mysteries of Christ our Savior's Body and Blood—such people can rise to heaven directly, with no hindrances, and the holy angels defend them, and the holy saints of God pray for their salvation, since they have lived righteously. No one, however, takes care of the wicked and depraved heretics, who do nothing useful during their lives, and live in disbelief and heresy. The angels can say nothing in their defense.

"'When a soul proves to be so sinful and impure before God that it has no hope of salvation, the evil spirits immediately bring it down into the abyss, where their own place of eternal torment is also. There the lost souls are kept until the time of the Lord's second coming. Then they will unite with their bodies and will incur torment in fiery hell together with the devils. Note also,' said the angels, 'that this is the way by which only those who are enlightened by faith and holy baptism can rise and be tested in the stations of torment. The unbelievers do not come here. Their souls belong to hell even before they part from their bodies. When they die the devils take their souls with no need to test them. Such souls are their proper prey, and they take them down to the abyss.'"

FOURTEENTH TORMENT

"During our conversation we reached the torment of murder, where are accused not only men such as robbers, but even those who have in some way wounded another man, or given him a blow, or pushed him angrily, or shoved him. We gave a little and went on."

FIFTEENTH TORMENT

"We passed the torment of magic, sorcery, poisoning, and incantations. The spirits of this station resemble serpents, snakes, and toads. They are frightening and repulsive. By the grace of God, they found nothing of the kind in me, and we went on, accompanied by the shouts of the demons: 'Soon you will come to the torment of fornication; let us see how you will free yourself from it!'

"As we were rising, I dared to question the holy angels once more: 'Do all Christians pass these torments? Is there no possibility to pass by the torments and not be tested in any of the stations?' The angels replied, 'There is no other way for the souls that rise toward heaven. Every one goes this way, but not everyone is tormented like you; only sinners like you incur the torments, for they have not confessed their sins fully, and moved by a false sense of shame, have kept their really shameful deeds secret from their spiritual fathers. When a man wholeheartedly confesses his evil deeds and repents and regrets them, his sins are invisibly wiped out by God's mercy. When a repentant soul comes here, the tormentors of the air open their books but find nothing written there; the soul, then, joyfully ascends to the throne of God.

"'The evil spirits open their records but find nothing written there, for the Holy Spirit has made invisible all the writing. The spirits see this and know that what they have recorded has all been obliterated because of the soul's confession, and they are very much saddened by this. If the man is still alive when his confession has wiped out his sins, the spirits once again try to have an occasion to record some new sins of his.

"'Indeed, there is a great source of salvation for man in his confession! Confession saves him from many misfortunes and much unhappiness and gives him the opportunity to pass all the torments with no hindrance and to approach God. Some people do not confess their sins because they hope to have time for salvation and for a remittance of their sins; others are simply ashamed of telling their spiritual father about their sins. They will, however, be severely tested when they pass the stations of torment. There are still other people, who are ashamed of telling everything to one spiritual father. Therefore they choose several and reveal some of their sins to one and others to another, and so on; they will be punished for this kind of confession and will suffer a great deal as they pass from one torment into another.

"'If you, too, had made a complete confession of your sins and had been granted remission of them, and had then done all you could to make up for them by good deeds—if you had done all this, you would not have been subjected to such terrible torments in the stations. You were, however, greatly helped by the fact that you have long ago ceased to commit deadly sins and have spent the rest of your life in virtue. You have been helped especially by the prayers of God's holy man Basil, whom you have served greatly and diligently.'"

SIXTEENTH TORMENT

"During our conversation, we approached the torment of fornication, where souls are accused not only of actual fornication but also of amorous daydreaming, of finding such thoughts sweet, of impure glances, lustful touches, and passionate strokings. The prince of this torment was clothed in a dirty and stenchful garment befouled by a bloody foam, and there was a multitude of demons standing around him. When they saw me, they marveled that I had already passed so many torments. They brought out the records of all my deeds of fornication and accused me by pointing out the persons, the places, and the times: with whom, when, and where I sinned in my youth. I kept silent and was trembling with shame and fear. The holy angels, however, said to the devils, 'Long ago has she left her deeds of fornication and has spent the remainder of her life in purity, abstinence, and fasting.' But the demons replied, 'We, too, know that she has long ago ceased sinning, but she has not sincerely confessed to her spiritual father and has not received from him proper directions for the penance she should make for her sins. Therefore she is ours! Either leave her to us or ransom her with good deeds.' The angels put down many of my good deeds but even more did they take from the gift given us by the holy man Basil; barely did I save myself from great grief."

SEVENTEENTH TORMENT

"We reached the torment of adultery, where are accused of their sins those who are married but do not observe marital fidelity toward each other and do not keep their marriage bed undefiled; here, too, rapes are punished. Besides, here are strictly punished those who have devoted themselves to

God and promised to live for Christ alone, but have fallen and failed to keep their purity. I, too, had a great debt here; the evil spirits already had accused me and were about to tear me from the arms of the angels, but the angels began to argue with them and show them all my later labors and good deeds. After some time they rescued me, but with difficulty, and not so much by my good deeds—all of which, down to the last, they deposited here—but rather by the treasure of my father Basil, from which they also took very much to put on the scale to balance my iniquities. Then they took me and we went on."

EIGHTEENTH TORMENT

"We approached the station of the Sodomic sins; here souls are accused of all unnatural sins, incest, and other revolting deeds performed in secret— shameful and frightening even to think about. The prince of this torment was more disgusting than any other devil; he was befouled by pus and full of stench. His servants were just like him. The stench that came from them was not to be endured, their ugliness was unimaginable, their cruelty and ruthlessness not to be expressed. They surrounded us but by the grace of God found nothing in me and ran away from us in their shame. We went on.

"The holy angels said to me: 'You have seen, Theodora, the frightening and disgusting torments of fornication! Know then that few are the souls that pass them without stopping and paying their ransom, for the whole world lies immersed in the evils of seductive foulness, and all mankind is sensuous. Few guard against the impurities of fornication and deaden the desire of their own flesh. And this is the reason why few pass here freely; many come as far as this place but perish here. The rulers of the torments of fornication boast that they, more than any of the others, fill the fiery abyss of hell with the souls of men. But you, Theodora, must thank God that you have already passed the torments of fornication by the prayers of the holy man Basil, your father. Now you will no longer fear.'"

NINETEENTH TORMENT

"Thereafter we came to the torment of heresies, where are punished those whose reasonings about faith are not right, and also those who turn away from the Orthodox confession of faith, who lack faith, have doubts about it, deny holy things or show a negative attitude toward them, and other sins of this kind. I passed this torment without being tested; we were no longer far from the gates of heaven.

TWENTIETH TORMENT

"But here we were met by the evil spirits of the last torment, the station that tests lack of compassion and cruelty of heart. Cruel are the tormentors of this place, and their prince is terrible; dried-up and depressed is his appearance. Here the souls of the unmerciful are tormented without mercy. Even if a man performs the most outstanding deeds, mortifies himself by fasting, prays ceaselessly, and guards and keeps the purity of his body, but is merciless— from this station he is cast down into the abyss of hell and will receive no mercy in all eternity. We, however, by the grace of Christ, passed this place without trouble, for we were helped by the prayers of the holy man Basil.

"Now we approached the gates of heaven. We entered joyfully, for we had passed unharmed through the bitter tests of the torments. The gates resembled crystal, and the buildings that stood there glistened like stars. The youths who stood there were wearing golden garments. They joyfully received us, for they saw that a soul had escaped from the bitter tests of the torments of the air.

"As we were walking in heaven, joyful and glad to be saved, the water that was above the earth parted, and then it closed again behind us. We came to a very awesome place where there were very beautiful youths in fiery garments. They saw the angels carrying me and met us with joy at the salvation of my soul for the kingdom of God. They went together with us and sang the divine song.

"As we continued walking, a cloud descended on us, and then another cloud. When we had gone somewhat farther, we saw an inexplicable height on which was the throne of God; it was very white and enlightened all who stood before it. Around it stood very beautiful youths, who were shining and clothed in red. Why should I, my child Gregory, tell you about it? There are things that cannot be either understood or explained. Reason is clouded by incapacity to understand fully, and memory vanishes there; I forgot where I was.

"The holy angels who had brought me there led me to the throne of God, and here I bowed before the Unseen God; and then I heard a voice which said, 'Go with her and show her all the souls of the blessed and of the sinners, all the dwellings of the saints that are in Paradise, and the dwellings in the nether regions of hell; then grant her rest wherever my follower Basil will indicate.'

"We went on a road unknown to me and came to the dwellings of the saints. What shall I say about them? I am in confusion. There are various chambers arranged artfully and beautifully. Of course they are created by

God's hand and are what the Scripture calls 'a temperate place, a place of verdure, a place of repose.' [allusion to the Orthodox funeral service, Rev 21:4, and Isa 32:18]

"When I saw all this I marveled and was very joyous and happily looked at everything. A holy angel who was showing these things to me explained, 'This is the abode of the apostles; that one—of the prophets and other martyrs; those others—of the holy bishops, holy monks, and the holy righteous.' All these were in their breadth and length like a king's city.

"When we entered and found ourselves inside these lovely dwellings, the saints met us and kissed us in spirit and rejoiced in my salvation. Then they took me to the abode of the patriarch Abraham and showed me everything that was there. Everything was full of glory and of spiritual joy; of fragrant flowers, myrrh, and sweet odors.

"There were various chambers, which are made and upheld by God's Spirit alone. We saw there a multitude of infants who were happy and rejoicing. I asked my angel leaders, 'Who are these infants gathered here, bathed in light, rejoicing around this holy old man?' The angels replied that this was the patriarch Abraham, and that the multitude was composed of Christian infants.

"Then we went to see the surroundings of Paradise; but their beauty simply cannot be described. If I should begin to tell all that I saw and heard there, I should be filled with fear and trembling.

"Then I was led into the nether reaches of hell, where the Lord has bound and imprisoned Satan. There I saw frightening torments. Thence they led me westward, and there, too, I saw similar horrible torments, ready for sinners. As the angels showed all this to me, they said, 'Do you see from what misfortunes you have been saved by the prayers of the holy man?'

"The sinners in their horrible torments were shrieking and begging for mercy. I saw torments of such a kind that it is excruciating even to tell about them. When we had passed and examined all this, one of the angels who accompanied me said, 'You know, Theodora, that in the world there is the custom to remember the dead on the fortieth day after their death; today the holy man Basil remembers you on earth in his prayers.'

"Yes, my spiritual child Gregory, forty days have now passed since the time when my soul parted from my body, and I am in the place which is ready also for our holy father Basil. You are still in the world, and so is holy Basil, but he shows the way of truth to all who come to him, and by compelling them to repent he makes many turn to the Lord.

"Come with me. We shall enter my inner chamber and you will look at it. Not long before you came, the holy man Basil was also here." I went after her and we entered together. As we were walking along I saw that her garments were as white as snow. We entered a palace decorated with gold. In its midst there were various trees that bore splendid fruit. When I looked east I saw luxurious halls, light and high. There was a large table on which stood golden vessels; they looked very expensive and were wondrous to look at. In the vessels were vegetables of all sorts, and fragrance issued from them.

The holy man Basil was there, sitting on a marvelous throne. Near the table there stood people, but they were unlike those who live on earth and have bodies: they were surrounded as if by the rays of the sun, but they still looked human. As they ate the food that was on the table, the amount of the food became replenished of itself. Beautiful youths were serving them. When any of those who were at the table wished to drink, a youth poured a liquid into his mouth and experienced a spiritual sweetness. They spent long hours at this table. The youths who were serving them were girded with golden belts, and on their heads were crowns made from a precious stones.

Theodora approached the holy man and begged him for me. The holy man looked at me and joyfully called me to himself. I approached and bowed before him to the ground, as was our custom. He quietly told me, "God will be merciful to you and forgive you, my child! He is the all-merciful; He will reward you with all the heavenly goods." He lifted me from the ground and continued: "Here is Theodora. You very much wished to see her and asked me for this so intently: now you do see her, and you see where she is and of what destiny her soul has been found worthy in this, our life beyond death. Look at her well."

Theodora looked at me and said, "My brother Gregory! Because you thought about me humbly, the merciful Lord has fulfilled your wish through the prayer of our father, the holy man Basil." The holy man turned to Theodora and said, "Go with him and show him my garden. Let him see its beauty." She took me by my right hand and brought me to a wall in which there was a golden gate. After she had opened the gate, she led me inside the garden. There I saw trees of a marvelous beauty. Their leaves were golden, they were full of flowers and emitted an unusually pleasant fragrance.

There was a countless number of such lovely trees. Their branches were bowed to the ground because of the weight of the fruit. All this astonished me. Theodora turned toward me and asked: "Why do you wonder? How much would you marvel if you saw the garden called Paradise, which the Lord Himself planted in the East!? You would be astonished at its greatness and beauty. As compared to it, this garden is nothing." I begged Theodora to tell me who had planted this garden, for I had never seen anything like it. She replied that it was obvious that I never had, for I was still living on earth; here, however, everything was other than earthly, and the life led here was other than earthly.

"God grants such dwellings in the life beyond death, but only to those who have led a life full of labors and sweat, such as the life our holy father Basil has led from his youth to his deep old age. Such dwellings are granted to those who pray zealously and deny their desires, as he has done when he slept on bare ground, endured intense heat and frost, ate on occasion nothing except grass. This was the kind of life which he led before he came to Constantinople, but this life was a source of salvation to himself, and through him, to many others. This kind of life, and prayers of holy men like Basil, enable the departed to enter the abodes of the blessed.

"He who during his earthly life endures many griefs and misfortunes; he who strictly keeps the Lord's commandments and does not swerve from them—he receives his reward and his comfort in the life beyond death. The holy author of the Psalms, David, said about the difficult life on earth that pleases God: 'For thou shalt eat the fruit of thy labors; blessed art thou, and it shall be well with thee'" (Ps 127:2).

When Theodora told me that life in heaven is different from life on earth, I could not help touching myself, for I seemed eager to know if I was still in the flesh, which, of course, I was. My feelings and thoughts were pure, and my spirit rejoiced in all that I had seen. I wished to return to the palace by the same gate through which I had entered. When, however, I had returned to the palace, I no longer found anyone at the table. I bowed to Theodora and returned home; and at that very moment I awoke and thought to myself: where had I been and what was all that which I had seen and heard?

I rose from my bed and went to the holy Basil in order to learn from him whether my vision was from God or from the devils. When I came to him, I, according to our custom, bowed to the ground. He blessed me, bade me to sit near him, and asked me: "Do you know, my child, where you were this night?"

I pretended to know nothing and replied: "My father, I have been nowhere; I was sleeping on my bed." The holy man said, "This is true. Your body actually was asleep on your bed, but your spirit was elsewhere, and you still know everything that was revealed to you this night. You have seen Theodora. When you approached the gates of the heavenly kingdom, she met you joyfully, led you inside the house, showed you everything, told you about her death and about all the torments that she had passed.

"Was it not at my bidding that you went into the court where you saw a marvelous table and its wondrous arrangement? Did you not see the vegetables placed there, and did you not recognize their sweetness and see the flowers, and what the feasters drank, and what youths were serving them? Did you not stand still and look at the beauty of those halls? When I came, did I not tell you to look at Theodora, since you had so much wished to see her and learn from her how she had been rewarded for her saintly life? Did she then not lead you at my bidding within the sacred enclosure? Did you not see all this in your vision this night? How is it then that you are saying that you have seen nothing?"

When I heard the saint saying all this, I no longer doubted that this was no delusion, no dream, but an actual vision sent to me by the Lord God. I said to myself, how great must this holy man be before God! He himself was there in both his body and his soul, and now he knows all that I have seen and heard there! My eyes filled with tears and I said, "It is true, my holy father; everything was such as you have said. I thank the lover of men, the Lord our God Jesus Christ, Who has granted it to me to see all this and has put it in my thoughts to take recourse to you, so that I can constantly be under the protection of your prayers and can be filled with the sweetness of my vision, in which such great marvels have been revealed to me."

The saint said to me, "If, my child Gregory, you will complete your earthly journey rightly and will not swerve from the divine commandments, the evil spirits of the torments in the air will be unable after your death to harm you. You have heard this from Theodora: you will pass the stations of torment and will be blessed. Joyfully will you be met where you have been this night and have seen Theodora, and where I, sinner that I am, also hope to be admitted to the abode which you have seen; for I place my hope upon Christ, Who has promised to give His grace to me.

"Listen, my child, to what I am saying to you, but keep the secret of your father. I wish to die before you, and you will follow me after a long time, when you will have perfected yourself in good works. This has been revealed to me by the Lord. Keep secret all that I have told you, while I am alive; let no one find out anything of what you have heard. When I am dead, if you should wish to undertake the labor and not to leave my humble life without remembrance, describe it as it is customary to describe the lives of those who have exerted themselves in virtue. Describe, that is, not so much my life but that divine grace which has led and strengthened me throughout my entire life, and given me the ability to perform not only good deeds but even miracles.

"Represent all that you seen and heard, and let it benefit those who will read or listen to your account. But be careful to state, first of all, that the Lord, when He so deigns, helps any man to do great wonders; and tell everything about these wonders witnessed by you, so that those who will learn about them from you may praise God, Who is generous with what is good. Beware of the traps of the evil one at all times of day and night until the Lord should call you." All this and many other things did the holy man tell me. Then he prayed and dismissed me.

From *Lives of the Saints* for March 26.

CHAPTER 20

Testimony of the Departed About the Immortality of the Soul and the Afterlife

The blessed Augustine tells about a physician named Gennadius who doubted the immortality of the soul and the existence of a future life. Once in a dream he saw a youth who said to him, "Follow me." He followed and came to a city. After some time the same youth appeared to him once more in a dream and asked, "Do you know me?"—"Very well do I know you," replied the physician. "How is it that you know me?"—"You took me to a city where I heard unusually pleasant singing."

"Did you see the city and hear the singing in a dream or in a waking state?"—"In a dream."—"And how about your perception of me now? Do you hear me speaking in a dream or awake?"—"In a dream," replied Gennadius.

"Where is your body at this moment?"—"In my bed."—"Do you realize that at this moment you see nothing with your bodily eyes?"—"Yes, I do."—"What then are those eyes with which you now see me?" The physician did not know what to reply, but the youth said to him, "Just as now you see and hear me although your eyes are closed and all your feelings are inactive, so will you live after death: you will see, but only with your spiritual eyes. Do not doubt that after this life there will be another."

From the works of A. Calmet, p. 95.

* * *

A highly educated man who deserves fullest confidence, A. N. S-in, tells the following occurrence from his own life.

"Several years ago I fell in love with a girl whom I intended to marry; the day of our wedding was already set. A few days before the wedding, however, my betrothed caught a cold, fell ill with a rapidly progressing variety of consumption, and died after three or four months. The blow was very great, but time did its duty. I forgot my betrothed, or rather, no longer grieved for her as I used to right after her death.

"Once it so happened that, because of my profession, I had to undertake a trip and pass through one of the cities of our province of Y. There I had some relatives, and I stopped with them for a day. I was given a room in which to spend the night. I had with me an intelligent and devoted dog. I still remember that the night was very bright; the moon was shining so clearly that it was possible to read by its light. I was just beginning to fall asleep when I heard my dog growl. I knew that it never growled without reason, and therefore thought that probably a cat happened to be in the room when the door was closed, or that a mouse had run across the floor. I rose slightly from my bed but noted nothing, although the dog continued growling more and more. It was obviously afraid of something: when I looked at it, I saw its hair standing on end. I tried to calm it, but it grew more and more afraid. Now I, too, felt fear, even though I did not know what it was that frightened me. It was not my nature to be a coward; but now I was so frightened that my own hair stood on end. It is remarkable that my fear grew together with the fear of my dog; finally it reached such a degree that it seemed I would faint in a moment.

"But then my dog calmed down, and so did I; and at the same time I began to feel some presence in the room. I felt myself waiting for its appearance, although I did not know who it was. When I grew quite calm, my betrothed suddenly approached me, kissed me, and said, 'Hail, A. N.! You do not believe that there is life beyond the grave; see, I have now appeared to you. Look at me; you see that I am alive, that I am even kissing you. Believe, my friend, that man's life does not cease with death.' And then she pointed out to me what I should read in the Holy Scripture about the afterlife; and what I should read in other writings dealing with spiritual questions. Then she told me some things which she forbade me to tell others. When I got up on the following morning, I discovered that my hair had turned completely white in that one night, so that my relatives were frightened when they saw me at breakfast. And I must confess that before this event I believed in nothing: neither in God, nor in the immortality of the soul, nor in the afterlife. For several years I had not been to church and had remained without confession and holy communion. I laughed at everything sacred, and the fasts, holidays, and sacred customs of the Orthodox Church did not exist for me. Now, however, by God's grace, I have once more become a Christian and a believer. I do not know how to thank the Lord that He has saved me from the abyss of destructive error."

To this we can add that at the time he wrote this A. N. S-in was a justice of the peace in one of the provincial towns in the Northwest. He became so pious that he apparently never missed a single church service.

* * *

A parish priest tells the following: "In the year 1864, there arrived at our village a young man, about twenty-five years of age, who settled in a small house. At first he went nowhere, but in about two weeks I saw him in church. Although he was young, his face did not look fresh, and in places was full of folds and wrinkles. Apparently his youth had not passed without storms and upheavals. He began to visit our church often; not only on holidays but also on weekdays one could see him praying somewhere in a corner, by the weak light of a holy lamp. He always came early, left later than anyone else, and every time kissed the cross with unusual reverence.

"Eventually the young man told me the following story: 'My father was a small landowner in the canton D. of the province of Y. He owned only one village, and that was small. My life took a quiet and smooth course; I was an exemplary child. When, however, I turned ten, I was placed in a secular secondary school. It was difficult for me to become used to my new life. In this institution I no longer received the warm, truly religious upbringing to which I had been exposed in my home at every step. At first I was religious and frequently prayed, but my prayers often were the object of my comrades' ridicule. All the students at this institution, being far removed from their parents, were terrible blasphemers, and their acid jests fell on me like hailstones, merely because I was religious. I had no one to support me, and my desire to pray grew weaker day by day, at first because I was shamed by my comrades, and then because it became a habit not to pray. I joined my comrades, and after a while it did not even occur to me to pray. Our talks and conversations were of the most sordid and ungodly kind. Ridicule of the Holy Scripture, of the church service, of the diligence and piety of some priests and the common people—these formed the subject of our conversations. At first I felt very uneasy at all this. Later, time and the surroundings dulled my feeling of discomfort, and the last manifestations of the good upbringing which I had received at home died down. Still, although I had changed for the worse in this society, I was conscious of my sin before God; but I still continued to do as my comrades did.

"'Time passed. In my last year at school I fell completely. My former jests about sacred customs and the piety of some people now passed into complete ridicule of divine religion in its entirety. I became a convinced materialist.

The existence of God, the immortality of the soul, the future life—all this I held to be fantasy and wickedly laughed at it all. I threw from me my cross, that instrument of our salvation, and looked at it with derision and disgust. When I was in church—for the students were expected to attend church—I ridiculed and laughed at the entire divine service. When days of fasting came, I purposely made all attempts to eat something forbidden, in order to show how fully I despised the rules of the Church. The holy icons and the lives of the saints were the principal objects of my insults. Before taking holy communion, I made all efforts to eat something, and only then would I go to communion. In short, at that time I was some sort of monster, not a human being.

"'The time came for me to leave the institution. I threw myself with all my strength into the abyss of destruction; and many, many were the pure and innocent souls that I dragged after me!

"'In one and the same year both my good parents died of cholera. It must have been their warm prayer before the throne of the Almighty that brought their erring son to better himself. When I received the news of their death, I went to their village in order to visit the grave. It is strange that I should have done so. Even though I had become bad and had nothing but laughter for all of man's sacred feelings, still my affection for my parents remained, and my cold and debased reason yielded to the voice of my heart; it did not laugh at my heart's desire to visit the grave. I ascribe this to a special influence of God's providence, for my journey home was the beginning of my improvement. When I came to my native village, I asked the church caretaker where was the grave of such and such people. Not even having crossed myself at the church, I went to the place indicated.

"'The grave was only ten steps or so from me. I already saw the fresh soil, and . . . my eyes grew dark, my breath stopped, my heart turned, and I fell on the ground unconscious. I do not know what happened next. I regained consciousness at the rooms which my servant had rented from a peasant. He told me how everyone thought that I had a stroke, for when they found me unconscious, my face was red, and there was foam on my lips. On the following day, I got up and felt completely well. No matter how I strained my mind, I could not explain my seizure. At the same time of day, I once more went to the grave; but how great do you suppose my surprise was when once again the same thing happened as on the preceding day? I thought that I had fallen ill with epilepsy and that the illness returned to me during certain hours of the day. On the third day, therefore, I stayed home. There was no seizure. On the fourth day, I went to the grave again; as soon as I began approaching it the seizure recurred. When I got up on the following day, I saw that my servant was frightened of me. As I found out later, he had decided that these seizures meant something very bad: I must have been a great sinner, he thought, if the Lord did not let me approach the grave of my parents. My servant was happier than I: he possessed faith in divine providence, in God; I, on the other hand, was a miserable man who did not want to acknowledge in all these events the finger of God. Still, I, too, was mystified by these strange seizures, and I sent for the nearest doctor. The doctor promised to come the next day, and I decided to wait for him. Around twelve o'clock at night I fell asleep. Early in the morning I awoke; but, oh my God! I shudder to think of it: I could not move, my tongue did not obey me, I lay there as if I were paralyzed, my whole body seemed to burn, my lips were dry, I felt a terrible thirst, and I was very despondent.

"'The doctor came, examined me, and gave me medicine. He began to treat me. At first he prescribed various medicines with no difficulty. Then he would spend a long, long time sitting at my bedside and biting his lips. Finally, after he had been treating me for six weeks, he wrote me a note: "Whenever I have anything to do with a man, I always openly speak about his illness, even when it is very dangerous. Your illness, however, cannot be explained, in spite of my efforts to understand it. Since I do not expect to be successful in my labors, I am leaving you. See if the illness will perhaps reveal its identity."

"'How great was my terror when human assistance gave me up, the only assistance in which I had hope! Others hope for help from above, but I rejected this. Every day my illness grew more intense and complicated. There appeared on my body pimples, which then turned into foul-smelling wounds full of pus. I did not know what to do. I did not sleep at night and found no rest.

"'Once—I was just going to sleep—I felt someone's hand on mine. I started, opened my eyes and—oh my God!—my mother was standing before me. I could not imagine how she could be there. After all, she is dead, I thought; how can she appear to me? My heart, however, was beating violently. My mother was all dressed in white, and only at one place was there a black spot. Her face was dismal, and she was surrounded by some kind of twilight. "I am your mother," she said; "your iniquities and your undisciplined life, full of disbelief and ungodliness, have come to the Lord, and He was about to destroy you from the face of the earth. You not only have destroyed yourself but have even spotted us; this black spot on my soul is made of your heavy sins. The Lord was about to destroy you, I say, but your father and I prayed before the throne of the Almighty for you, and He wished to turn you to Himself; not by His mercy, which you would not be able to understand, but by His severity. He knew that only our grave here was dear to you, and He consequently did not allow you to visit it, but instead has inflicted on you a supernatural disease, so that you should recognize a supreme power which you have rejected; but you still have not turned to God. Now the Lord has sent me to you. This is the last means to make you better your life. You did not acknowledge God, the future life, the immortality of the soul; but here you have a proof of life beyond death: I am dead, yet I have appeared and am speaking to you. Believe in God Whom you have denied! Remember your mother who, not sparing herself, attempted to make you a true Christian!"

" 'Her face at these words grew even darker, her sobs resounded throughout the room and shook my whole soul. "I entreat you once more," said my mother, "turn to God. You do not believe me or, perhaps, you think to explain my appearance to you as a creation of your disturbed imagination. You must know that your explanations are false, and I am standing before you in my own spiritual being. As proof of this, take this cross which you have rejected; take it or you will perish. Believe, and your illness will be miraculously cured. But if you reject me, destruction and eternal hell will be your lot!"

" 'So spoke my mother and disappeared. I came to my senses and saw in my hand a small cross. All this upheaved my soul down to its most secret depths. My conscience rose with all its strength; my former convictions fell. In one minute I seemed to experience a complete rebirth. A sweet feeling which I could not explain appeared in my breast, and I was about to thank God for His mercy. At this moment my servant came into the room carrying a teacup full of water. "Drink this, dear master, and perhaps you will be better," he said; "this is holy water from the immersion of the life-giving cross." I joyfully accepted this suggestion. He helped me to raise myself, and I drank the water. Oh Lord! I cannot recollect that wonderful moment without being deeply moved. I immediately felt healthy. My limbs once more obeyed me, my tongue moved freely in speech, and instead of the sores only spots remained. I rose, and first of all prayed before the icon brought by my servant. After this, I went to church and prayed there; and how much sincere feeling was there in my heartfelt prayer! I went to the dear grave, kissed it and wept on it, and my burning tears were washing away my former life; they were the repentance of the prodigal son.' "

From "Diocesan Announcements of Nijni-Novgorod," 1885, no. 24.

* * *

A certain priest lost his intelligent and pious wife after sixteen years of marriage. He was very affected by his loss. Deep sorrow and inexpressible sadness took possession of him. He became despondent, became infirm in his purpose, and went downhill. He began to drink. "I do not know," says the widowed priest, "how long I would have continued along this dangerous path if my departed wife herself did not stop me. She appeared to me in a dream and said to me with deep compassion for my condition, 'My friend! What has happened to you? You have chosen a dangerous way on which you will lose people's respect, and what is more important, lose God's blessing, which until now has rested on our house. Your position is such that even a small blemish on your reputation can seem great. Everyone sees you everywhere. Besides, you have six children, like six fledglings that have not yet learned how to fly; for them you must be both father and mother. Have you so entirely ceased to value your position, your merits, and that honor which everyone used to render to you? Do you think that your honor, your life, your merits were needed by your wife alone? Think, my friend, about this; I entreat and beseech you, judge the situation sensibly and hasten to leave this road along which, to my great sorrow, you have been going. You are sad because you have parted with me; but, as you see, our union is not broken: we can even now be in spiritual communion with each other. If you will be found worthy, in our future life we can be eternally reunited. You complain about the emptiness in your heart. Fill this emptiness with love for God, for your children, for your brethren; feed your soul with the bread of the angels, as you used to call the word of God—you always used to feed yourself and your children with it. Pray to God for me and for yourself and for our children, and for the souls entrusted to you.' The voice of my beloved wife penetrated deeply into my soul and affected me for the better. I accepted it as the voice of my guardian angel, or even as the voice of God Himself, Who was bringing me to my senses. I decided to resist temptation with all my strength. I have now, God be thanked, through His help surmounted temptation, and am firmly standing on the right way."

From *The Pilgrim*, July 1865.

* * *

An official relates the following. "My father was very ill and asked that I should visit him. He lived quite far from me, in Chicago. He believed that the departed souls can return to earth, but he never was successful in persuading me of this. When I came to him on this occasion, he told me that he was particularly glad to see me because he would not live on earth much longer.

"'How can this be?' I said. 'Do you really think that you will soon die?'— 'No,' he replied, 'I shall not die but leave my earthly body. Soon I shall go to the world of the spirits and there be clothed in a spiritual body. I wanted to see you in order to ask you for a promise. When I shall depart to the other world I shall come and show myself to you. Promise me this: when you see and recognize me, you will believe that souls can return; and you will testify to this.'

"To this I replied: 'All right, father; but now you should not speak about death. Perhaps you will grow well and still live a long time.'—'I am telling you that I shall not die now,' he objected, 'but you will no longer see me in my earthly guise after this our meeting. Do not forget your promise.'

"When I parted from him, he was relaxed and felt well, but he repeated that he would soon go into the world of the spirits and then would come to me. Ten days after I had returned home I decided to give a dinner for several of my friends, for there had been no bad news about my father. I spent the whole day in the fulfillment of various duties. When I went to bed I was thinking about the next day and the preparations for the dinner.

"No sooner had I fallen asleep when I suddenly woke up, without the interval that was usual for me, between deep sleep and awakening. I looked around, trying to find out what it was that had wakened me. At the opposite end of the room I saw a bright light, something like a light spot the size of my palm. I began to look at it closely and became convinced that this light could not penetrate from the outside. This was a delicate, white light, very much like moonlight; it moved in waves and trembled like a living thing. Soon the light spot began to draw near me. At the same time it grew larger and larger in size. It seemed to be moving toward me. When it had approached, I began to distinguish in it an entire human figure. This person stood before me so that I was able to distinguish all his features. Nothing in him had changed, only his face seemed younger and less tired than it was during our last meeting, and his figure was more straight and vigorous. He began to speak, and his voice was so much like the voice of my father that I no longer could doubt that this was he. He said with his gentle smile, 'Do you remember your promise? I have come to you as I promised.'—'Father, did you die?' I asked him. 'No,' he objected, 'I did not die; I am alive, but I have left my earthly body and am now clothed in a spiritual body. I am at peace and rest. But you must not forget your promise.'

"I do not know why I suddenly asked him: 'Father, what time is it now?'—'Exactly four minutes after midnight,' he said. 'So you died in the night?' I asked.—'I am telling you,' he said, 'I have not died, I am quite alive, I want you to fulfill your promise and believe that the spirits of those whom you love can return to earth.'

"Then he parted from me, and his entire figure seemed to dissolve into a light cloud; gradually it disappeared in the same way in which it had appeared; it seemed swallowed by darkness.

"On the following day, when my friends came to dinner, the bell suddenly rang and I was given a telegram which said, 'Father died today at midnight.' I feel, or rather, I am convinced that I saw my father. My supposition, however, cannot be verified, and his appearance remains to me a mystery."

From *Rebus*, 1889, no. 49.

* * *

When the Russian Prince Vladimir Sergeevich Dolgoruki held the position of ambassador at the court of Prussia, he was infected there with free thinking. He no longer believed in God and in life after death. When his brother Prince Peter found out about it, he began to write letters to him in which he implored him, "Believe me, my brother; without true faith there is no happiness on earth; faith is absolutely necessary for future life"; and other things to this effect. But everything was in vain. Prince Vladimir Sergeevich laughed at the convictions of his pious brother.

Returning from Prussia, and because he was feeling very tired, he quickly undressed, threw himself on his bed, and soon fell asleep. Suddenly he heard someone pulling away his draperies, approaching him, and touching him with a cold hand; he even felt a handshake. He looked up and saw his brother, who said to him: "Believe!" The prince, overjoyed at his brother's sudden appearance, was about to throw himself into his arms when suddenly the apparition disappeared. He asked his servants, "Where did my brother go?" but heard from them that they had seen no one. He tried to convince himself that this was a dream, but the word "believe" did not cease to ring in his ears. He had no peace of mind.

He wrote down the day, hour, and minute of the vision. Soon he received news that on that very day, hour, and minute, his brother Peter Sergeevich had died. From that time on he became a pious and believing Christian and frequently told others about his vision.

From *How Our Departed Live* by the Hieromonk Mitrophanes, vol. 1.

* * *

In his recollections, which came out after his death, the protopriest N. Sokolov tells the following. "I had a comrade at the seminary. We were good friends and roomed together during our course of theological studies. He was a son of the priest of Bolhovo, and his name was Nicholas Semenovich Veselov. After we graduated from the seminary, he remained behind and became a teacher at the local school. I became a priest at Cherson.

"Once I dreamed about him in such a way that I understood that he no longer was alive. I wrote to his father and received the reply that his son had died, and died on exactly that day and at that hour when I dreamed about him. My dream had been as follows.

"I seemed to be at the Cherson cemetery near an ancient monument in the shape of a pyramid. Some stones had fallen out of the monument, and there was in it an opening about five inches wide. I became curious and climbed through the opening into the monument. When, however, I wanted to climb out again, I could not find the opening in the darkness. I began to break the stones; finally there appeared light. After I had enlarged the opening, I climbed out and discovered that I was in a beautiful garden. When I turned into one of the walks, Veselov came toward me.

"'Nicholas Semenovich, how is it that I find you here?' I exclaimed.

"'I have died, you see . . .' he replied.

"His face was shining, his eyes were brilliant, his neck and breast were bare. I rushed toward him to kiss him, but he jumped back and stretched out his arms to keep me away. 'I have died,' he said, 'do not approach me.' I indeed believed that he was in another world, and grew afraid. When, however, I looked at him and saw his joyful face, my fear disappeared. Veselov and I went side by side without touching.

"'I am alive, even though I have died; to be dead and to be alive is the same thing,' he said. His words appeared to me so logical that I had nothing to say to them. When we approached the old monument in the shape of a pyramid, Veselov said, 'Farewell, you will now go home,' and pointed to the opening. I climbed into it and immediately became awake."

From "Appendix to the Diocesan Announcements of Chersonese," 1891, no. 11.

* * *

Archbishop Nilus of Jaroslavl tells the following: "In 1871 a man by the name of A. Y., who was one of our choir singers and had reached the age of only twenty-four, died in an epidemic of cholera. Ten days after his death, on the morning on the July 16, he appeared to me in a dream. He was wearing a coat in which I had seen him before, only this coat had become much longer and reached to the ground. At the moment when he appeared I was sitting at the window of my sitting room. He came from the hall fairly quickly, as he always did. After he had bowed, he came to the table, and without saying a word, began to throw on it from his waistcoat pockets some copper money, among which there were also some silver coins.

"I was amazed and asked him: 'What does this mean?' He replied: 'This is to pay my debt.' (It must be noted here that the day before, someone came to me from the photographer G. and said that, according to their books, Y. owed them four rubles.) I was very surprised and kept repeating: 'No, no, I do not need your money, I shall pay your debt myself.' At my words, Y. quietly said to me, 'Speak more softly, please, so that the others will not hear you.'

"As to my willingness to pay his debt, he did not object. He immediately collected the money from the table, but I could not tell where he put it; the money seemed simply to disappear suddenly. I rose from my chair and asked Y., 'Where are you now that you have left us?'—'As if in a closed castle.'—'Do you have any communication with the angels?'—'We are strangers to the angels.'—'Do you have any relationship with God?'—'I shall tell you some other time.'

"'Is not Misha together with you?' (Misha was also a singer, a boy who used to live in the same room with Y. and died about four years before.)—'No.'—'Who then is with you?'—'All sorts of rabble.'—'Have you any entertainment?'—'None. There is even no sound, for spirits do not talk among themselves.'—'Have the spirits any food?'—'No, none....' This he said with apparent displeasure, probably because my question was inappropriate.

"'How do you feel?'—'I am sad.'—'How can you be helped?'—'Pray for me. To this day no liturgies have been offered for the salvation of my soul.' My soul was disturbed at these words, and I began to apologize to the departed man, and promised definitely to take care that forty such liturgies should be offered. My words seemed to reassure him.

"Then he asked my blessing. I asked him: 'Must you ask anyone for leave?' His reply was one word only: 'Yes.' This word sounded sad, drawn out, and forced. He asked my blessing a second time and I gave it to him. He left through the door toward the hill of Tugova, on which he had been buried.

From *Salubrious Reflections*, 1881.

CHAPTER 21

The Deaths of the Christian Boys

Mrs. Bernasconi, at the age of sixty-five, told the following story. "In the 1860s, I lived in the village of Krasnoe, on the estate of the Raevski family. My son Victor was with me. He was a wonderful child, agile, intelligent, developed beyond his years, and was remarkable for his piety. Everyone loved him, including the simple people of the village. When he turned five, he fell ill with diphtheria. One morning he said to me: 'Mama, I must die today. Get ready for me a bathtub and bathe me, so that I will come to God all clean.' I began to tell him that he would get worse: he might get a cold if I washed him. But he continued to demand his bathtub, and I yielded to his request. I washed him, dressed him in clean linen, and put him in his bed.

" 'Now, mama, give me that little icon which I love so much,' he asked, and I gave it to him.

" 'Hurry, mama, give me a candle to hold in my hand; I am going to die this moment,' said the child, and I lighted a wax taper and put it in his hand. 'Farewell now, mama!' These were the child's last words. He closed his eyes and immediately departed.

"The loss of this child was a source of unquenchable sorrow to me. I cried day and night and found comfort in nothing. One winter morning I woke and heard on the left side of my bed the voice of my child Victor. He was calling me: 'Mama, mama, are you awake?'

"I was astounded and said, 'Yes, I am awake.' I turned my head in the direction of the voice and—O wonder of wonders!—saw my Victor, who was standing there in light clothing and sadly looking at me. Light appeared to be coming directly from him, for the room was still so dark that without this light I would not have been able to see him. He stood so near me that my first impulse was to throw myself toward him and press him to my heart. But as soon as this thought appeared in my mind, he

123

warned me: 'Do not touch me, mama; I should not be touched,' and moved back. I looked at him fondly but kept silent; he meanwhile continued to speak: 'Mama, you are still crying for me; but why? I am happy there, but I would be even happier if you did not cry so much. Do not cry.' He suddenly disappeared.

"Two years later, Victor appeared to me once again, when I was awake in my bedroom. 'Mama, you do not need Olya, why should you have her?' he said. (Olya was my daughter; at that time she was about a year old.) When I asked him: 'Are you going to take her too?' he replied: 'You do not need her,' and disappeared. Two weeks before she died he appeared again and said, 'Mama, you do not need Olya; the rest of your children are all big, she will just get in your way.' I was convinced that my daughter would die. Two weeks later, I was not at all surprised when I came home and heard from the nurse that the child had a fever. In two days my Olya was dead."

From *Rebus*, 1893, no. 2.

* * *

Count M. V. Tolstoy related the following: "In the night between the 28th and the 29th of September, I dreamed that I was standing in my hall and that I heard the voices of my children from the drawing room. As I looked on, the children came into the hall, among them our departed son Volodya. I happily rushed toward him; he smiled at me with his angelic smile, just as he used to. I stretched my arms toward him. 'Is this you, Volodya?' I asked. He rushed to me, threw his arms around my neck, and embraced me very closely.

"'Where are you, my joy? Are you with God?'—'No, I am not yet with God, but soon I shall be with God.'—'Are you happy?'—'Yes, happier than here. But I frequently am here, all the time near you. Almost always I am alone, but sometimes Mary Magdalene is with me. Sometimes I am sad.'

"'When are you sad?'—'Especially when anyone is weeping for me. It comforts me when people pray for me or give something to the needy on my behalf. I pray all the time; I pray for mother, for you, for my brothers, for Pasha (his sister), for everyone who loves me. Embrace my dear mama for me, closely, like this.'

"'You ought to see her, my joy.'—'I shall, I definitely shall.'—'When?'—'When she will stop weeping.' At this point I heard my wife's voice from the corridor, turned toward her, then looked back—but he no longer was there.

"I woke up. My heart was beating fast, and I was so moved that I could not keep myself from sobbing loudly, so that my wife woke up. I immediately wrote down what I had dreamed, word for word."

From *Simple Accounts of Complex Things*, in Russian, by M. Pogodin.

* * *

A priest, Father Nicholas Orloff of the city of Tver, tells about the following marvelous occurrence. In September 1860, the children of the Tverian townsman Sergius P. Blinoff were very ill with scarlet fever. On the 15th, his little son Arsenius, who was one year old, died of this disease; a week later he lost his daughter Mary, who was three years old; finally, about three days later, on the 25th of the month, his 12-year-old son Nicholas also approached death.

It must be noted that Nicholas was the eldest son in the family and greatly helped his father in his business. His mind was quick beyond his years; a kind heart was combined in him with a sincere love and tenderness toward his parents, sisters, and brothers. In his contacts with everyone else, but especially with those who were older than he, he was unusually, but very attractively, sweet in speech and most respectful. Thus everyone loved him: his parents, relatives, and all who knew him.

It was very bitter for the parents to see their dear son during the last hours of his life. Still, they kept concealing their bitter tears from the dying boy and diligently continued praying to the Lord for his life. He expressed a wish to confess and to take holy communion as soon as possible. The priest was called. When he came in, the boy rose from his bed, and standing upright, confessed wholeheartedly and touchingly; later he attentively listened to the brief prayers before communion and also prayed very diligently. When the priest told him to repeat the words that he was reciting—"I believe, O Lord, and I confess that Thou art truly the Christ, the Son of the Living God ..." and "Of Thy Mystical Supper, O Son of God, accept me today as a communicant ..." and so on—the ill boy made the sign of the cross and then, as if inspired, pronounced these prayers with such a fire of love and faith in God's Son Jesus Christ, and with so strong a desire of eternal life and union with God, that the priest was amazed. After he had taken holy communion, the boy turned to an icon of the Savior and with a deep feeling of gratitude said, "I thank Thee, O God! I thank Thee."

After a prayer of thanks, the priest wished him to be well in body and soul and said, "Many people who during their sickness take holy communion with faith soon get well of their illness. You, too, will now get well according to your faith. May God make you well. You must live. You are still young." But God's young elect, although he thanked the priest for his good wishes, said to him: "No, Father, I am not going to live in this world; I shall die, surely I shall die."

"How can you say that you will die?" the priest retorted. "How can you know? God alone knows such things and appoints to every man his own time of life and his own time of death." But the boy said, "So it is, father. But I know from none but God that I shall die. He is calling me, and I shall go to Him."

The priest saw that the child was weakening and therefore, having taken leave of him and his parents, left him to rest. The ill boy lay down on his bed. This was at half past six in the evening. No later than half an hour after this, the boy, still lying in bed, began to recite quietly but in a hurried and very diligent way all those prayers that he knew—prayers to the Savior and to His Mother and the holy men—and finally, having made the sign of the cross, he began to grow weak. He fell as into a sleep, then he stopped breathing; finally, his eyes assumed a staring expression, and he died.

His parents, who until this time were barely able to restrain themselves from weeping loudly, now gave full vent to their tears and moans. The father, the mother, the mother's sister and her brother, and finally all the other relatives who were present loudly complained to one another about the loss forever of their dear, cherished son and nephew. He whom they so mourned was lying breathless and senseless and did not hear those who were weeping and moaning.

About an hour passed thus. Finally, the mother became somewhat calmer and began to look attentively at the face of her dead son, as if she wished now, at her final parting with him, to imprint his features on her heart. The father went into another room to have a look at his two other ill children and give them the prescribed medicine.

As her eyes were resting on her dead son, the mother suddenly noticed that his breast seemed to move slightly. She thought that she was mistaken because her eyes were full of tears and because the candles and the holy lamps before the icons gave an inconstant, wavering light; however, she continued looking at him fixedly. The dead boy's breast once more moved; it kept on moving, although only slightly. She went to her husband and quietly told him of this. Hardly daring to breathe, they both attentively watched their son's remains. Another half a minute—and he actually sighed; obviously, the boy was alive. After a few more seconds he quietly opened his eyes.

They did not wish to upset him by their disquieting appearance. Therefore they stepped aside so that he might not see them. But he made attempts to see them, then rose with some effort, sat on the bed, and said to his father, "Father, come closer to me! I must say a few words to you."

When his father approached, the boy said, "I have returned here to take leave of you. I have seen Mary and Arsenius and Sasha" (this was a sister of his who had died ten years before, at age seven) "and my godfather" (who had died twelve years before) "and talked to them all. Do you think that they are dead? No! They are all alive! And how lovely is the place where they live!

"How brilliantly light it is there, how beautifully colored are the flowers and trees, and how large the stars! What is our house compared to what I have seen there! Each star there is three times the size of our house, and all the stars shine so joyously! I saw there my dear little sisters and my brother, and my godfather, and when I came near them, my godfather said to me, 'There you are, Nicolya! How did you get here?'—'I have come to visit you, to see you,' I said. 'This is good,' he said. 'Stay here and visit with your sisters and your brother; or you may even stay with us always.'—'Stay with us!' said my sisters and my brother. 'You see how wonderful it is here!'—'Indeed I shall stay,' I said; 'it is wonderful here.'

"Sister Mary took me by the hand and said, 'How wonderful it is that Nicolya is staying with us!' and led me happily along a meadow full of flowers past some tall green trees such as I have never seen. Together with us also went Arsinka and Sasha.

"But suddenly I remembered you, Father and Mother, and said, 'Oh, I have not yet taken leave of Father and Mother. Wait here; I shall go to them and ask their blessing to live here with you. I shall immediately return to you.'—'Go and do that!' they said, 'but come back as soon as you can. We'll wait for you.'

"And so I have come to you, my dear parents, in order to take leave of you and to ask your parental blessing; please let me live with my dear little sisters and brother. Let me go, dear Father and Mother; please bless me!"

During this tale, the father, mother, and the other relatives listened to him carefully. When he ended, his father thought that the boy had said all these things in high fever. To test this he said, "Nicolya, do you know who I am?" He looked at his father, smiled slightly, and said, "How can I help knowing you, my own father! You are Sergius Pavlovich Blinoff, my father!" The father pointed to the mother and said, "And who is this?"—"This is my dear mother, Alexandra Mihailovna Blinova," he said. And then he named all his other relatives who were there.

The father whispered to his wife that she should ask their son to tell them once again where he was and what he had seen. She did; and the boy repeated his own words, and much to the amazement of all, told exactly the same story as he had before.

Finally he said, "Father, do you really not believe me? Do you not see that I am in full possession of my reason; that I remember everything and am fully conscious? If you are still in doubt, here is a sign of the fact that I am speaking the truth: in a day, Xenia, the daughter of our former servant, will come to our house, although you have not seen her for many years. She will ask you about your health and that of your children and will be very surprised to learn that all your children are ill and that three of them have already died, and will say that she has heard nothing of this." (This woman actually came to them on the day of the boy's funeral and actually was surprised that three of the children had died.) "Then," he continued, "you will believe everything that I have told you. But now I ask you, I beg you, my dear parents, not to keep me here but to let me go as soon as possible. Please bless me!"

His father finally became convinced of the truthfulness of his words. With all the power of his parental love, he began to talk to him and try to convince him that he should stay and continue being his intelligent and useful helper in his business and all his occupations. But the boy said to his father, "Father, it is not worth living here. Everything here is so bad, so dirty. I entreat you to let me go. Do not wish and do not pray that I should stay here. You, too, will not live forever; you, too, will pass to that other world. If you let me go, I shall pray to God to receive you into His light and His joy."

His father was not only convinced but even reassured by such words. Unable to argue further, he blessed his son and wished that he should live in a bright place where there is no sickness, sorrow, or lamentation. After this the boy grew calm. With great joy he many times kissed his parents; then he lay back again and said, "Farewell! My time has come. They are waiting for me. God be with you. Farewell!" With these words he crossed himself, peacefully closed his eyes, and having folded his arms crosswise on his breast, departed forever from this world to the domain of the Father of light where "the righteous shall shine forth as the sun" (Matt 13:43). During the funeral, which took place on September 26, the face of this boy shone with a joyous quiet smile.

From *The Pilgrim*, 1864, pp. 18–24.

CHAPTER 22

Two Visions of the Heavenly Kingdom

Many holy men have been taken by the Holy Spirit to Paradise and from there have penetrated to heaven, to the heaven of heavens, to the very throne of the Lord, Who is surrounded by fiery seraphim and cherubim. Thus the holy man Symeon the Stylite saw in Paradise marvelous gardens, and in them the soul of the first man Adam, and the soul of the repentant thief who turned to Christ on the cross and was the first of all men who was led by God into Paradise after Christ's work of redemption was complete (*The Life of St Symeon the Stylite*, May 24).

Of all the visions of the holy fathers that are known to us, the most vivid and detailed vision of Paradise is that which appeared to St Andrew, a fool-for-Christ, who for two weeks supernaturally contemplated the invisible Paradise. He told his vision to a man who knew his secrets, Nicephorus.

"I saw that I was in a beautiful and most marvelous garden. My spirit was exalted, and I thought: what is this? I know that I am living in Constantinople; how then can I be here? I cannot understand this. I was truly amazed and did not know whether I was in the body or outside my body; only God knows. But I saw myself dressed in a most light garment which seemed woven from lightning; on my head was a crown made of large flowers, and I was girded with a belt worthy of a king. I rejoiced in this beauty, marveled at it with my mind, and rejoiced in my heart at the sweetness of God's Paradise as I walked through it. I saw many gardens with tall trees which moved their tops and were pleasant to look at; their branches emitted a wonderful fragrance. Some of the trees were perpetually in bloom; others were full of golden leaves; still others bore various fruit of unspeakable beauty and sweetness. It is impossible to compare these trees to any that grow on earth, for it was God's hand, and not that of any man, that had planted them. There were countless multitudes of birds in these gardens. Some were sitting on the branches of the trees and sang beautifully—so beautifully that I did not remember who I was, so sweetly was my heart affected. It seemed to me that their song reached the very height of heaven. These beautiful gardens were growing in rows, like armies lined up against each other.

"As I was walking there and felt my heart expand, I saw a great river that was flowing in the midst of the gardens and watering them. On the other bank there was a vineyard. Its vines were full of golden leaves and golden bunches of grapes, and they were great and broad. From all four sides there blew quiet fragrant winds, and the gardens moved in the breeze and created a wonderful sound with their rustling leaves."

St Andrew was taken up not only into Paradise but also, like the holy Apostle Paul, even up to the third heaven. He went on as follows: "After this, I grew afraid and felt that I was standing higher than the surface of heaven. A youth whose face was like the sun was walking before me. I was following him. Finally I saw a beautiful and great cross which resembled a rainbow in its colors.

"Around it were standing flamelike singers who sang a sweet song of praise to the crucified Lord. The youth who had led me approached the cross, kissed it, and made a sign to me that I should do likewise. I fell before the cross with great fear and joy and carefully kissed it. As I was doing so, I was filled with unspeakable spiritual sweetness and sensed a much greater fragrance than that of Paradise.

"Once past the cross, I looked down and saw an abyss under me, for it seemed to me that I was walking on air. I grew afraid and cried out to my guide, 'I am afraid of falling into the abyss!' He turned to me and said, 'Fear not, we must rise higher,' and gave me his hand. As I took it I saw that we were above the second surface of heaven. There I saw marvelous men and their great peace, and the joy of their perpetual festival, which is inexpressible in the tongues of men.

"After this we entered a wonderful flame which did not burn but only enlightened us. I once again became afraid, and once again he who led me turned to me and gave me his hand and said, 'We must rise to the third heaven, and even higher.' At this word we were already above third heaven, and there I heard many heavenly powers, who were singing and praising God.

"We approached a curtain that shone like lightning. Before it stood great youths who were like flames of fire. Their faces shone more brilliantly than the sun, and in their hands they held fiery weapons. They were surrounded by countless numbers of the heavenly host. The youth who was leading me said, 'When the curtain will be removed and you will see the Lord Christ, bow before the throne of His glory.'

"When I heard this, I trembled with joy. Horror, but also an inexplicable happiness, filled me. I stood there and looked at the curtain. A fiery hand removed it, and I saw my Lord as the Prophet Isaiah once saw him, sitting on a high, elevated throne, surrounded by the seraphim. He was clothed in a crimson garment, His face was shining with unspeakable light; with great love He turned His eyes on me.

"When I saw Him, I fell on my face before Him and bowed before the radiant and terrifying throne of His glory. It is impossible to tell how great a joy filled me when I saw His face. Even now, as I remember this vision, I am filled with indescribable sweetness. I lay before the Lord trembling and amazed at His mercy: how did He allow me, a sinful and impure man, to come before Him and see His divine beauty?

"I was full of great tenderness but also of a realization of my unworthiness. As I contemplated the greatness of my Lord, I repeated to myself the words of the Prophet Isaiah: 'Woe is me, for I am undone! Because I am a man of unclean lips, and I dwell in the midst of a people of unclean lips; for my eyes have seen the King, the Lord of hosts' (Isa 6:5).

"Then I heard how my all-merciful Creator said to me through His most pure and sweet lips three divine words which filled my heart with such sweetness and burned in me with so great a love for Him that I felt myself melting like wax with the warmth of my spirit; the words of David came to pass for me: 'My heart also in the midst of my body is even like melting wax' (Ps 21:15).

"Then all the hosts of heaven sang a most marvelous song, impossible to recount. Then—I do not know how—I found myself once more walking in Paradise. The thought came to me that I had not seen the Lady, the Most Holy Mother of God. And then I saw a man, brilliantly light like a cloud, who was carrying a cross. He said to me: 'You wish you had seen here the Most Holy Queen of heavenly hosts? She is not here now. She has gone to the troubled world in order to help men and to comfort those of them who are in pain. I would show you her holy abode, but now there is no time: you must return to that place from which you have come. Thus the Lord commands.' When he said this, it seemed to me that I was in that same place where I had been before my vision."

From *Lives of the Saints* for October 2.

* * *

We may compare to the preceding account the experience of St Euphrosinus. The blessed Euphrosinus was born to simple parents, but he surpassed in virtue all who were noble and wellborn. It often happens that people who come of an illustrious family possess no virtue and therefore fall into the depths of hell. On the other hand, people of humble descent rise to God's Paradise because of their outstanding humility. Thus this man also, the blessed Euphrosinus, rose to Paradise and sojourned there while he was still alive, and after death he inherited Paradise by his holy life. Here we shall tell of a vision in which a priest saw Euphrosinus in Paradise while he was still alive.

Euphrosinus was a monk, and in his monastery he served the other brethren in the kitchen. He served them not as one serves people but as one must serve God—in great humility and obedience. Day and night he performed his allotted tasks while never forgetting prayer and fasting. His patience was astounding, for he constantly suffered great troubles: ill treatment, bad words, and other annoyances. Yet while he was keeping up in the kitchen the material fire, he was aflame with the spiritual fire of love of God, and his heart was burning with zeal for Him. While he was preparing food for his brethren, he prepared for himself by his virtuous life a place in the heavenly kingdom, where he might sate himself with heavenly blessedness with those about whom it has been said, "Blessed is he who shall eat bread in the kingdom of God" (Luke 14:15). He served the Lord in secret in order to be rewarded clearly and manifestly; and rewarded he was, for the Lord revealed the deserts of His servant Euphrosinus.

An abbot, Blasius, who lived in the same monastery as Euphrosinus, always prayed to God with the desire that God might reveal to his senses those future blessings that are prepared for those who love God. One night he had a vision: he seemed to stand in Paradise and see, fearfully yet full of joy, its unspeakable beauty, and there he saw the monastery cook Euphrosinus.

Blasius approached and asked, "Brother Euphrosinus, what is this? Can this be Paradise?" Euphrosinus replied, "Yes, father, this is Paradise."— "How is it that you are here?"—"Because of God's great grace I come to dwell here, for this is the realm of God's chosen," Euphrosinus replied.

Blasius asked, "Have you any power over all this beauty?"—"I have some power to give of these things that you see here."—"Can you give me something of these good things?"—"By God's grace, take whatever you wish." Then Blasius pointed to some apples and asked for them. Euphrosinus plucked off three apples, put them in Blasius's garment, and said, "Take what you asked for and enjoy it."

At this moment, the hour of matins was struck. The abbot woke up and thought that he had been dreaming; but when he felt his garments, he found in them those apples which he had received in his vision from Euphrosinus. He felt that a great fragrance was issuing from the apples and was greatly surprised. Finally, he rose from his bed, put the apples on it, and went to church. There he saw Euphrosinus who had already arrived for the morning service. Blasius approached him and entreated him to reveal where he had been the previous night.

Euphrosinus replied, "Forgive me, father; this past night I was where you saw me." The abbot said, "This is the reason why I am entreating you by the Lord to reveal God's deeds and not to conceal the truth." Then humbly Euphrosinus said, "You, father, have asked the Lord to show to your senses how His chosen will be rewarded; the Lord has deigned to reveal this to your reverence through me, an evil and unworthy man; thus you saw me in my God's Paradise."

The abbot asked, "What was it you gave me, father, in Paradise at my request?" Euphrosinus replied, "I gave you three apples, the same apples that you have put on the bed in your cell; but forgive me, father, for I am but a worm, not a man."

At the end of matins, the abbot gathered the brethren, and after showing them the three apples of Paradise, told them in detail all that he had seen. All smelled the indescribable fragrance that issued from the apples; they were full of spiritual joy and touched and surprised at what the abbot had told them. They went to the kitchen, for they wished to bow before Euphrosinus, the servant of God, but they did not find him there: he had left the church and vanished. He escaped from the praise of men, and no one was able to find him. Where did he vanish to? There is no need to investigate: if Paradise was open for him, where else would he have gone? The apples were divided among the brethren, and portions of them were given as a blessing to many others, especially because of their healing powers, for those sick who tasted them were healed of their illnesses. Many men greatly benefited from this gift of Euphrosinus the saint and kept this marvelous vision alive not only in writing but also within their hearts. Inspired by it, they aspired to great good deeds and pleased God.

May the Lord, through the prayers of the venerable Euphrosinus, find us also worthy of His Paradise!

From the *Alphabetical Patericon*.

CHAPTER 23

Two Marvelous Occurrences

In 1871, during a severe epidemic of cholera, one of the churches in the Moscow suburbs lost Father Deacon I. S., my brother. Although he was young and strong, within only a few hours of the beginning of his illness he was already lying in his coffin. I had loved him very much, and his loss was a great grief to me. My sorrow developed into a feeling of despondency which left me only during sleep and prayer. With all my heart, I prayed for his soul. I was moved to do so not only by my love for the departed brother but also by a realization that his last confession was incomplete, for it was made during the highly painful cholera cramps. Soon after his death he appeared to me in a dream. He seemed to be alive, but I realized that he now belonged to a different world.

I began to talk about the torments of the air. "I suppose that you are now passing through torments?" I asked. "Yes," he replied.—"Tell me, how are you passing them?"—"With great difficulty," he said; "and the reason is this: I have discovered that the devils have written records of all the sins that anyone has ever committed; even momentary thoughts are recorded there, those thoughts that involuntarily arise on occasion and then pass with lightning speed. We never paid attention to such thoughts, forgot them, and never repented of them. But these involuntary and passing sins are also pointed out to us during the torments, and the souls themselves remember them and recognize them as actual occurrences." At these words he took out from under his clothes a tablet, seemingly made of cardboard, somewhat larger than a sheet of letter paper. This tablet was completely covered on one side with a record of his sins, and these were written there so densely and in so small a script that the tablet seemed to be covered with black poppy seeds. "There were twenty-five tablets of this kind to my record," he continued, "but seven of these I obliterated by my confession before death. Eighteen still remain." I next asked him if the departed were allowed to return and see whomever they might wish. "Yes, they are," he said.—"In that case, come to me more often," I said to him, but he immediately disappeared into a hole which seemed to form in the floor. After this vision I prayed for him all the more diligently, but he did not come to me for many years.

When the Lord deigned to allow me the grace of priesthood, I made use of my greater proximity to God's throne than I enjoyed while I was a deacon. Even more diligently now I began to pray for the soul of my beloved brother. During the fifth year of my priesthood he appeared—but not to me. Instead he came to a woman of my congregation, K. M., whose life was distinguished by her piety and her particularly diligent prayers for the departed. One morning she unexpectedly sent someone to ask me to come to her and talk about a very important matter. She began thus: "Did you, father, ever have a brother who died while belonging to the clergy?"—"Yes, I had a brother who was a deacon," I replied. She began to describe his outward appearance so precisely it was as if she saw him before her, and then said, "This past night he appeared to me and said, 'Tell my brother that five more tablets have been obliterated.'—'Who is your brother?' I asked. 'He is the local priest.'— 'What tablets are these you mention?'—'He will know what I mean, but be sure to tell him.'—'Why did you not appear to him instead?'—'I shall appear to him when all the tablets will be obliterated,' he said; and then disappeared. This, then, is the reason why I sent for you," said the pious woman. "I wished to learn the mystery behind this dream. Is it a true dream or not?" I told her how my brother appeared to me soon after his death and told me about the tablets. At this point I recognized that his appearance to me was not a figment of my imagination, as I considered it before, but full of significance. I began to wait for his appearance to me, which he promised me through this woman. Five years later I received news about his second appearance to this same woman, through whom he asked me to pray for him most assiduously on Great Thursday. "I need this for my sins," he said. Of course I obeyed his injunction most zealously and continued to offer special prayers for him every year on this great day which commemorates our Lord's institution of the bloodless sacrifice for our sins. His request was a sacred duty for me. Still eight years later (consequently, eighteen years after I began to wait for his personal appearance), my brother appeared to me in a dream, as he had promised, and informed me of his freedom from his sins. (It is remarkable that the number of years during which I prayed for him was the same as the number of tablets on which the records of sins had not been obliterated.) This time his appearance was very brief. I was sitting at my desk. Suddenly my brother came in from the next room. He was wearing his deacon's garment and seemed to be alive. As he was passing behind my chair, he said distinctly, "Now I am free," and became invisible. Does not this orderly series of the departed man's appearances serve as an obvious proof of a connection that exists between the world beyond and the one on earth? His appearances are clearly extraordinary. Should they not be regarded as intended to persuade those who still live on earth that our souls do not cease to exist but pass at death into another, spiritual, world, where they are to pass through torments and will be accused of their most minute sins and impure thoughts, even those thoughts that were swift to pass; and that prayers offered for the dead assist them to gain forgiveness of their sins and freedom from suffering, especially if such prayers are offered at the bloodless sacrifice?

From Priest I. Sharov in *Salubrious Reflections*, 1898.

* * *

An old monk had a vision which lasted about three hours, that is, almost throughout matins, and resembled the marvelous vision of blessed Andrew, the fool-for-Christ, who is remembered by the Church on October 2. The vision of this old monk of Mt Athos happened in March of the year 1854. It clearly reveals the error of the various Protestant sects, as well as of other people who, like the Stundists, the Baptists, the Pashkovites, and many others, deny the intercession for us of God's Mother and of the saints before the throne of the Trinity. In order to refute these sects and to establish and confirm the Orthodox in their holy faith, we shall here recount the vision of the old monk of Athos in its entirety. This is what he said about it.

"One Thursday at six o'clock at night, after the sun of the previous day had set, I got up for matins and, having entered the church and gone to my place as the brethren were already beginning the midnight prayers, I began to think about the incomprehensible depths of God's Being and to consider that He alone is the Lord, Creator, and Supporter of the whole universe; and that, for the sake of human salvation, He has taken upon Himself our nature, become a man, been crucified and buried. At these reflections I felt such sweetness in my heart and so great a joy enveloped my soul and put to rest my reason that tears began to flow copiously from my eyes. A limitless love of God filled all my being to ecstasy, but at the same time my humility, too, was limitless.

"Then my heart was opened. One single road seemed to go from my heart to God's throne. United with my reason and all my senses, my heart gave full freedom to a fiery prayer, and every word of this prayer came from deep within my soul. I felt love for all other men and began to pray for those who had hurt me or censured me; and my soul, because of the joy which I felt in my heart, was in ecstasy. But in this my condition I felt that I was still inside the church, and I saw how the brethren were praying. When I no longer had the strength to stand on my feet, I lowered the folding bench and sat down, but I did not cease to pray inwardly. I was so intent on God's love that I was unable to rest on earth. The more love I felt and the more I dared to love the Lord, the less grew my fear of Him and the more did my soul rejoice, so that I was unable to continue either the prayer which I had begun or any other prayer. All I felt was a sincere desire for God's love, a desire that burned in my heart like a fiery flame. My soul was clinging to God and was intent on Him only. Tears continued streaming from my eyes, and I continued in full ecstasy and humility. Then unexpectedly I lapsed into some kind of forgetfulness and no longer saw the church or the assembled brethren, and no longer heard what was being read. I discovered that I was in the midst of a large, luxurious meadow, full of beautiful trees and flowers, from which there issued a marvelous fragrance. It is impossible to describe or to tell of the beauty and loveliness of this field, for it was full of such light as if seven suns were shining, and from a distance there could be seen a countless multitude of people, young and brilliantly dressed, who were very comely, and whose faces shone more than the sun; and although they were walking, they made no noise.

"My soul was joyful at this sight. Astounded, I asked myself: whose is this garden, who are these people, and how did they get here?! With this thought I proceeded, and saw yet another multitude. Those who composed it all shone together with one brilliance. They were clothed like warriors. They were all young, although of different ages; their bodies looked strong but their faces were humble. Their beauty was so brilliant that it shone more than the sun.

"When I saw these people, I stopped and was overjoyed in my soul at their comeliness and their ornaments. Then I saw a voice issuing from their midst and naming me: 'As we all know, our brother ... has a great desire to approach the King. Who of us will be his guide?' One of them declared himself ready. He was young and more beautiful and powerful than all the rest. He shone among them as the moon shines among the stars and seemed their superior. Addressing the whole crowd, he said, 'I shall be his guide, for you know that he has particular love toward me and has been begging me day and night for this, and I have interceded for him before God many a time.' After he said this, he started toward me;

meanwhile I thought in my amazement: I have never seen these people, yet they must have seen me, for they know my name and have found out that I have a wish to come to the King. Yet how can they have found this out? And when the glorious warrior approached me and said, his whole face expressing joy, 'Follow me; let us go to the King,' I begged him to leave me and said that I was in no way worthy of standing before the King. I also asked him what this King wished of me, and what kind of King He was. He slightly smiled and then cheerfully continued: 'Apparently you are jesting when you say that you do not recognize the King to Whom I am to take you. And do you not know me, you who love me and pray to me day and night? I now have come in order to conduct you to the King, and I could not leave you even if I should wish to do so. Therefore follow me.' I had nothing to reply and therefore followed him. I was very eager to find out who he was, since he was doing me so much good. I still could not recognize him and was hesitant to ask, for I thought that I would find out later. I was awed by the prospect of meeting him and felt some trepidation at the thought of seeing him near me.

"After we had gone a considerable distance away from that luxurious garden, there was no one near, and my guide and I were alone. We approached a narrow way which extended so far into the distance that its end could not be seen. Enclosed between two high walls, this road barely allowed one man to pass. I was somewhat taken aback, for this place was too dangerous to pass without assistance. However, as I looked at my guide, I once again grew calm. He slackened his pace and, looking at me affectionately, began to admonish me: 'My brother, why is your soul confused, and why has sorrow taken hold of you? Why is your mind not wholly directed in prayer to God? Do you not know how much a man loses when he forgets to pray and his thoughts are occupied only with himself? Or how much he gains if he constantly takes recourse to the redeeming name of Jesus Christ? A man who does this becomes freed from suffering and from his sins; he contains the Holy Trinity in himself and attains divine love in that perfection in which you, too, unexpectedly took part, due to God's grace. But now that you have attained to this blessedness, why do you not take care not to lose it? How long will you endure in this deep sleep of indolence? Remember, my brother, your former eagerness which you have now totally renounced. Before, without any constraint put on you by God, you yourself willingly put your trust in the Ever-Virgin Mother of God and entrusted her with intercession for your salvation. Have you not become now unworthy of Her merciful efforts? Apparently you prefer sloth to God's love. But do you really know how much inexpressible mercy the Lord has poured out on you; and how great is His love for you, despite your carelessness?!'

"As my guide was speaking, his words penetrated to the very depths of my soul. Full of contrition, I repeated, 'Lord Jesus Christ, have mercy on me!' This sincere prayer, remote from any distracting thoughts, filled my entire mind and was so full of divine love, of joyful feelings, and of power, that it instantly dispersed all my fears. Then my guide once more addressed me and said, 'Now you see yourself that it is better to keep praying. If you wish always to remain in this spiritual state and to gain salvation, flee from destructive sloth, and putting all your trust in the name of Jesus Christ and in our Lady, the Mother of God, attempt to conduct your life as you always used to: ever exerting yourself in good deeds in accordance with divine commandments. Remember and keep well my advice and always, whenever something befalls you, confess your troubles completely and hide nothing from your spiritual father.'

"And then we entered the narrow gorge. As I ascended, I saw before me a cross which seemed to point the way to us. When we approached this cross, the guide and I stopped and, having thrice put the sign of the cross on us and having prayed, 'Before Thy cross we bow down in worship O Master, and Thy holy resurrection we glorify,' we went on. After a long time we came to the end of the road. From that point I saw a place such that anyone who should see it would be held by fear and trembling: this was a deep ravine, so terrible and dark in its depths that it seemed to be like a bottomless abyss, and it was difficult to ascertain how long, wide, and deep it was. On the other side of it there was a high mountain which touched the sky.

"Instead of a bridge, there was put across this ravine a round thin log, one end which touched our road and the other which rested at the foot of the mountain opposite us. It was especially terrifying to cross here because the log shook over the abyss, moving in the wind like a leaf on a tree. When we came near this abyss and this crossing, fear and trembling took hold of me again, for I saw the need to cross by means of the log: no matter where and how long I looked, there was no other crossing except by the log. My guide addressed me somewhat reproachfully: 'Again,' he said, 'you take no care of prayer and again you are fearful! Give me your hand.' I gave him my right hand and we began to cross the horrible bridge, which at our first few steps began to move like a leaf on a tree. When I looked right and left into the abyss, my soul shrank in fear. I hesitated, and only the presence of my guide, who was holding me by the hand, inspired me once more, and so we continued.

"We stopped after some time, and my guide bade me to cross myself and to invoke the name of our Lady, the Mother of God, the Ever-Virgin Mary, and said that Her name was very powerful in that place. O wonder! When I did as I was told by the guide and repeated time and again, 'Most Holy Mother of God, help me!' I grew so brave that I felt a great calmness, even though the bridge was bending under our feet like a cobweb. Once we reached the end of the bridge, we came to the foot of the mountain. My guide let go my hand and added that now there was nothing to fear. Because of the love which I felt for him I did not wish to separate myself from him, and I continued to hold his hand as we went along. After a while, we began to ascend the mountain, but I could not see the top, no matter how hard I looked. The mountain was very precipitous, but its environs were charming, and when we stopped after a while, I was surprised to find all the sides of the mountain covered with olive trees. I was amazed and kept thinking: How can so many olive trees grow here?

"Soon we reached the summit. As we continued on our way we came to a great gate which was open. The guide, and then I too, put thrice the sign of the cross on ourselves and then passed through the gate inside. Before us was once again a large field, as spacious as heaven itself: none of its limits could be seen, and none could tell how wide or how long it was. As for its beauty and magnificence, they are inexpressible, for the tongue of man cannot explain or put into words what this field is like, nor human intelligence comprehend its perfection. This field is planted with excellent trees of all kinds and beautified with magnificent flowers, full of marvelously pleasant fragrance. The sun that shone there was not like the ordinary sun but like seven such suns; and the place was so happy that my heart grew full of it and I wished to stay there. But my guide said to me, 'Hence you will go through still other places much more wonderful than this one, and will finally see the King Himself.'

"I was happy to hear this, and we went through a lovely garden where I saw from afar a multitude of people clothed in monk's raiment, but the color of their clothes was crimson instead of black, and these clothes shone like the sun. Their faces shone also, more brightly than the sun, and the whole appearance and beauty of these monks were beyond comprehension. Some of them were young, others were advanced in years. When we approached they joyfully received us and greeted my guide saying 'Joy to you, great martyr George, the beloved of Christ!' My guide in his turn greeted them: 'Joy to you also, beloved of Christ, holy monks!' Then they called me by name and joyfully addressed me: 'Our son ... consider what use has man if he gains the whole world but loses his soul! No matter how long he should live, how well his wishes should be fulfilled, and how many worldly pleasures he should experience—the hour of his death will strike, and his entire life will have passed like a dream. You, too, will discover that your life is but a shadow, if only you will shake off your sloth and begin to live as piously as you once lived before, and then you will please the Lord and be found worthy of the heavenly kingdom and eternal bliss with us. But if you should end your life in carelessness ... you know what slothful and unrepentant sinners must expect. Our son! No longer prefer the dark abyss to this kingdom. Do not cling to sloth in preference to the love of Jesus Christ, Who has prepared everything that you have seen especially for your salvation. Remember from what degree of perfection you have fallen, how much you have lost, and where you have sunk! Come back and turn to God's mercy, and we shall not cease to pray to the Lord for your salvation.' Then they once more turned to my guide and said, 'George, beloved of Christ, take complete care of this soul and put it before the King; the more so since you have great daring before Him'.

"We left them and went on. Since I had heard that my guide was the great martyr George, I now recognized him and understood the words that pertained to me when he first declared himself ready to lead me and to the question 'who of us will be his leader?' replied, 'I shall be his leader, for you know that he has particular love for me and has been begging me day and night for this, and I have interceded for him before God many a time.' For indeed, from my earliest childhood I honored the great martyr George more than other saints and often asked him to intercede for me before God in the matter of my salvation.

"Having now recognized in my guide the holy great martyr George, at first I grew somewhat afraid, but then a feeling of sweetness and love and gratitude filled my heart, and I embraced him and kissed him time after time. Then we went on, and after a while I saw from a distance a small number of the blessed. They, too, were clothed like monks and were similar to the ones whom we saw before, but they were more glorious and their faces were more radiant. I asked my guide who they were and why they were clothed in so great a glory. 'These are monks of the present time,' St George replied, 'who have no guides to advise them, and yet they are full of good will and therefore vie with the godliness of the monks of former times. They have ended their life in good deeds and have pleased the Lord.' I then asked how it was that such chosen people lived on earth in the present time, for good deeds have all but disappeared now from the world. 'Indeed,' said my guide, 'there are very few such people now in the world. But in these days whoever will do even a little good, in accordance with his powers, will please God and be called great in the heavenly kingdom: for the small good deed done willingly, of one's own accord, is accepted by the Lord like a great good.

"'My brother,' he continued, 'at the present time, good deeds have become scarce, immorality has increased, injustice has taken root, love is forgotten, faithfulness has become lost, and the word of God has dried up in the mouths of men. Falsehood and godlessness are everywhere triumphant, enmity has taken the place of love, cruelty has displaced mercy, truth has been conquered by falsehood. Men's minds are full of evil thoughts, and their evil deeds have so increased that they all are clinging to what is wicked, and there is almost none who lives piously. This is the reason why those who do even a little good now are yet found worthy of much reward.' We continued on our journey while we were thus conversing. Having proceeded eastward through the garden we saw a tall, spacious, and magnificent palace. Its walls could not be compared to anything we know on earth. They seemed to be made of pure gold, and their brilliance illuminated everything far and wide. The glory and magnificence of this palace are incomprehensible for human intelligence. I asked my guide about this most unusual palace, and he replied that this was the King's palace. We soon came to the high gates of this palace. They were open. We thrice placed the sign of the cross on ourselves and passed through the gates to an open space from which the whole surface of the mountain could be seen, and all its surroundings, although they are limitless. As I looked at beauty such as never had been seen by human eyes, I was greatly astounded. Here were countless saints, all of them full of great glory. My guide took me by my right hand and we passed through yet another gate eastward. This gate was artfully constructed of precious stones. At the right side of the gate there was an icon representing the Savior sitting on a throne; and on the left side there was one of the Mother of God. As I passed under the gate, I saw once more a multitude of people who were holding crosses and branches in their hands. They were all dressed alike, in crimson monk's habit as brilliant as lightning, and their faces were indescribably beautiful. When they saw us appear, they met us with great joy and sweetly greeted me saying, 'Brother, how long shall we wait for you? Why do you yourself make no efforts to be in our company?' Then they turned to my guide and said, 'George! You have taken him under your tutelage. When will you bring him to us?'—'When God's will may allow,' said George. They took my hands, caressed and comforted me. St George drew near to the icon of the Most Holy Mother of God and began singing most soulfully 'It is truly meet to call Thee blessed....' After he had ended the troparion, we thrice put the sign of the cross on ourselves and bowed before the icon of the Mother of God. St George took me by the hand and said, 'Everything that you see now is so only in order that you may not doubt what you have now seen and heard and may not consider it all to be a temptation of the devil.'

"All the blessed stepped away from us, but my guide and I remained at the gate, which suddenly opened of its own accord. We heard a voice: 'Great is Thy mercy, O Lord, to the sons of men!' Standing at the gate, I was in ecstasy at all I saw and heard. After the gate was opened, I saw a great church full of ineffable light. In the middle of the church there stood a high and wonderful throne on which sat the King of Glory, surrounded by a numerous throng of saints: holy priest monks and other monks were clothed in white garments, others looked like an armed host. The King's countenance was like that of the Savior on the icon at the gate which we had passed: he was young and of indescribable beauty, dressed in the garments of a bishop and bearing on his head a crown of precious stones. It is impossible either to describe or to express by a human tongue the beauty, greatness, and glory of the King. The whole temple was lighted by the light that issued from the King's countenance, and the assembly of the blessed seemed to be embraced by the same brilliance as that of the King. If thousands and millions of millions of suns could possibly be gathered in one place, even then no such brightness could be created as the brightness of the King's face.

"As I stood at the doors of the church and looked at that which no glance can comprehend, my guide went into the church to bow before the King. When St George returned he said to me, 'Why are you standing here? Come with me and bow to the Lord.' But the instant that I was about to enter the church, I heard the King's voice: 'George, leave him at the door. He is unworthy of entering, for he does not have a wedding garment.' This voice inspired some fear in me, but then I grew completely calm, for the love that was filling my soul left there no room for fear. St George left me at the door and went once more into the church, where the crowd of saints met him with honor, like one of the King's grandees, and the King of Glory Himself stood up from His throne when George approached and joyfully kissed him on the face. Then my guide thrice bowed before the King and kissed his feet and humbly said, 'Lord! For the sake of the blood that Thou hast poured out on the cross for sinners, forgive him and put him on the road of salvation. Great is Thy mercy, Lord, and endless are the acts of Thy goodness!'—'George,' answered the Lord, 'you know My goodness which was granted to him from the very beginning, when I showed him the mysteries of My love, although others made greater efforts than did he and yet were not granted as much.

But he remained obdurate and has preferred to Me the treacherous loveliness of the world. He is unworthy of My goodness.'

"Then St George began to implore the Lord: 'Lord, I implore Thee, forgive him and make manifest on him Thy goodness and mercy, so that men will learn to praise Thy name. Do this even if he is found unworthy. Thou seest his good intention. Do not leave him!' And thus he continued for a long time to beg the Lord to forgive me. 'George, my beloved!' answered the Lord, 'I see how low the world has fallen: My commandments are not kept, impiety has taken the place of My word, hate has replaced love, and faithlessness has replaced truth. Faithfulness has become rare, humility has been rejected; lies, deceit, and pride are spreading. Instead of chastity there is fornication and adultery, and not only among men and women of the laity but even among priests and monks. The earth has become like Sodom; its people once again are nailing Me to the cross. But I endure it all meekly, without anger, for I am waiting for their repentance.' St George once again fell to the feet of the Lord and implored Him, 'Lord, remember the blood which I shed because of my love for Thee. I implore Thee, Lord, give me this soul, forgive it and make it worthy of the cup for which it is longing!'—'George,' said the Lord, 'let your wish be fulfilled.' Suddenly there appeared in the King's left hand a golden cup full of a drink like wine. He blessed it with His right hand and gave it to St George saying 'Give him to drink this cup of My love.' St George accepted the cup from the Lord and brought it to me. I thrice made the sign of the cross on myself and then drank it all. This drink was so sweet that it cannot be compared to anything earthly. My soul and my heart instantly went on fire with love for God.

"When St George returned the cup to the Lord and once more was standing before the King of Glory, I was no longer able to stay in my place. I dared to enter the temple, approached the King of Glory, and fell at His feet. I kissed His feet with joyful trepidation and my soul was so filled with love for God that I was no longer able to rise to my feet. Then I heard a voice addressing my guide: 'George! Take him and go. Let him completely purify himself in order to attain to My love, which he had lost, and let him accept the cup which I shall soon give him.' After this my guide lifted me by my right hand. We both thrice bowed to the ground before the King of Glory and then went out from the temple. The gate closed after us. On our return journey we were once more met by the saints whom we saw before. They said to us, 'Brother, make an effort; we shall wait for you.' I attempted to ask my guide to leave me with them and not to make me return again to earth. 'It is God's will,' he told me, 'that you should return to earth in order to be purified like gold by your good deeds, namely, by fulfilling the commandments of God.'

"After we had thrice made the sign of the cross on ourselves, we went back from the luxurious happy garden; and once more met the small crowd of monks, who greeted us joyfully. Then we found ourselves again on the top of the high mountain. There we stopped for some while, and I enjoyed a view of this mountain, which was all covered with olive trees. When we had descended, I again saw the terrible abyss which we passed on our way up. My guide took me by the hand and we began to cross the terrible log, but this time I felt no fear whatsoever. In the middle St George stopped and said to me, 'My most dear brother! Make an effort to gain the heavenly kingdom and fear to lose it. Did you see God's mercy to you? See to it then that you be not ungrateful toward your Savior, Who has revealed to you that which is invisible. Attempt to gain His love, and make ready to drink the cup which will be sent to you in accordance with our Lord's will—then God's grace and the protection of our heavenly Queen will always be with you; and I, too, will not leave you.' Then he made the sign of the cross over me thrice and said, 'Most Holy Mother of God, help Thy servant,' and became invisible, while I remained alone in the middle of the terrible log over the very abyss of hell.

"I suddenly heard a horrible thunder and a noise that came from the abyss, and then there was a savage and terrible cry: 'Now he is alone! Let us go and throw him down into the abyss! Let us go quickly, while George is not there!' And the log that crossed the abyss began to shake like a leaf on a tree. I looked right and left and thought, 'Lord! Who can help a man here!' and suddenly I heard a voice like thunder: 'Only good deeds and the mercy of the Most Holy Mother of God can help here!' At this moment the thunder and the noise and the horrible voices of the abyss and the gnashing of teeth— all grew quiet, and I came to my senses."

Such is the comforting and hope-inspiring tale of the old Romanian monk's instructive yet comforting vision.

* * *

Indeed, many Christians, both monks and laity, when they offer their prayers to the Lord God, also pray to the Mother of God and to the other holy inhabitants of heaven, choosing of their number some whom they invoke particularly zealously. This choice is determined either by some incident in men's lives or by the inclination of their heart. Thus, as Christians pray to the Lord God, they offer to Him as their intercessors, first, the Mother of God, then the incorporeal powers, their guardian angels, the saints whose names they bear, and some other saints in particular, and then all the other saints in general. Our divinely inspired father, the monk Theognostos, says, "If you wish, I shall show you another road to salvation, or rather, to dispassionate calm: tire your Creator by prayers, wear Him out by your persistence, pray as much as you possibly can. And in order not to sway from your ultimate goal, offer to Him as your intercessors all the heavenly powers and all the saints, and especially the Most Holy Mother of God."

CHAPTER 24

The Miraculous Dream of the Novice Thecla

Another vivid vision of the afterlife was given to the novice Thecla in a dream: I fell asleep and dreamed that my sister Pelagia, who had died thirteen years earlier of consumption, was coming toward me. At the time of her death she had been a girl of sixteen. Now I saw her wearing a small crown on her head and a white dress. She smiled at me and said, "Let us go." I went with her. After we had crossed a field we came to a very dark place, so dark that it is difficult to describe the darkness, and saw that there were deep ravines on both sides. Monks were falling into one of them and rising from the other. My sister disappeared at this point, and I was approached by two youths so beautiful and glorious that none can exist on earth. They said, "Come." I asked them why the monks were falling into the ravine, and the youths replied, "This happens because of their careless and slothful life. They keep falling and getting up again because at present there are on earth no proper teachers and guides, and one can be saved only through illnesses and suffering."

One of the youths disappeared, but the other stayed with me and said, "Be attentive; cross yourself and come with me." He took me firmly by the hand, and we went on. The place through which we were passing was narrow and dark, and he was walking very rapidly, so that I could barely keep up with him. All of a sudden monsters (demons) appeared. They were holding a long list in their hands, and this list was full of writing. They brought it near my eyes, and here I saw all my sins, recorded from the time of my earliest youth.

At this moment there appeared still another youth. I saw that he was winged and guessed that this was my guardian angel. He said in a severe voice, "Dare not frighten this soul today: she has partaken of the holy sacrament. Do not appear before us." Then I saw how the list became completely clean, all my sins were obliterated, and the monsters disappeared.

Together with the first youth, I went on while my guardian angel disappeared. The road was very confining, so that I had much trouble walking and had to walk sideways behind my guide up a dark stairway. Here, too, monsters appeared, but they made no attempt to catch me. The youth and I approached three large furnaces surrounded by monsters. They kept running around the furnaces with hooks in their hands. On grates inside the furnaces there seemed to be wood burning; the monsters kept pulling the logs out of the ovens and striking them with hammers, and then I saw that the logs were really people, for after they had been struck with hammers, they cried out and roaring threw themselves back into the furnaces. I grew very much afraid of being thrown into one of these, but the youth smiled and said to me, "Cross yourself and come." When we drew away from the furnaces, I asked, "Why have these people been put into those horrible furnaces?" The youth replied, "All Christians come here if they are Christians in name only, rather than also in deed: they have not honored holy days, have used indecent language, have feasted since early morning. As for you, be brave and cross yourself." And thus we went on.

Then we came to a very dark forest, where I saw two tall ladders on which there were very many demons. On the one side of these ladders was an abyss, and on the other side a large vat of boiling pitch. They threw a man into the vat; the man was groaning horribly, and there were many people around the vat. I asked the youth, "Why are people here being thrown into the vat?" He said, "Because they are wicked and proud, and these sins are bad enough but not as bad as those that seek to gain. Those who are guilty of calumny and condemn others go into the abyss."

We continued along the same road and finally came to a chamber which had no roof or ceiling. From it we heard loud screams and whining, and when we entered we saw many people. Some of them were very poorly dressed, and others were completely naked and were sitting back to back, and appeared not to see one another. Suddenly the chamber began to shake and bubble, and I asked the youth why this was so. The youth replied, "A sinful soul has come here." To my question about why these people were sitting here as if they did not see one another, the youth replied, "They used to live on earth carelessly, without doing evil or good; now no one remembers them in his prayers, and they have neither torment nor joy here. They could be released by prayer, but there is no one to pray for them."

We left this chamber and continued along the same narrow path, and I still heard the noise and the whining. When we approached another chamber I saw again a great number of people, who were sitting with their heads lowered. Here the youth left me and I was very frightened when I saw monsters who were trying to grasp me with their long hands and throw me on a balance that stood in the middle of the chamber, and on which the good and the evil deeds of every soul were being weighed. I grew very much afraid and began to tremble. Suddenly I saw my guardian angel appear with a kerchief which at one time I had given to a beggar. He threw it on the balance and it outweighed all my evil deeds, but I eagerly left the chamber. My guardian angel once again disappeared, the youth returned to me, and we went on, but he was walking so fast that I could not keep up with him and was worn with fatigue. The youth kept comforting me saying, "Cross yourself and be attentive." I crossed myself and felt better.

Once again we came to a chamber surrounded with stench and whining. I saw a woman sitting in it. Her dress was all covered with blood spots, her head was surrounded with a snake as if with a crown, and there were also many worms on her head. Her neck, too, was surrounded with a snake which was sucking her lips and buffeting her ears with its tail. Another large snake entwined itself around her feet but reached with its mouth to her breast and ate its way into her breast. The woman beckoned to me and asked me to help her. Near her there was chained someone who looked like a ram but had a man's face. I became frightened and begged my guide not to leave me. Together with him I left this chamber. I asked him who this woman was. He replied, "She is an adulteress. On earth she had given herself completely over to her passions, and here she receives punishment for her deeds."

As we continued on our way, we once more came to a very large and high chamber. Below there was a deep abyss in which there burned a great flame. In the middle of the chamber there stood a column entwined with snakes, and on this column there were some sort of shelves. They kept shaking, although there was a great number of people on them, all of the people very horrible. Monsters kept throwing these people into the abyss, tearing their clothes, and even pulling them with hooks from this abyss to one still deeper and lower, a bottomless pit, where they drowned. I was very much afraid that I, too, would be thrown there. The stench here was so strong that I could not breathe. The snakes opened their mouths and seemed about to swallow me. One of them even had three heads. Suddenly the great martyr Barbara appeared in the air, holding a cup in her hands, and the youth left me. She said to me, "Fear not." Then my guardian angel again appeared to me and said, "There is much meaning in fasting on Mondays for the sake of all the angels." I asked about the sins for which these people were suffering. He said, "For sodomy."

Then the youth brought me to gates of glass, through which I saw an enormous room in the middle of which stood covered tables, and on them I saw everything prepared for tea, including also wines; but on plates I saw mice, frogs, and all kinds of disgusting things. People were sitting around these tables, and still others were dancing in the midst of flames, and all these people were crying out constantly, as if pleading for something, but the monsters kept scalding them with boiling water. To my question the youth replied, "They did not honor holy days, and early, while the liturgy was being celebrated, they were eating, drinking, and intoxicating themselves." Not far from these people there was a whole crowd dancing in the midst of flames, and whenever they stopped dancing, the demons forced them to it again. "The reason," said the youth, "is that they danced and played during church services."

Near this chamber I saw a woman who was walking back and forth, her teeth clattering. A poison was in her mouth but she was able neither to spit it out nor to swallow it. The youth explained that this was a punishment for love of sweets.

Once more we came to a chamber, this time a small one. There I saw several people who were hung to the ceiling by their tongues and the middle of their bellies. I was very much afraid, for they were groaning horribly. I asked the youth why they were so hung. He said, "These people were godfathers and godmothers of the same children, but disregarding these spiritual ties, they loved each other as flesh."

After this we once more went on our narrow and dark journey and once again approached a chamber and entered it. In the middle of it I saw standing a man whose ears were pierced with red-hot chains whose ends were fastened to two opposite walls. His tongue was being pulled out, and two monsters were cutting him with a dull, hot knife. There was another man here too, and fire was coming from his ears. In great fear I asked the youth to tell me the reason for such torments. He replied, "The first of these talked in church during services, and this is the reason why they are sawing his tongue. The other one stood in church without paying attention to the service, did not hear the singing and the reading, kept turning his head, and now is being punished by these chains which keep his head fastened in one position. The third one has flames coming out of his ears because he heard calumny and passed it on."

From this chamber we came to a well of ice. A woman was sitting on the edge and pouring water with a dipper to the right and to the left. I asked the youth what she was doing. He said, "During her life she sold milk diluted with water. Here she is forced to separate water from milk."

The path after this was especially dark and narrow. The youth was walking so fast that he seemed to be flying. He was dragging me by the hand, for I no longer was able to follow him. When I told him as much, he said, "Be attentive, cross yourself, and go on." I felt myself going up a stairway, but no sooner had we gone up two steps and onto the third, when a man fell at our feet and then rolled down into the abyss under the stairs. The monsters began to appear again, and I was very much afraid. When we had passed the stairway, I asked my guide who the man was that was thrown into the abyss. He replied, "This man has passed all the stations of torment except this one, for he was cruel and merciless."

After we had gone up the stairway, I once more was scarcely able to keep up with the youth, for he was walking very fast. Suddenly I heard a horrible noise and saw a fire before me. My guide disappeared at this point, and I found myself near a river of flame. The waters were very stormy, but the waves were unlike those that the wind rouses. Instead they whirled around in strange ways. There were very many people in this river, but across it were thrown only two very thin planks. I saw my guide on the other side of the river saying, "Come here." I told him that I was afraid of falling into the river and that I was unable to cross it. "Come and be not afraid," said the youth, "for you know me." "No, I do not know you," I said. "There is no one like you where I come from." But he said once more, "You know me and have loved me since your childhood. You prayed to me and I have brought you to the convent and helped you to be accepted there; but now you have forgotten me and have not prayed to me for two years." "No, I do not know you," I said again. "I am the great martyr George," he said, and once again approached me.

Before this, the monsters were pressing me and telling me that no one can avoid this river, but now the holy great martyr George took me by the hand and led me across the river. An angel flew across with us. Walls formed on both sides, so that I did not see the river and fearlessly crossed to the other side together with the holy great martyr George. As we were walking along the bank on the other side, I saw a great number of people inside, and all of them seemed eager to jump out. But they all kept falling in again and continuously exclaimed, "O, woe is me, woe is me."

In the river I saw a peasant from our village, who shouted to me, "Why are you here? Go away, you will not endure even one spark of this fire." At this point I started at a spark that fell on my left hand. I asked the holy great martyr George who these people were and what their sins were. He replied,

"Here will be all suicides and all those who only called themselves Christians but did not act as Christians should. All such will be immersed in this river, even deeper than are the infidels. It is very difficult to free a soul from this river; much prayer and labor is needed to free it."

We continued walking along the bank. There were fewer and fewer people in the river below; finally we came to a wide bridge and crossed it. Suddenly I saw deep snow, and there started a powerful wind that drove the snow before it. I went on with great difficulty, scarcely able to pull my feet out of the snow. I was terribly cold and felt all my limbs becoming rigid. But the holy great martyr George said to me, "Be attentive and cross yourself." We finally drew near a large field covered with ice. The ice was very thick, and the snow was blowing with all its force; St George vanished from my sight. Here I saw some people in monastic habit. They were sitting on the ice, their hair was unkempt, they were trembling, and their teeth were chattering. I felt sorry for them and was wondering why these monks were there. And since I did not see St George, I began to fear for my own sake and thought that, perhaps, I, too, would have to remain there. But then I felt something warm and suddenly saw near me St George, who said to me, "These monks lived in their monasteries and wore the cloak of the Queen of heaven; but they lived carelessly, were disgruntled when they had to work for the monastery, and were dissatisfied with their food. While they were on earth, they kept chattering with their tongues; therefore here the Lord has made their teeth chatter. However, because of the prayers of the Queen of heaven, they are spared the eternal flame."

We went on and left this field. I felt that it was getting warmer and warmer. A marvelous light was spreading over the places which we passed. And then I saw an enormous field covered with grass and flowers, in the middle of which was flowing a small river. St George said, "This is the Promised Land: the righteous will inherit it."

I felt carefree and happy and began smiling. As we went along, the grass and the flowers were getting more and more beautiful. It was so bright that it seemed as if not one but several suns were shining. In the middle of this field, a very large temple was standing, and near it there was a passage in which were hung many black cloaks like those in which monks are buried. Some of these were changed to white, but not all the monks were found worthy; the rest of the cloaks remained as black as firebrands. I saw several of these but did not recognize the faces above the cloaks. These people were subject neither to pain nor to fire, but they were found unworthy, and their hands remained bound.

We came to the platform before the church, where I heard singing so marvelous that I find no words to express it. They were singing "Holy, Holy, Holy" and "Having Beheld the Resurrection of Christ." The temple was so beautiful inside that no one can tell of it: the doors seemed to be made of small pearls and were brilliant with variously colored fires. There were very many columns, and around them nuns were standing; they seemed to be few in comparison with the great size of the temple. I recognized several of our nuns and novices who are still alive, but St George said to me, "When you return to the stormy sea of your life, do not tell any of the living about these whom you see here; for if they find out about themselves, they may become proud. But anything that I do not forbid you, you may tell."

It was so wonderful in the temple that I unwittingly exclaimed, "O Lord, You are here!" In the middle of the temple was an enormous mountain, like crystal, and it shone and glistened with rainbows of all colors. When I felt the wish to look up, I saw a light so great that I instantly was blinded and quickly lowered my head. St George said to me, "This temple is made ready for the last monks, but there will be few of them. There are no longer on earth teachers and guides for them, and few people can save their souls; but how great a beatitude has the Lord prepared for them!" As I marveled at all this beauty, I was able to say nothing but "Lord, Lord."

Suddenly St George said, "Look, look, the Queen of heaven is descending." I looked up and saw a majestic woman of inexpressible beauty, wearing a crown and a royal mantle. She descended through the air, smiled, and flew very close to me, so close that I wished to grasp her with both my hands. I exclaimed, "O my heavenly Queen!" She smiled, made the sign of the cross over me three times, and said quietly, "St George, return this soul to earth."

St George said to me, "Pray to Her, pray to Her always. She is the protectress of all Christians; day and night She prays before Her Son and God, and especially for the monks, that they may not do shame to Her mantle, which they wear." Here I saw that all were forming into pairs and going to the front part of the church in order to kiss the Gospel and an icon of the Mother of God "Of the Sign"; and I went there too with St George.

When we came out of the temple, we went into another temple nearby. It was smaller than the other one; inside there were three tables, and around them were beautiful youths. Boys were sitting around the tables and winding crowns of various blossoms that lay on the tables in great profusion. The youths were teaching the boys how to wind the crowns, and all of them together were beautifully singing "alleluia."

Among these boys I saw my nephew, who died this year. When he saw me, he smiled but did not come to me, and I felt very much hurt that he did not speak to me. I stood there a long time and did not wish to go away, but St George finally took me by the hand and led me out of the temple. To my question, "For whom are the crowns intended?" St George replied, "For the blessed."

Not far from this temple I saw three habitations. St George told me that these were the habitations of the abbesses of the Presentation Convent. When we drew near them, our abbess Raphaela, who had died not long ago, came out of one of these. She addressed me and said, "So you, my dear Thecla, are you here already? I shall not yet take you in, for you must still labor in the convent." She asked me how all the nuns were, and when I told her she said, "I know, I know everything. May the Lord help Mother Apollinaria; I pray for her and for all the sisters."

When the abbess left me, I went to a beautiful little house, at the door of which I saw my elder, the nun Liudmila. She opened the door and joyfully said, "Ah, you, too, have come here; but it is too early for you, and I shall not yet take you in." She brought me to her cell, where I saw very many icons. The whole cell was very pleasant. She sat down at the table and began to write something. Then we heard a ringing of bells, and the elder said, "Go home now, for I must go to the liturgy."

When I left her, I met Mother Polyxenia. She was very glad to see me and said, "Ah, my dear little Thecla, are you here already? It is too early for you." She firmly embraced me and showed me her cell; it was a beautiful one-story little house. She said, "I know everything and pray for my cell mates and feel for them."

When she was gone, I met my first elder, who had been the first in charge at the dairy. She, too, was very glad, embraced me firmly, and said, "You, too, my dear little Thecla, have come to us?" I asked her, "Mother, you are dead; are you happy here?"—"At first I was not," she said. "You know how it was; I used to be much among people of all sorts, and so there was much sin; but the sisters prayed for me for six weeks and within that time placated God for me. Now I am happy."

She left me, and I remained standing in the middle of a field. St George came to me, and we went on. The field was getting more and more beautiful. From afar I saw a gate. Suddenly I saw how through the field were monks walking, all in troops, dressed in brilliant garments of white brocade, and in golden and silver crowns. Among them were many bishops in golden robes, crowns, and with crosses around their necks. In the fifth troop I saw my priest, who had been a notably good man.

Abbesses, leaning on their staffs, were walking in front of their nuns. I recognized many of my departed sisters. Some of them were wearing white cloaks and golden crowns, others were dressed in white but with silver crowns; some of them were carrying marvelous flowers. All the nuns whom I knew bowed to me and smiled. One novice said, "My little Thecla, you, too, have come to us! But no, you still have to return."

At the head of the priests I saw a bishop wearing a miter; he was all dressed in gold and in his hand there was a crucifix. In the fifth troop I also recognized three priests, monks of the great monastery of Tikhvin, among them Father Claudian; all had crucifixes in their hands. They all looked happy and all seemed to be of the same age, about thirty years old. Laymen were walking on both sides of the troops of priests, and there were so many laymen that they made me think of mosquitoes in the air. They all passed through the gate.

At this moment I saw beside me a white-haired old man in brilliant garments decorated with crosses. I recognized him as St Nicholas. "Come," he said, "you must go back." I went with him. I saw no one until we came to another field, very much like our meadow, called "Plan," where we make hay, but the river seemed to flow from a different direction, from the east. On this field I saw nuns and novices whom I knew. Some were mowing hay; others were raking it. This place was very radiant, and they were singing a very good spiritual song, "My Most Radiant Lord's Angel."

Suddenly something glistened in the air, and I saw a small crown in the air above the place where our nuns were working. It was a golden crown and was getting larger and larger until it was hanging over the entire field; now it rose, now it lowered itself. From the east an abbess seemed to come with her staff, but I could not see which one of the abbesses she was; I only saw her making the sign of the cross over everyone.

Here I looked back across the river and saw that everything was dark there. On the other bank I saw other inhabitants of our convent. Their hair was disheveled; they seemed very anxious to cross the river, but when they would come to the very edge of the bank, the ground would begin to slip from under their feet, and instead of getting closer they kept drawing farther away. I felt very sorry for them. Suddenly Father Claudian appeared to me, wearing his priest's garments and holding a crucifix, and said, "Tell no one whom you saw on the other side of the river; they may still, through God's grace, repent."

After these words, I once again saw St Nicholas near me. He said, "Come now, I shall conduct you." And indeed, we came to my cell, I lay down on my bed, and he disappeared in the corner. At this point, the door of my cell opened and our departed Mother Abbess Raphaela came in wearing a brilliant brocade mantle and a crown on her head. Behind her another nun, tall and dark, came in, and her garments were even more brilliant, and she, too, had a crown on her head. She stood behind the mother abbess and kept smiling. The mother came near me and said, "Now that you are ill, see that holy unction is performed over you, and you will get well." She crossed me three times. I asked: "Mother, who is with you?" Mother replied, "This is our blessed queen, the schema-nun Daria." While the other nun was standing there and smiling, she made the sign of the cross over me again from a distance, and then they both disappeared.

After this I woke up, looked over my whole cell, and found it very dirty and dismal after all that I had seen. At first I could not recognize any of the people who were around me, for they, too, seemed to me evil and black after those whom I had seen in the field and those who had walked there in troops. After some time had passed, I began to recognize what was around me, recognized all present, and said to them: "My girls, do no evil. It is terrible even to think how all evil will be punished in the other world."

* * *

Here the tale of the novice Thecla ends. After her dream, she lay in bed for fifteen days and was very weak; she was so ill that she could indeed be said to sway between life and death. Her fear was so great that a lamp was kept at her side every night, and every night two or three nuns came to sleep in her cell, for she was too frightened to stay just with her elder. She was so weak that when she had to get up from her bed, she fell to the floor unless she was supported.

On the 19th day in the evening, the sacrament of holy unction was performed on her. She was barely able to stand during it, and while the Gospel was read she had to be supported. After the reading, however, she felt strong, extraordinarily vigorous, and on her way to recovery. At present she is completely healthy and does all work assigned to her. Her fear has also passed. She is still alive.

At the time of this writing, Thecla has been living in the convent for seventeen years. She is almost illiterate and can barely read the Psalms; all day long she works; her behavior is the best, her diligence is great; she is modest and humble, and briefly put, she lives in fear of God. At present she is thirty-three years old. She has spent several years with an ailing elder and taken care of her without ever complaining. When she first entered the convent,

she was difficult to understand, for she came from the government of Olo-
netz, and in her village there is a peculiar dialect. She had not much of a
concept of the fate of the righteous and of sinners, and thus her vision cannot
have been influenced by her imagination.

Derived from a brochure published at Pochaev, and also from a brochure
published on Mt Athos at the monastery of the Ascension, the latter being
marked "Reprinted from a publication allowed by censorship."

CHAPTER 25

The Clairvoyant Girl

We shall now tell the beautiful story of a clairvoyant girl, abridging it from the book of the well-known Russo-Galician protopriest, John Naumovich.

An old villager, Onouphry, once told his grandson Nicholas the following story about the clairvoyant daughter of his landlord.

"One day the news spread throughout the neighborhood that our young lady Anna was ill, but with no ordinary illness: for even though she seemed asleep, she had knowledge of everything and spoke strange things. All the people went in crowds to see her; everyone, but everyone, was going to our landlord's estate as if to a fair or to a church where a miraculous icon had been found. I did not believe the rumor at first, for I knew how people will often say stupid things and add all sorts of miracles to what has actually happened. Later, however, I, too, became curious and went to the estate. On the way there I met the late Father Andrew Levitsky, our priest, who asked me, 'Have you been at the house and seen the young lady, Anna?'

"'I was just going there,' I said. 'But, Father, I cannot properly understand why people are all going to her, and why there seems to be no end to this.'

"'There is a good reason, my good man! There is much to see and to hear there. It is not often that one can see and hear anything of the kind.'

"'Well, what is it?' I said. 'My dear father, is she a saint?'

"'A saint indeed, for her soul is pure and pious,' replied the priest. 'Whatever sin there may have been in her was quite ordinary, and she has removed it by her good deeds. You see, she is clairvoyant.'

"'What does this mean, clairvoyant? I don't understand this word.'

"'My son, there have always been pious men who did good and were pure before God and to whom God gave the grace not only to see more clearly what is here on earth, but even while they were still alive on earth, they rose in their spirit above the earth and contemplated the world beyond this life. Anna is such a clairvoyant. You see, she has always been living in God, praying and doing good deeds of mercy and pity, and has never been of this world. For our world is a world of evil, falsehood, impurity, and sin. She has come to us for a short time only, in order to show to others how to live so as to please God. Now the end of her earthly life is approaching, and she will soon go to her real home in heaven where she will join the pure and radiant spirits. But while she is still here, she talks to us about heaven, so that we might repent and change our lives, and have the desire to be saved.'

" 'Have you already seen her, Father?'

" 'Yes, I have. The very first day that she felt ill she asked for me, and asked me then not to leave her. I have spent four days with her, but now I can no longer endure hearing what she says. All who have heard her have been unable to keep back their tears.'

" 'What did she say?'

" 'The first day of her illness, as soon as she fell into her deep sleep, she called her father, the landlord, and her mother, and all the servants in the house, and told me that she would definitely die, but that she would like no one to weep for her, for she would go where there is no grief and no sorrow. Instead of mourning her, we should live like good Christians, pray, love one another, and do good and holy deeds.'

" ' "Here you are, Father Andrew," she said. "Thank you for coming to see me!" And then she spoke to her servant Timothy: "Come closer, dear Timothy, you my faithful servant and friend, my dear brother! Don't cry, why should you cry? Why are all of you crying? You too, Father Andrew?"

" 'I was unable to say a word, tears were choking me, and infinite sorrow was burning my soul. After I had given full vent to my tears, I collected my strength and said, "How can one help crying for you when you are so ill. All of us love you so much, our dear mistress! My soul is in pain for you!"

" ' "Don't call me a lady or a mistress," she said. "These are words of this earth. There are no such words where I am going. God alone is the Lord, and we all are brothers and sisters, and you are my brother." '

"I asked him then, 'Did she say all this with her eyes closed?'

" 'All the time while she was in that dream her eyes were closed, but she saw everyone who approached her and recognized everyone, and had something different to say to everyone. We even gave her books and unopened letters, and she read them with her fingers, although not with her eyes. Perhaps I should say that she was reading not so much with her fingers as with her spirit or some special sense. This is the reason why people who are in this kind of condition are called clairvoyant, for they clearly see things that others cannot: they can see into a book through its cover, and they can see through stone walls into the street outside, and can see what is happening across thousands of miles.'"

At this point, the old man's grandson Nicholas said, "These are strange things that you are telling me, grandfather! And what else did the late Father Andrew tell you?"

"I shall tell you only briefly, since there is so much to tell that I should not have the time for it all. He told me how Anna for three days continued telling those around her about hell. The first day of her illness an angelic spirit came to guide her through the realm of suffering which we call hell. She kept telling about the darkness and the terrible torments in which the great sinners must endure: those, that is, who even while they were alive kept resisting God and His commandments. She was unable to look at them for long, but all the while she repeated, 'My dear people, you are all brothers. You must revere that image of God, your soul, must love God and your neighbor, must praise God and uphold His commandments, in order not to come to this wretched place! Everyone who will come here will repent without end, all the time, and curse his own foolishness, for here a sinner curses the hour when he was born, but most of all those are tormented who brought others to sin and directed them toward evil.' While she was speaking about those torments, tears were flowing down her cheeks, and those who heard her also were weeping, and many sincerely repented."

"Did she speak about heaven also?" asked Nicholas.

"I am going to tell you her words now as an eyewitness, for I was with her myself, together with Father Levitsky, on the fourth day of her illness. When we entered, she was lying as if asleep, with her eyes closed, but she instantly recognized us both and pronounced our names in a whisper. We came near her. She was lying on her back with her arms crossed, like a dead body; and her breathing was barely perceptible. Then she suddenly began to speak: 'Ah, I see light—glorious light. Oh, how sweet and lovely it is here. I hear low sounds at a distance; ah, what beautiful singing! But these are not voices of this earth. I cannot tell you about this singing; there are no words in human speech to describe it!' Her appearance changed. Her breast was rising quietly, and on her face we saw the expression of great and blessed happiness. The late Father Andrew began to question her:

"'Is your guide with you now, Anna?'

"'Yes, but he is no longer sorrowful, as he used to be when we were passing through dark places and were among dark and unhappy spirits. Now he is so lovely and brilliant! I cannot drink in and be sated with that love of which this heavenly air is full.'

" 'Do you, Anna, see any of the blessed spirits?'

" 'Yes, I do, and I am among them myself.'

" 'Do you see anyone you know?'

" 'Yes, many of those.'

" 'Whom do you see?'

" 'I see the old woman Semenova whom we buried not long ago. I remember how no one wanted to come to her burial, for she had been poor and therefore there was to be no food and no brandy for the funeral guests. How wretched people were! They should have gone to her burial like good Christians. She is talking to me. Here she is not old at all, but beautiful; marvelously beautiful and transfigured!'

" 'How did you recognize her?'

" 'All souls recognize one another here, for they all see everything very clearly.'

" 'What is she saying to you?'

" 'She is thanking me for having sewn a shroud for her and gone to her funeral, even as far as her grave.'

" 'Is it then so good a deed to accompany the dead to their grave?'

" 'Yes, for such a deed signifies love, and love is more important than anything else.'

"Then she kept quiet for a while, as if tired, and only then did her breathing again become normal and she spoke once more.

" 'My brothers, dear people! How many are among you who sin, who never think about the life to come, who do not go to church because they are too slothful, who never pray, who occupy themselves with bad thoughts, who do evil, and who never care for anything except their flesh. But our flesh is only an unimportant cover, like the one which a winged insect throws off when it flies into the free air. How I should like to tell you about everything that I see here, but I cannot!'

" 'Why not, Anna?' asked the late Father Andrew. 'Tell us everything; please tell us everything. We wish to know what awaits us there.'

" 'It is impossible to tell of such things. You have no words on earth to express these things, and I have no strength. Even if every drop of my blood turned into a thousand tongues, and I could talk with each tongue as well as St John Chrysostom could, I still would not be able to express even a hundred-thousandth of the happiness and beauty that I see here. Oh let me implore you—forgive your brothers, your neighbors, your friends, and beg them and entreat them to leave their sinful life, repent, and begin once more an honest Christian life. If they do this, they all will be blessedly happy.'

"'What is this happiness like, Anna? What forms this happiness?'

"'Love, love! Holy love, which here reigns over all the blessed spirits!'

"'And what else?'

"'Beauty and greatness, limitless depth and height and the breadth of God's works! On earth you seek to study the starry heaven by calculating and measuring it; you guess about it and still know very little of it, but here everything is clearly seen. How numberless are these lights with their beauty and greatness! Blessedness is as limitless and impossible to measure as they are, and blessedness is to see and recognize God's works and praise Him.'

"'Can the spirits rise toward those lights? Can they go wherever they may wish?'

"'Yes, they can go wherever they may wish, but they can rise only to that height to which their strength will allow them. There is beauty such as even a pure spirit cannot endure before it becomes even more highly purified and even more closely approaches God.'

"'Do you see far?'

"'No, not far yet, for I am not yet quite freed from my body. My body still drags me down to your earth. Tomorrow my body will become even weaker, and then my guide will take me higher. Oh, how I long to see all the marvels of beauty which I cannot yet endure to see!'

"'What do you mean when you say that you would not be able to endure them?'

"'I am like a worm that from the beginning of its life is used to digging in the ground. An earthworm cannot endure the light of the sun, and should it happen to be in the sun, it turns and twists and perishes. Thus a soul born on earth cannot at once endure the view of the highest celestial beauty and blessedness.'

"'Are all equal there?'

"'All are equal in love, but not all are equal in perfection. There are degrees of perfection and degrees of blessedness.'

"'And who is at the highest degree of perfection?'

"'Even in that heaven where I am now, I see some crowned spirits. They shine here more than all the others. My guide says that these are the teachers and enlighteners of the nations. Their deserts are the greatest before God, and theirs is the highest honor. But these are the teachers who taught with their entire mental effort and with all their heart; they taught others to recognize what is true and good, and they did this not only in church but also in schools; not only in writing but also by word of mouth. They spread God's light and God's love and love for one's neighbor among individuals and nations. But woe to that teacher and that spiritual leader who occupies his position in vain or teaches badly, or gives a bad example to others! Such will never come here!'

"When she had said this, I remembered our departed teacher Leonovich and asked her: 'Anna, tell me if you see there my teacher Leonovich?'

" 'No, I do not.'

" 'Why?'

" 'Because he is higher, much higher. So my guide tells me. But he can be called to come here.'

" 'How is that?'

" 'The spirits that dwell in the higher heavens can descend to the lower degrees, but the lower ones cannot ascend.'

" 'And you will call him, Anna?'

" 'My guide will call him. Three minutes are needed for this.'

"Father Levitsky looked at his watch, and when three minutes exactly had passed, she said, 'I see him! He is beautiful and beautifully crowned. All the spirits around me honor him and praise him in their songs. Ah, how marvelous and lovely it all is, I cannot tell you how lovely! Oh, if only I could describe to you even a part of all that I see here! But this is impossible, this is nothing for you who are on earth.'

" 'Do spirits ever come to us, to this world, from their world?'

" 'Yes, they do, and they appear in dreams to some who deserve to see them. They are present at church services said for their souls, even though they need no prayers of ours, but they rejoice in our love. Oh, now I am going up and farther up, and even better do I feel the indescribable happiness and blessedness of these regions! Wake me, for I no longer have the strength to endure this happiness.'

"Father Levitsky touched her chest with a glass, for nothing else would wake her, and she opened her eyes. When we began to tell her of her words, it turned out that she did not remember any of them and was unable to repeat any, for her soul had returned to her body and now saw only this world: her room, her bed, and the people around her.

"She was very tired and weak, but she refused food when it was offered to her, so that it is difficult to understand how she went on living. But, my dear, I never would finish if I were going to tell you everything. For three more days our young lady Anna continued telling us about heaven and continued rising higher and higher. She told us about the saints whom she saw there, and instructed us to honor their memory and follow their teachings in order to achieve eternal salvation and heavenly life. Who can tell everything that we heard! Even the most hardened and unfeeling sinner could not keep from tears at her words. Such sinners wept like children, and many turned to the right way: drunkards stopped drinking, and violent and deceitful men and other sinners grew penitent.

"Toward the evening of the fourth day, the sick girl said that her soul would completely leave its body at five minutes past seven o'clock. She ordered us to wake her at that time. When we did, she called Father Levitsky to her bed and kissed his hand; then she kissed her faithful friend and tireless nurse, the head maid Maria. She told us to embrace and kiss her father and mother for her, comfort them and ask them not to weep for her (they both were ill in bed, and the doctors allowed no one near them). Then she took leave of everyone else, asked the servants to be called to her, thanked them for their service, and blessed them all. Everyone was crying; tears were streaming down my face too, for I had never seen anyone die as this girl did. When it was precisely five minutes after seven by the clock, the invalid gave a deep sigh, and her soul left her beautiful earthly body. I have never seen a face so lovely and so angelic; never seen a dead face lighted by so joyful a smile as was that of our mistress Anna, dressed in a white dress, covered with flowers...."

At Anna's funeral there was a great crowd of people who had come from all the villages near and far, and many of the gentry came too, some of them from a great distance; and everyone was weeping, for in her person they had lost an angel on earth.

Abridged from the book of the protopriest I. G. Naumovich, *Four Guides to a Good Life*.

CHAPTER 26

The Experience of a Certain Ascetic

"Blessed father, is there any recompense in the future life for the good and the wicked?" Such was the question put to a certain great ascetic. "Indeed," he said, "there is recompense even for all that we think, be it in the daytime or at night; and the more so for all our deeds, both good and evil." In support of his statement, he raised his hands to heaven and swore that he would tell the truth about the revelations that some people had. He could not refrain from weeping as he began to tell the story told to him by a certain priest of this country, an admirable man who had spent much time in self-mortification and had with great diligence read the Holy Scriptures.

"I had a sister, a young girl who was nevertheless as reasonable as an old person. She spent her life in fasting and continence. Once she was sitting near me, when suddenly she reclined on her back and lay thus, speechless and breathless, for a whole day and night. The following day at the same time when she had fallen into this state, she rose as if she had been sleeping, but she was terrified. When I asked what had happened to her, she begged me to leave her alone and to permit her not to speak until her terror should subside. For, she said, that which she had seen was beyond vision and beyond hearing. She spent many days weeping. She did not wish to listen to anyone, did not even speak to those closest to her, but often remembered them by name and while she did so, groaned and wept. I had a strong desire to know what she had seen, but she could hardly be moved to yield to my pleas. Finally, she spoke.

"'At the time when I was sitting near you, two white-haired men of dignified appearance, dressed in white, came, took me by my right hand, and bade me follow them. One of them was holding in his hand a staff. He raised it and opened heaven with it; thus we were able to enter. They brought me to some place where a great multitude of angels were standing before the doors of a building. These doors were so impressive that they cannot be described in words. When I entered I saw a high throne surrounded by many persons, all of them more beautiful and grand than the ones who were standing outside. I saw sitting on the throne someone Who illumined all with His light. All bowed and fell down before Him.

"'My guides told me, too, to bow before Him. Then I heard how He ordered them to lead me forth and show me everything, so that I might inform and persuade those who were still alive. They took me by the hand and did as He had told them. They brought me to some place where I saw a great multitude of God's creatures, all of them inexpressably beautiful. They were clothed differently, but all were shining with gold and precious jewels. I saw various dwellings and the men and women who inhabited them in honor and glory. As I was shown each dwelling, my guides told me, "These are bishops who have guided their charges holily and justly; these are clerics; those are laymen; some of them have shone forth in their office, others have simply lived in purity and righteousness."

"'There, my brother, I saw also the priest of this village, as well as clerics whom both you and I know. I saw a great number of virgins and widows, and wives who had honorably lived in wedlock. Many of them were our acquaintances; some came from our village, others from other places, and I remembered meeting them at the festivals of various martyrs. Still others I did not know, but I asked my guides to tell me something about them. They said, "These come from different towns and villages. Some of them have exercised themselves in asceticism, others lived simply in the condition to which they were born; some of them spent the greater part of their lives in widowhood and have been oppressed by sorrows and many misfortunes. There are among them some who at first fell into sin in their maidenhood or in their widowhood, but they repented and wept much, and thus they were restored to their former condition." Then they took me again and brought me to some places of horrible appearance, terrifying to our eyes, filled with all sorts of groans and weeping and sobbing.'

"As she was about to begin telling about these places, she again was so terrified that her tears began to come down in streams; her voice faltered while she was speaking, her tongue stumbled and moved without producing a sound. Yet, urged on by me, she resumed: 'I saw places so fearsome and horrible that neither sight nor hearing can give an adequate idea of them. My guides told me that these were prepared for all the impure and lawless and for those who called themselves Christians in this world but committed much evil. There I saw a lighted oven from which issued a horrible kind of bubbling. When I saw it and grew afraid, I asked, "For whom is this prepared?"

They said, "For those who, being clerics, insult God's Church by their love of money and by their carelessness and spend their lives shamelessly and do not repent." They clearly named some who belonged to my own church, and others who lived in the city; you yourself have heard that they led shameful lives. I trembled and cried out, "Can it be that clerics and celibates will be destined to such suffering?" I heard a reply from some distance: "Maiden, they are destined to suffering that corresponds to their vileness before God and their injustice toward their neighbors. For he does not leave unpunished those who do deeds that displease Him. The all-powerful God gives to each according to his good or evil deserts."

" 'We went on for some distance and stopped at a place full of deep darkness. There I heard nothing but moans, gnashing of teeth, and confused sounds of all sorts, for the place was full of sorrowful voices and horrible groans. There, O my brother, I saw many virgins and widows who had not fulfilled their vows, or wandered from one place to another and ruined the reputation of others by their undisciplined lives; or were eager for wine and enjoyment but paid no attention to the singing of psalms, prayers, and fasting, although they had vowed to be one with Christ. Of some of them I heard that they had been telling tales about others' intentions, and even if the tales were true, they proved a stumbling block to some and they became subverted; and those who had been spreading tales proved to be guilty of their ruin. When I witnessed their great tears and groans, I was seized by a fear no less than theirs. When I looked more closely, I saw two maidens of whom I used to be fond. They were surrounded with fire and suffering, although you, my brother, together with me have often offered them good advice and talked to them in order to correct them, for you, too, were fond of them because of their friendship to me. When I saw them there I groaned myself and called one of them by name. They looked up and their faces reflected the shame which they felt because of their punishment. They were suffering from this shame even more than from the punishment itself, and finally lowered their eyes. I, however, tearfully kept questioning them about what they had done so secretly that no one knew of it, and what were their evil deeds for which they were being punished here. They said, "Why do you ask us when our punishment accuses us and reveals our deeds? Yet why should we seek to conceal our troubles? We ruined our virginity, and when we became pregnant, we decided on murdering our infants. Before others we seemed continent and devoted to fasting, but our secret actions were different. We only sought glory among men and paid no attention to what would threaten us here. But our suffering here has revealed what we have

been doing in secret. Now we have our meet punishment for the blandishments to which we fell prey! Now we endure shame which befits our vanity
while we were alive! Our shame is just and we deserve it for our actions.
Our former friends cannot help us here, but if you have any power and any
daring before God because of your upright life, help us in this suffering
which surrounds us!"'"

    Thus the great ascetic ended his story.

CHAPTER 27

An Ancient Tale

A nother old ascetic has left us the following tale about a very elderly virgin, who had been living in the fear of God. When he asked what had caused her to become a nun, she sighed and shared the following story.

"Most honored father, my parents died when I was still a child. My father was a modest and quiet man, but his constitution was weak and sickly. Throughout his life he so intently devoted himself to his salvation that even people who lived in the same village scarcely ever saw him. At those infrequent times when he felt somewhat healthier, he brought home what he earned for his labor, but most of his time was spent in fasting and suffering. He was so silent that those who did not know him could take him to be mute. My mother, on the contrary, led a life entirely dissipated. She was so dissolute a woman that there was probably none like her in the whole country. Her speech was so copious that it seemed as if her tongue was the most important part of her. Unceasingly she started quarrels with everyone. Her time was spent in drinking with the most incontinent men. She wasted all the property belonging to our family. It was very considerable but it did not suffice us for our wants, for my father had entrusted her with caring for it. She misused her body and befouled it with impurities of all sorts, so that there were few men in our village who were able to avoid fornication with her. She never suffered even the least amount of pain: from the day she was born to her old age she enjoyed perfect health. Such were my parents.

"Finally my father died, worn out by a long-lasting illness. As soon as his soul departed, the air grew dark, it began raining, there was lightning and thunder, and this storm continued for three days and three nights. Because of such weather, his burial took place could not take place for three days, so that the villagers shook their heads and said with surprise: this man must have displeased God so much that even earth does not receive his body in burial. So that his body should not putrefy in our house, he was buried somehow or other, although the rain and the thunderstorm did not cease. My mother now became still freer in her actions and even further abandoned herself to the misuse of her body. She made our house into a house of vice and spent her time in greatest luxury and the enjoyment of various pleasures. When her time came to die, she was buried magnificently, and the very weather seemed to contribute toward making the last rites beautiful. Upon her death I remained alone, an adolescent whose flesh began to clamor for pleasure. One evening I began to contemplate the life of my parents. Whom should I follow: my father, who lived modestly, quietly, and continently, but all his life did not see any personal happiness, and having spent his life in sickness and sorrow, was not even received properly by the earth? If such a life pleased God, why did my father, who chose this kind of life for himself, endure such misfortunes? It seemed to me better to live like my mother, to devote myself to luxury, lust, and pleasures of the flesh. There was no vileness which my mother did not commit, she spent her life drinking, yet she was always healthy and happy. I should live as my mother did. It would be better to believe the evidence of my eyes and to enjoy that which is apparent and obvious, rather than to believe that which cannot be seen, and for its sake give up everything. Thus I, wretch that I was, decided in my soul to choose my mother's life. The night came, and I fell asleep. In my dream I saw some tall person, terrible in appearance. He directed at me a horrible glance and asked me angrily and sternly to confess to him what I had been thinking. I was terrified and did not dare to look at him. He even more loudly repeated his bidding that I should confess what kind of life pleased me best.

"Confused with fear, I forgot everything and said that I had been thinking of nothing at all. But he reminded me of all my secret thoughts. I saw myself discovered, began entreating him to pardon me, and explained the reason for my thoughts. He said, 'Come and look at both your father and your mother, and then choose a life for yourself.' Seizing me by the hand, he led me away to a large field of unspeakable beauty. There I saw many gardens full of various fruit-bearing trees. He led me into these gardens, and there I was met by my father. He embraced and kissed me and called me his daughter. I put my arms around him and asked his permission to stay there. He replied, 'You cannot do so now, but if you follow in my footsteps you will come here in a relatively short time.' When I asked him again to allow me, the man who had shown my father to me seized me by the hand again and led me away saying, 'Come, I shall show you your mother also. When you see her burning in the fire, you will know which of your parents to choose as a model for yourself.' He put me down in a dark and dismal place where there was sorrow and gnashing of teeth. There he showed me an oven burning with fire and boiling with pitch, and near the opening there were some kind of monsters. I looked inside the oven and saw my mother: she had sunk into the fire up to her neck, her teeth were gnashing, and her whole body was being consumed by the fire; the never-dying worm spread around a heavy stench. When she saw me she cried out and called me her daughter: 'Alas, woe is me, my daughter!' she cried. 'These sufferings are the fruit of my own actions. When I was alive, continence and the other virtues seemed to me worthy of laughter. I thought that my life of lust and vice would never end, and I did not consider drinking and gluttony to be sinful. But you see, I have inherited hell, and for my brief enjoyment of sin I have subjected myself to these deadly punishments. For my short-lasting joys I am now paying with eternal torments. You see what reward I have for despising God! All kinds of unending griefs embrace me. Now is the time to help me! Remember now that my breast has nursed you! Prove grateful to me now if you have ever received any benefit from me! Be merciful! This fire burns me but will never consume. Be merciful! Despair consumes me in the midst of these torments. Take pity on me, my daughter, give me your hand and lead me away from here.' I refused to do so, for I was afraid of those terrible guardians who were standing there, but she began once more: 'O my daughter, help me! Do not despise the tears of your own mother! Remember how I suffered when I gave birth to you! Do not despise me, else I shall perish in this hellish fire.'

"I wept at her cries and also began groaning, sobbing, and crying. These sobs and tears woke the others in the house. They lighted a lamp and began asking me why I was groaning so loudly. I told them what I had seen. Thereupon I chose to follow my father, for I was certain, through the grace of God, that those who lead a sinful life come to suffer for it."

CHAPTER 28

The Soldier Taxiotes

There lived in Carthage a man named Taxiotes. He was a soldier and led a dissolute, sinful life. Once, however, when Carthage was struck by an epidemic and many people were dying, Taxiotes was frightened. He turned to God and repented of his sins. He and his wife left the city, went to a village, and lived there devoting themselves to contemplation. After some time, however, the devil tempted him, and he committed adultery with the wife of his neighbor, a farmer. A few days after he had made himself guilty of this sin, a snake bit him and he died.

There was a monastery a mile's distance from the village. Taxiotes's wife went there and asked the monks to come for the dead man's body and to bury it in their church. At nine o'clock in the morning they buried him, but at three o'clock in the afternoon they heard a loud voice from the grave: "Have mercy on me, O have mercy on me!" The monks approached the grave, and since these cries continued, they uncovered it and found Taxiotes alive. They were terrified and kept asking him what had happened and how he had come back to life. He, however, was weeping and crying so desperately that he was unable to tell them anything. They only understood that he was asking them to take him to their bishop, Tarasius; and so they did.

For three days the bishop kept asking him to speak about his experience, but Taxiotes could speak only on the fourth day, and this is what he said, weeping greatly as he spoke: "As I lay dying, I saw demons standing before me. My soul was troubled at their horrifying appearance. But when I saw two beautiful youths, my soul went out to them, and we immediately began to rise to heaven, as if earth no longer mattered to us. On our way we met various stations of trial, where every man was kept back and his soul was examined for the presence of various sins: untruthfulness, envy, pride, and so on. Every sin has its testers. I saw how angels were holding a box full of my good deeds, which they offered for comparison with the wicked ones.

"We gradually passed most of these stations, but when we were already near the heavenly gates, we came to the station of adultery. Its keepers did not let me pass and began revealing all my sinful deeds of adultery and fornication, beginning with my childhood and continuing to the time of my death. The angels who were leading me said, 'God has forgiven you all your sins which you committed in the city, for you have repented of them.' But the evil spirits said to me, 'After you left the city, you committed adultery out in the field with the farmer's wife.' When the angels heard this, they could find no good deed which they might balance against that sin, and they went away. Then the evil spirits took me and began to beat me. They led me down into the earth, which had parted to receive us. I was conducted through narrow entrances and confining, evil-smelling cracks. When I reached the very depths of hell, I saw there the souls of sinners, confined in eternal darkness. Existence there cannot be called life, for it consists of nothing but suffering, tears that find no comfort, and a gnashing of teeth that can find no description. That place is forever full of the desperate cry: 'Woe, woe! Alas, alas!' It is impossible to describe all the suffering which hell contains, all its torments and pains. The departed groan from the depths of their heart, but no one pities them; they weep, but no one comforts them; they beg, but no one listens to them and delivers them. I, too, was confined in those dark regions, full of terrible sorrow, and wept and bitterly sobbed for six hours. After this time I saw some light and the two angels who had come in. I diligently prayed them to take me away from that place of suffering and give me an opportunity for repentance before God.

"The angels said, 'Your prayers are in vain, for no one goes hence until the time of the general resurrection of the dead.' But I continued praying and begging even more intently and promised to repent of my sins. One angel said to the other, 'Will you stand surety for this man's repentance, and promise that he will repent with all his heart, as he says?' The other said, 'I shall,' and gave him his hand. Then they led me out to the surface of the earth, brought me to the tomb where my body was, and said, 'Enter that which you have left.'

"I saw that my soul was as shining as a pearl, while my dead body was as black and rank as dirt, and I was reluctant to enter it. The angels said to me, 'You cannot repent without your body, by means of which you sinned.' But I kept entreating them to let me not enter my body. 'Enter it,' said the angels, 'or else we shall take you back to that place from which we brought you up.' Then I entered, revived, and began crying, 'Have mercy on me!' "

Having heard his story, Bishop Tarasius said, "Eat some food." Taxiotes refused, for his mind was set on something else. He wandered from church to church, and in each church he would prostrate himself, weep, and sighing deeply, confess his sins. He exhorted others to repent and would speak to them in words like these: "Woe to sinners! Eternal suffering awaits them. Woe to those who do not repent while they have the time to do so! Woe to those who make foul their own bodies!"

Taxiotes lived for forty days after his resurrection, during which time he purified himself by confession and repentance. Three days before he died, the time of his death was revealed to him. He departed to the merciful and compassionate God, Who can make a soul go down into hell yet save it, and Who is praised forever. Amen.

From *Lives of the Saints* for March 28.

CHAPTER 29

The Tale of Gabriel Ivanovich Gonchar

At the church in N., there served for a long time a churchwarden, Gabriel Ivanovich Gonchar. He held this office for almost fifty years. There passed no church election at which the parishioners would not say something to the effect of "We have here no man more just than Gabriel Ivanovich, nor anyone more diligent at attending church. We are afraid of even thinking that he might be displaced; we beg him to stay in office all his life." And so he did, until his very end, which came on Easter Friday.

He was an ideal honest man, infinitely meek, and a true Christian in his love for everyone. God granted him no children. He lived with his wife, his brother, and a nephew. No one ever saw him idle, and—God knows—he was perpetually engaged in silent prayer. He looked like the holy Father Seraphim of Sarov; and it so happened that he died the year when St Seraphim was canonized.

He used no alcohol and no tobacco, and he always gently reproached others about their intoxication or their pipe-smoking. Even when he received the Holy Mysteries, he drank only pure water afterward. I knew him only during the last years of his life, but I heard everyone say that he had always known Grandfather Gabriel to be a total abstainer.

Several times I asked him why he was so strict in this respect; for when he was ill he even disobeyed the doctor and took no medicine which contained alcohol. I asked him whether he had ever drunk wine. Grandfather would avoid the issue and change the subject. Once, however, a year before he died, as we were going to town together, he spoke. A short time before, Grandfather had deposited a small sum of money for the perpetual use of our church, so that he might be remembered and prayed for. He was usually taciturn, but on this occasion he became talkative and told many stories about the Holy Land and Mt Athos, where on his pilgrimage he had become ill and therefore stayed for about a month. As an abstainer, he had been surprised that the monks there were served wine at every meal. So was he; "But I could not drink it," he said.

I again asked Grandfather to tell me why he could not take even a small glass of weak wine mixed with water (as was the wine served to monks). This is what he told me:

"I was my father's only son, and our family was prosperous. My parents brought me up well and were strict with me. Still, young blood is unruly. The young men in the village used to go to evening gatherings, hire musicians, and drink vodka; and to have money for the vodka and for gifts to give girls, they used to steal grain from their fathers. So did I. My father punished me time and again, but often my stealing passed unnoticed, for we had everything in plenty and it was possible to go on stealing for a long time and not be caught. I kept going to parties, but they became dull for me without vodka. At this point my father died. I became my own master and did not listen to my mother. Thinking that I would improve with marriage, my mother found me a wife, but I became completely lost, and would be lost forever if the Lord had not looked upon me.

"Once I went to town to sell a wagonload of flour. When I had sold it I got drunk. I went home with my friends and kept drinking all the way. I do not remember how we got home. Father, there are some people who do not believe in future punishment and in the fire of hell. They say that there is no hell, but I know. I, poor sinner that I am, have suffered those hellish pains already here on earth; and although a long time has passed since then, I still remember at every moment how I burned in the fire of hell.

"I woke and saw fire all around me. I felt that I was bound and could move neither my hands nor my feet. Around me were standing..." (He never named the devil but only paused and crossed himself.) "They were burning me with fire, but the fire was not at all like what it is on earth; you can endure this fire, but that was much worse. It hurt so much and was so hot" (at this point he was practically weeping) "and I still remember how it all was, although more than fifty years have passed since the night when I was in such suffering! The fire was so horrible, and it burned and scorched me; and they themselves ... they were such that I cannot tell about them!

"O my Savior! O Mother of God! I cried out to Them, but my suffering had no end. I thought that a whole century had passed, but actually it was only one hour. It would seem that the Lord punished me in order to make me a reasonable man. Suddenly all this disappeared and I felt that my hands and feet got untied. I turned and saw a lamp burning before the icons (this was the very day of the Dormition); my mother was kneeling before the icons and praying and weeping. I remembered everything and understood how rightly it is said that 'A mother's prayer raises even from the bottom of the sea.' Thus my mother's prayer set me free from the hellish suffering.

"I got up as healthy as if I had not touched a drop of alcohol. My mother told me that my horse had brought me home unconscious. They had picked me up like a dead man, carried me in, and put me on a bench; they thought I had stopped breathing. My mother, all in tears, started praying.... I cannot forget that hour and never shall. How will it be with us sinners if we must thus suffer for all eternity! Merciful Lord, You have punished me here on earth; punish me again and again, but save me from eternal suffering."

I asked him: "Did you, Grandfather, tell anyone of this?" He replied, "Yes, besides my confessor, I told a man in Kiev" (every Lent he went to the Laura in Kiev, but in his own church, too, he communicated very often), "but that man laughed and told me that I had only a drunken dream. May God forgive him, but I never told anyone again, only now I have told you, Father." Grandfather was right to tell no one. He was glad that the Lord had made him reasonable, and did not wish to let the enemy of man raise fruitless thoughts and explanations which might lead him astray once more.

Such events happen often, but they just as often pass without leaving a trace behind. Those to whom they happen try to explain them by finding natural explanations for them, but they forget that everything in the world, and particularly in every man's life, happens not merely because of natural causes, but through God's providence.

Told by a priest in *The Helmsman*, a Russian journal, no. 18.

CHAPTER 30

A Tale from the Holy Mountain

There is a holy tale, preserved by the Father of the Holy Mountain, which tells us how grave are the sufferings experienced in hell. There were two friends, one of whom was moved by the word of God to enter a monastery. There he spent his life in tearful penance. The other friend remained in the world, led a life full of distractions, and finally his heart became so hardened that he began insolently to deride the Gospel.

Death came to him in the midst of such a life. When his friend the monk learned about his death, he, obeying the dictates of friendship, began to pray to God that the state of his departed friend might be revealed to him.

After some time, when the monk had sunk into a light sleep, his friend appeared to him. "How are you? Is it well with you?" asked the monk.

"Woe is me! The never-resting worm is consuming me and will give me no rest for all time."

"What is the suffering of hell like?" the monk continued.

"This suffering is unbearable!" the departed exclaimed. "But it is impossible to avoid God's anger. Because of your prayers, I have been temporarily set free. If you wish, I shall show you my suffering. Were I to reveal it to you in its entirety, you would not be able to bear the view; but recognize it at least partly." At these words the dead man raised his clothes to his knees. O horror! His legs were completely covered with frightful worms that were eating his flesh. Such a stench issued from his wounds that the horrified monk instantly woke up. But his whole cell was filled with the hellish stench, and the odor was so strong that the monk in his horror jumped out. But he forgot to close the door, and the stench penetrated the whole monastery. All the cells were filled with it, and time did nothing to take it away. Thus the monks were forced to leave their monastery and to wander to a different place. As for the monk who had seen the prisoner of hell and his terrible suffering, all his life he was unable to free himself from the evil odor that kept clinging to him. He could neither wash it off nor cover it with any perfumes.

From *Eternal Mysteries Beyond the Grave*, printed in Russian by the monastery of St Panteleimon on Mt Athos.

CHAPTER 31

The Suffering Paralytic

There was once a paralytic who, becoming impatient of his suffering, cried out to the Lord and asked that his miserable life might end. An angel appeared to him and said, "Very well. Since the Lord is ineffably good, He will respond to your prayer. He will put an end to your life on earth, but on one condition. Will you consent to spend three hours in hell instead of suffering one more year on earth? Hell cleanses every man, as gold is purified in the fire, and your sins need cleansing. You were destined to suffer from your illness one more year, so that the paralysis of your body might cleanse you of your sins. Like all believers, you have no road to heaven except the way of the cross, opened by the sinless God-Man. This road seems to have tired you here on earth; well then, experience what hell is, where all sinners go. Yet you must experience it for three hours only, and then you will be saved through the prayers of Holy Church."

The sufferer thought about these words. A year of suffering on earth seemed an unbearably long time. "I would rather endure the three hours," he finally said to the angel. The angel quietly took up his suffering soul, enclosed it in the abyss of hell, and then departed, saying, "In three hours I shall appear again and take you away from here."

The darkness that reigned all around, the closeness, the indescribable sounds of the cries emitted by sinners, the sight of the evil spirits in all their hellish ugliness—all this formed for the miserable sufferer one overwhelming feeling of fear and sickness.

Everything that he saw or heard was full of suffering, and there was no hint of any happy sound throughout the limitless abyss of hell. He saw nothing except the fiery eyes of demons glistening in the darkness, and their gigantic shadows, which seemed about to oppress, devour, and burn him with their hellish breath. The poor sufferer trembled and cried out, but there was no response to his cries except an echo which died down somewhere in the far distance of the abyss, and the bubbling of the hellish fire. It seemed to him that whole centuries of suffering had already passed, and from one moment to the next he was waiting for the light-bearing angel.

Finally the sufferer despaired of the angel's coming. Gnashing his teeth, he groaned, he roared with all his strength, but no one listened to him. All the sinners who were languishing in the dark abyss were occupied with themselves and thought only of their own suffering.

After some time, however, the calm light of angelic glory spread over the abyss. The angel approached our sufferer and with a celestial smile asked him: "How are you, brother?"

"I never thought that an angel's tongue was capable of a lie," the sufferer whispered with a barely audible voice which was breaking with suffering.

"What do you mean?" the angel asked.

"How can you ask?" the sufferer said. "You promised to take me away from here after three hours, but now whole years, perhaps whole centuries, have passed, filled for me with unspeakable suffering!"

"What years? What centuries?" the angel asked, mildly smiling. "Only an hour has passed since I left you here, and two more hours remain."

"Two more?" the sufferer asked alarmed. "Two more hours? I cannot endure them, I have no strength left! If only it may be possible, if only this is the Lord's will, I beg you to take me away from here! I should rather suffer for years and centuries on earth, even to the last day, to the time of Christ's coming at the last judgment; but do take me away. I cannot stay here! Take pity on me!" Thus the sufferer groaned and cried out, stretching his arms to the angel of light.

"Good," said the angel. "God, the Father of mercy and of comfort, will reveal His mercy to you."

At these words the sufferer opened his eyes and saw himself once again lying on his bed. All his senses were extremely weary, and the suffering of his body had affected his spirit as well. Yet from that time he sweetly endured his suffering on earth, for he bore in memory the horror of suffering in hell, and thanked the Lord, Who is merciful to all.

From "The Letters of Our Father of the Holy Mountain," Letter 15, 1883.

PART IV

PRAYING FOR THOSE IN ETERNITY

CHAPTER 32

How Important It Is to Remember the Dead

The Holy Orthodox Church, like a careful and kind mother, takes care of her children. While they are alive, she asks God to grant them good health, success in all their good undertakings, and forgiveness of sins. After their death, she often raises her prayers for them to God. Thus the departed are remembered by the Church during the midnight service, matins, vespers, and compline. The Church prays to God to forgive their sins and to repose their souls with the saints.

But it is especially during the Divine Liturgy that the holy Church cries out to God for the departed, for it firmly believes that the blessed Blood of our divine Redeemer, the Lord Jesus Christ, washes away the sins of all who are thus remembered at the liturgy. Such remembrance is particularly important during the first forty days after a person's death, for on the fortieth day God pronounces the future destiny of each soul, which is then to last until the last judgment. This is the reason why the Church advises the survivors to take care that such remembrance should take place. The importance, usefulness, and power of such remembrance are indicated by many occurrences about which we learn not only in the lives of the saints but also from other oral and written reports. Such reports extend from the beginnings of Christianity to our own times.

Once the great ascetic St Macarius of Egypt was wandering in the desert. On his path he saw a human skull lying on the ground. "I touched it with my palm stick," he said, "and the skull said something. I asked him, 'Who are you?' The skull answered, 'I used to be the chief of the pagan priests.'— 'How do you pagans fare in the other world?'—'We are burning in the fire,' said the skull, 'flames surround us from head to foot, and we cannot see one another. But when you are praying for us, we can get a glimpse of one another, and this brings us some measure of happiness" (*Christian Reading*, part 2, 1821).

St Gregory the Dialogist tells the following. A monk of his monastery did not keep his vow to own no money. When he died, the authorities, in order to set an example for the others, refused to allow him church burial, as well as prayer. This lasted for thirty days, after which the authorities relented and pitied his soul. For thirty more days, the church prayed and offered the bloodless sacrifice for him. On the last of these days, the departed man appeared in a vision to his brother, who was still alive, and said, "I have suffered cruelly until now, but now I am happy, and I dwell in the light; for today I have entered into communion." Thus the departed monk was spared punishment because the soul-saving bloodless sacrifice had been offered for him (*Sermons of St Gregory the Dialogist*, bk. 4, ch. 55).

St Gregory also tells how, in the time of St Benedict, there were two women who excelled in fasting, but, although they had a reputation for the holiness of their lives, they had an unfortunate passion for talk and used to say much that was untrue and harmful. The holy old man begged them to restrain their tongues and when they disobeyed he even threatened to excommunicate them. But their passion for lies had taken so deep a root that even threats did not stop them. A few days later they died.

These fasters were buried in a church. When, during the liturgy, the deacon would say: "Catechumens depart," they, since they had been excommunicated, would get out of their graves and go out. Some pious Christians saw them doing this. When St Benedict had been told of this, the holy man sent a eucharistic bread (prosphoron) to the church where the women had been buried, and ordered a part of the bread to be taken out for their souls. After this no one saw them again coming out of the church, and the true believers understood that their prayers for the dead women had made God merciful, and He forgave them (*Sermons of St Gregory the Dialogist*, bk. 2, ch. 23).

The *Prologos* tells us that the blessed monk Luke had a brother who became a monk but took little care of his own soul. Death came upon him in this state of carelessness. Blessed Luke was distressed that his brother had not prepared properly for death. He therefore prayed God to reveal to him his brother's destiny. Thereupon the old man saw his brother's soul in the power of evil spirits. Immediately after this vision he sent some men to inspect his brother's cell. They found there money and some other things. Luke then understood that his brother's soul was suffering for breaking the vow of poverty, as well as for other sins. He took everything that had been found and gave it away to beggars for the sake of his brother's salvation.

Some time later, when the blessed Luke was at prayer, he had another revelation. He saw a judgment seat at which the angels of light were disputing with the evil spirits over possession of the dead monk's soul. Luke heard the evil spirits cry out, "This soul is ours, for it used to do deeds inspired by us!" But the angels said to them that the soul was saved from their power because of the alms that had been given for its sake. The evil spirits retorted, "Did the dead man himself give alms? Was it not the old monk who did so?" and they pointed to the blessed Luke. The monk said, "Yes, it was I who gave alms, but I did not do so for my own sake but for the sake of this soul." The spirits, put to shame at the monk's reply, dispersed. Luke, however, was put at ease by his vision and ceased mourning his brother's lot (*Prologos* for August 12).

Lives of the Saints gives us the following account. The Reverend Abbess Athanasia told the sisters of her convent that after her death they should for her sake feed beggars for forty days. But when she died, the sisters invited beggars for ten days only, and after that were too indolent to do the bidding of their departed abbess. But the matter did not rest here. Athanasia appeared to the sisters and said, "Let everyone know that alms given for a departed soul during the forty days after death, as well as food then offered to the hungry, appease God. If the departed souls are sinful, they are thus pardoned by God of their sins; if they are righteous, the good deeds thus performed serve to save the souls of the survivors who perform them" (*Lives of the Saints* for April 12).

There are many testimonies to the expectation which the departed have of prayers for their sake. They appear to the survivors in dreams or in visions and assure them that they need to be remembered in prayers. Sometimes they persistently ask for prayers and make their need obvious by acting in various ways on the senses of those to whom they appear.

Thus St Gregory the Dialogist tells of a certain priest who was accustomed to visiting warm baths. Once when he came to the baths he found there a man whom he did not know, yet this man began helping the priest to undress. He took off the priest's boots and clothes with the promise that he would keep them safe. When the priest came out of the bath, the strange man gave him a piece of linen to wipe off his sweat, helped him to dress, and assisted him in all ways with the utmost respect.

This happened several times when the priest came to the baths, and was met by the stranger and assisted by him. Finally, the priest wished to express his gratitude for this diligence. Once when he came to the baths he brought two eucharistic breads (prosphora) in order to give them to the stranger. He met the man as usual and after the bath asked him to accept the breads as a sign of affection.

The stranger began to weep and said, "Father, why do you give me these? I cannot eat. Once I was the proprietor of this place, but for my sins I have been condemned to stay here. If you wish to do something for me, offer this bread for me to the all-powerful God and pray for my sins. If you come here and do not find me, you may know that your prayer has been heard by God." Having said this, the stranger instantly became invisible.

The priest then understood that the strange man who assisted him at the baths was a spirit. The priest spent a whole week weeping and praying God to forgive that man's sins, and every day he offered for him the bloodless sacrifice. After a week he came again to the baths, but he no longer saw the stranger there and never met him again (*Sermons of St Gregory the Dialogist*, bk. 4. ch. 55).

CHAPTER 33

The Departed Request the Living to Pray
for Them and Are Grateful

Here we shall cite a few more accounts dealing with the appearance of the departed to the living. From these accounts it can be seen how anxious the departed are to be remembered in our prayers.

A. T. B. tells the following story. "I came home from church one Easter morning and went to bed. As soon as I fell asleep, I heard someone crying bitterly at the head of my bed. My heart went out to this voice. I was afraid to open my eyes and timidly asked, 'Nadya, my dear, is it you?' I feared the answer that would follow, for it occurred to me that this was my sister Nadya, who had died long ago. Perhaps she did not attain to bliss in life eternal and had now come to ask me for my prayers. But what I heard in response to my question was, 'No, I am not Nadya.' These words were uttered in a girl's voice, sad and sweet, and trembling with emotion.

"'Who are you then?' I asked. 'Tell me what you need. I shall do everything you ask me.' My visitor broke into sobs and answered, 'I am Barbara N. For God's sake, pray for me and have me remembered at the liturgy.' I promised to do this, and the sobs died away. I opened my eyes and saw that the room was already light and that no one was there.

"When my husband's relatives came to visit, I asked my husband's brother-in-law: 'What was the name of your sister who has recently died in Moscow?' He said, 'Barbara Nikolayevna.' I then told him of my vision. He was struck by it and immediately took care that his sister should be remembered by the Church."

From *Salubrious Reflections,* 1882, issue 5.

* * *

Mrs. D. had this to say. "My niece Yulenka has been living with us for seven years. I took her in when she was three years old, after her mother, my

sister, died. Now she is past ten. Until recently she has been a healthy and carefree little girl. She never brooded and was a good student. One morning, however, she said to me, 'Auntie, I dreamed of my dear mother. She promised to come to me in broad daylight and told me not to be afraid of her.'

"Three days later, in the morning, when Yulenka was studying her geography lesson, she suddenly got up and went toward the door, as if to meet someone, and said, 'Mommy has come.' Then she put out her hand and raised her head as if to let someone kiss her. She sat down in a chair which was standing beside another, on which, as she said, her mother was sitting.

"Yulenka then said that her mother bade her tell me such and such things. She was speaking about things completely unknown to her and unfamiliar to any child of her age. She told me of certain facts from the past which were known only to my departed sister and to me, and passed on to me in my sister's name thoughts such as no ten-year-old child could possibly think of, or even set forth in due sequence. In time, my departed sister and I came to have entire conversations through Yulenka. These appearances of my sister occurred often throughout six months, and we got quite used to them. Our visitor seemed to have a liking for one particular spot in the room. There she usually sat down and began her conversations with her daughter.

"'Tell Auntie,' she once said, 'that I could become visible to her also, but she would not be able to endure this experience and would fall ill. This is the reason why I am talking to her through you: children are less afraid of us than are adults.' She very frequently asked us to pray for her, and on one occasion asked us to have a liturgy for the departed and a memorial service said for her.

"We all went to church to attend these services. Our priest was already accustomed to our accounts and no longer was surprised at them. As soon as the liturgy began, Yulenka said, 'Here is Mommy; she has come with her friend.' As usual, she approached someone whom we did not see, greeted this someone, and then, having returned to her place, added, 'They both are kneeling before the Holy Door.' At the beginning of the memorial service, Yulenka said to us, 'Mommy said she needs not this kind of memorial service but an intensive one.' I went to the priest and told him of my sister's request, and asked if an intensive kind of memorial service really existed. 'This is not the name for it,' the priest said, 'but I understand what it is you need. It is a very long service for the departed, and it is almost limited in its use to monasteries. But I can perform it.'

"When 'With the Saints Give Rest' was sung, Yulenka said, 'Mommy is weeping and praying; and she says she has no place with the saints, but she would like to find at least some rest.'

"During one of her appearances, my sister said to Yulenka, 'Your father will soon remarry, but you must not be afraid of this. Your stepmother will be a good woman, very fond of you. She will even leave you all her property.' This prediction came true in all respects.

"After six months, my sister told us that her aim was accomplished, and that she would no longer come. Toward the last of her visits she used to come with a friend of hers, who also was a departed soul. Yulenka had not known her at all, but I knew her well. She often greeted me through Yulenka. My sister constantly asked me to pray for her. Before her appearances our family was not very pious, but now, according to my sister's request, we began going to church very frequently" (*Rebus*, 1884, no. 41).

* * *

When Archimandrite Symeon was living in Yekaterinoslavl, he was the friend of a nobleman and his family. The father of the family died in February 1844. By this time, Father Symeon had been appointed to Voronezh. Among the nobleman's survivors there was a daughter, Lyubov, who was ill with consumption. On August 6, the ill girl took holy communion, but did not remove her mourning for the occasion. Her mother remarked that she should have done so, but the daughter said, "I shall dress up on the 15th." On that day, the feast of the Dormition of the Mother of God, she put on a bride's dress, sent for the priest, and again communicated. Then she asked him to read the prayers for a departing soul, and while this was being done, she addressed her departed father, who seemed to have appeared to her, and said, "Father, my dear father, wait for me." Her soul fled at the last word of the prayers.

At the same day and hour when she died in Yekaterinoslavl, Father Symeon, who was in Voronezh, saw in broad daylight the dead girl's father, who said, "You must comfort those who are in mourning in Yekaterinoslavl. My dear little Lyubov is with me, and you must not forget us too" (*Monastery Letters*, 1884, no. 17).

* * *

On July 2, 1893, the priest of the Church of Saints Peter and Paul, Father Dimitry Koiko, and a man well educated at a university, who lived in the same city, came to His Eminence Martinianus, the bishop of the Taurus and of Simferopol. They told the following story.

The night before July 30, the man accompanying the priest had had a strange dream. He saw an army officer with a bloody bandage on his head. This officer told him to ask the priest of the Church of Saints Peter and Paul why the priest was not praying for him, and also why the priest was not praying to those of God's saints whose relics were inside the icon given by the speaker to that church. He added that on July 20, the festival of St Elijah that icon would be 200 years old.

The man who had this dream went the next morning to the priest of the Church of Saints Peter and Paul and told him of his experience. Father Dimitri remarked that his church possessed no icon 200 years old, for the church itself existed only from 1805, and also that there was no icon containing relics. However, he was surprised by the vision, for there was in his church an icon which, according to his predecessor, the protopriest Rudnev (who was dead), had been brought by an unknown officer during the Crimean War. The officer had said that if he should return from Sebastopol, he would take the icon back, but if he should not return, he asked that it be accepted as his gift to the church.

The unknown officer never came back, and the icon stayed in the church. The points of resemblance between the dream and Father Rudnev's story caused Father Koiko to inspect the icon. Father Koiko told his visitor, and later told the bishop, that, although he had been serving this church for fourteen years, he had never opened up that icon. He sent for his deacon, and all three went to the church.

The icon was painted on a cypress board. It bore an old-style representation of the Holy Trinity, and also the faces of several saints. In a special hollowed-out place there was a silver cross. When with great effort it was removed, they discovered that it could be opened. Inside there were relics of St Lazarus, the Holy Great Martyr Theodore Stratelatos, the Apostle and Evangelist Luke, and the Holy First Martyr and Archdeacon Stephen.

Inscriptions testified that the cross contained other relics as well, among them those of the Holy First Martyr Thecla. Then there was discovered something even more marvelous: below the cross there was cut into the wood a barely visible inscription which said, "Year 7201 after the Creation of the World." Consequently, the icon would be 200 years old that very year.

When His Eminence Martinianus was told of this, the bishop ordered that there should be special prayers said every day in the Church of Saints Peter and Paul for the warriors who have fallen on the battle field for the sake of their faith, their sovereign, and their country.

From "Light," 1893.

* * *

A new priest came to a church to replace the old priest, who had died. But the newly appointed priest also died only a few days after he performed his first service in this church. The parishioners were deeply troubled.

Another priest was appointed. He went to church the first Sunday after he came, and was going to celebrate the divine service. When he entered the altar, he was struck by something terrible: another priest, whom he did not know, was standing near the altar. He was wearing all his vestments, but his hands and feet were bound with iron chains. The new priest did not understand what this all meant, but he nonetheless did not lose his self-control and began the service.

As soon as the service was over, the spirit disappeared. Only now did the priest fully understand that he had seen an inhabitant of another world. Yet he was unable to explain to himself what this unusual event meant, and why the other priest had appeared to him in so horrible a guise. He only recollected noting that, while the strangely bound priest had said not one word throughout the service, he had from time to time made efforts to point with his raised bound hands toward a particular area on the floor, although there seemed to be nothing there. At the following service the same thing happened again, only now the newly appointed priest, as soon as he entered the altar, looked in the direction in which the other one was pointing. In a corner near the sacrificial table he saw a little old bag. He untied it and discovered inside a great number of notes bearing the names of the dead and of the living. The notes were like those that are handed to the priest during the first part of the liturgy so that he may remember these persons in his prayers and offer the Sacrifice for them. As if enlightened from above, the new priest understood that the bound priest, who had served this church, had not read these notes during his life. As soon as he began the service, therefore, he first of all remembered in prayer the names of all the living and all the departed mentioned on the notes. He then saw how important his action was for the departed priest, for as soon as he had fulfilled the dead man's duties, the iron chains fell away from the hands and the feet of the prisoner, and he himself approached the newly appointed priest and, without saying a word, prostrated himself before him. Then he and his iron chains suddenly disappeared. The new priest never saw him again.

From "The Wanderer," 1867, vol. 1.

* * *

The secretary of the Department of Social Charity at Tver, Selinin, suddenly lost his father, the deacon of a country church, who died unexpectedly in 1850. When the son learned of his father's death, he was affected with profound sorrow. His heart stayed oppressed with it for a long time.

A year after his father's death, he was somewhat comforted by a visit to his native village. There Selinin saw the grave of his father, situated near that part of the church where his father used to sing. But although Selinin now felt better, he still was full of anxious thoughts about the state of his father's soul. He found no peace of mind until his father appeared to him.

This was on the day of the Holy Spirit. Selinin had gone to the liturgy and prayed especially diligently for his father. That very night the departed appeared to him in a dream. He seemed to come to his son and to bow low before him. "Dear father, why do you bow before your own son?" Selinin asked. But the old man did not answer. Instead he bowed a second and a third time, and only then he said, "I thank you, my dear son, for not abandoning me," and then disappeared.

From "The Wanderer," 1864.

* * *

On February 28, 1831, there died in Moscow the General Stephen Steph. Apraksin. From his youth he had been a close friend of Prince Basil Vladimir Dolgorukov. They both served in the same regiment: the one as colonel, and the other as major. Dolgorukov died in 1789 in extreme poverty, so that there was no money left for his burial. His friend Apraksin paid for the prince's burial and church services, and fulfilled this duty in such a way as if the prince had been his own brother.

The third day after the funeral, the departed Dolgorukov appeared to his benefactor to thank him. The mysterious visitor foretold his constant and merciful friend a long and happy life on earth, and promised to appear to him a short time before his death. After this experience, Apraksin, who was a good man, was particularly attentive to the needs of the poor and rejoiced every time when he had an occasion to be beneficent.

Forty-two years passed. True to his promise, Prince Dolgorukov again visited the general, now an old man. This happened at ten o'clock in the evening. First, the prince reminded Apraksin of himself and of the good deed which Apraksin had performed for him many years ago. Then he told his friend to prepare for death, which would occur in twenty days. He promised to visit him again three days before his death, and then suddenly went out from the room. Apraksin believed the words of his strange messenger from the other world. He confessed his sins, communicated, and received holy unction. Three days before his death he invited a friend to spend the night with him. At eleven o'clock, Dolgorukov appeared and began talking to Apraksin. Later the friend who witnessed their conversation told many persons about his involuntary fear during it. He did not see the prince, he said, but he heard his voice. Three days later Apraksin died. A long time after his death, stories were told throughout Moscow about his meetings with the dead Dolgorukov.

From *Salubrious Reflections*, 1867, pt. 1.

* * *

The blessed monk Luke tells us the following: "A prince of my country died and was buried according to custom. Once when I was passing the burial ground I saw a man as black as coal, standing near one of the graves. He called me. I approached and heard him saying, 'I asked in my last will that a sum of money specified by me should be given to the poor for the salvation of my soul, but this request in my will is as yet unfulfilled. Tell them to give the money instantly, or else I shall forever remain such as you see me now.'"

From *Prologos*, August 24.

* * *

Pliny the Younger tells about a beautiful house in Athens which was uninhabited because of a ghost that appeared there. Once the philosopher Athenagoras came to Athens. When he heard that this house was very cheap, he bought it and settled in it. The very first night, when Athenagoras, according to his custom, was reading and writing, he heard something that resembled the ringing of iron. A short time later he saw an old man bound in irons. The old man drew near Athenagoras, but the philosopher paid no attention and continued writing. The ghost made him a sign to follow, but Athenagoras in his turn made a sign to the old man telling him to wait, and continued writing. When he finished, he took a candle and followed the old man.

They came out into the garden, and here the ghost disappeared into the ground. Athenagoras felt no fear, but he made the spot recognizable by tearing out some grass over it. The next day he notified the city authorities. When they began digging on the indicated spot, they discovered the bones of a man bound in chains. The bones were duly buried, and the house ceased being haunted by the bound old man.

From *Salubrious Reflections*, 1883.

* * *

A certain priest was particularly diligent in praying for the dead whose names were given to him to be remembered at the liturgy. He used to copy out these names into his private notebook and pray for them all his life. The names accumulated, and eventually his notebook contained so many thousands of names that he was forced to divide it into sections and take up one section a day.

It so happened that he fell into some sin which threatened him with losing his priestly rank. This matter reached Philaret, the metropolitan of Moscow. As the metropolitan was about to sign a resolution stating that the priest should be removed from his duties, he suddenly felt his hand grow heavy. He thus postponed signing the document until the following day. In the night he dreamt of seeing a great crowd assemble under his windows. In the crowd there were people of all ages and walks of life. The crowd was agitated and finally addressed to the metropolitan some kind of plea.

"What do you need?" the bishop asked. "And who are you?"

"We are departed souls and have come to you to plead for our priest. Do not remove him from his office."

Philaret, greatly impressed by this dream, was unable to forget it after he woke up. He had the accused priest brought before him. When the priest came, the metropolitan asked him: "What good deeds have you done? Tell me."

"None, my Lord," the priest answered; "I deserve being punished."

"Do you pray for the departed?" asked the metropolitan.

"Why yes, my Lord, always; it is a rule with me always to remember all whose names are handed to me, and I always take out parts of the prosphora for all of them, so that my parishioners have begun complaining that my proskomide is longer than the liturgy itself. But I cannot do otherwise."

The metropolitan limited himself to transferring the priest to another parish, having first explained to him who had interceded for him.

From "The Wanderer," May 1862.

* * *

One of the novices at Mt Athos revealed the following to a monk of the Holy Mountain, the well-known Father Seraphim: "I became a monk because I saw in a dream the future destiny of sinners. This happened after I had been greatly weakened by an illness which lasted two months. I saw two youths who entered my room, took me by the hands and said, 'Follow us.' I no longer felt my illness. I got up, looked back at my bed, and saw my body lying there quietly. Then I understood that I had left the earthly life and had to appear in the other world.

"I recognized that the youths were angels. They showed me the places of torment, and I heard there the groans of the sufferers. As the angels showed me the flaming places appointed for various sins, they added, 'If you will not set aside your sinful habits, you, too, will have your punishment here!'

"One of the angels took up from the flames a man as black as coal. He was as burnt as a coal and bound in chains, hand and foot. Both angels approached the sufferer, unbound him, and his blackness disappeared with the chains. He became as pure and light as an angel. The angels clothed him in a brilliant cloak which looked like light.

"'What does this change mean?' I dared to ask. 'This sinful soul,' the angels answered, 'was separated from God for its sins and had to burn eternally in these flames. Meanwhile, this soul's parents kept giving alms for it, remembered it at liturgy, had *panikhidas* said for it, and now for the sake of the parents' prayers and those of the Holy Church, God has mercy on the soul and has completely pardoned it. It now is freed from eternal torments and will stand before the face of its Lord and be joyful with His saints.'

"When my vision was ended, I came to myself and saw people weeping around what they considered to be my dead body, which they were preparing for burial."

From "The Wanderer," May 1862.

CHAPTER 34

The Departed Appear to Their Relatives and Friends to Tell Them of Their Death

His Eminence Nicanor, the archbishop of Odessa, tells us about the following occurrence of which he heard from a layman who was a deep thinker widely read in theology. A certain Caucasian was one night sitting at home reading a book. When he raised his eyes he saw a mist in the opposite corner. He began waving his hand to make the mist disappear, but instead he saw the bright figure of his betrothed appear from the mist. At that time he knew her to be far away in Russia. He involuntarily fell on his knees before this shadow. His bride put a garland on his head and disappeared in the mist. He went to his parents and told them about his vision. They noted in writing the day and the hour of this vision. Later they discovered that his betrothed died the day of her appearance. For a long time after this he felt around his head something like the touch of a garland.

From "The Wanderer," 1887.

* * *

Archbishop Nicanor learned the following from a well-known and active member of the Slavic Philanthropic Society, who also had a good knowledge of the Scriptures, the canons of the Church, and the history of the Church. His brother, a military officer, was once going home with a comrade after an evening party. They were in the same carriage. He got out at his house, and his comrade went on home. When he, accompanied by his servant and his dog, came into his study, he saw his comrade sitting at the desk, his back turned to them. He was surprised, since he knew that he had just parted with his comrade. The servant said, "I did not see him coming in." Even the dog was clearly seeing a strange person. When they looked at the face of the man who was sitting at the desk, they saw that it was deathly pale. At this moment the comrade's servant ran in and told them that his master had just returned home and died as soon as he came in.

From "The Wanderer," September 1887.

* * *

   Eudokia Petrovna Yelagina had a child, Raphael, about two years old. He fell ill and was in great suffering. His mother, who had great love for him, was sitting all night at his little bed, unable to tear her eyes away from him. But by chance she looked at the door, and distinctly saw her friend Maria Andreevna Moyer, born Protasova, who was coming into the room. Eudokia Petrovna jumped up from her chair and ran to meet her, crying: "Masha!" But no one was there. Eudokia Petrovna felt unwell. That very night and that very hour Maria Andreevna died at Derpt, and only later did her friend hear of this.

From the *Works of V. A. Zhukovski*, vol. 4.

* * *

   An official by the name of Vladimir Engelhardt tells the following. "In 1858 I was working in Moscow. At the beginning of February I was sent to Archangel on business connected with my work. Before my departure I wrote to my mother, who was living in Petersburg, and asked her to bless me, as I was going on a journey. Then I left. During one of my stops at a station, while I was going to lie down on a couch and rest, I was greatly surprised at seeing a few steps from me my mother and also my sister, who had died in 1846. Struck by this unfathomable vision, I was unable to move from the spot. Intently and with some strange fear, I kept looking at these beloved women who so incomprehensibly appeared to me. My mother, like a real person, blessed me by making the sign of the cross over me. I suddenly took a match, lighted a candle, and the vision disappeared from the lighted room. This happened after two o'clock in the morning on February 13, 1858. When I arrived at Archangel, I received a letter from my brother-in-law, notifying me that my mother had died the night of February 13."

From *Salubrious Reflections*, 1870.

* * *

When the Russian scientist Lomonosov was sailing home from abroad, he dreamed of seeing his father shipwrecked at a spot on the shore of the White Sea. This spot was familiar to him, since when he was a boy he was once carried there by a storm, as he was accompanying his father during a fishing expedition. As soon as he got to St Petersburg, Lomonosov took care to find out about his father from his countrymen, and they told him that his father had gone out to fish last fall and had not returned since then. They thought that he had met with some misfortune.

Lomonosov was as struck by this news as he had been by his dream. He decided to return home to the White Sea, find his father's body on the island which appeared to him in his dream, and bury it with all honor. But since his duties in St Petersburg prevented Lomonosov from fulfilling his plan, he sent a letter to his relatives and gave it to merchants who were going from St Petersburg to his home country. In this letter, he asked his brother to take care of the matter.

That summer his wishes were followed. A group of fishermen from Kholmogory went to the island pointed out to them and found there the dead body of Vasiliy Lomonosov. They buried the body and put a large boulder over the grave.

From *The History of the Imperial Academy of Sciences in St Petersburg*, in Russian, vol. 2, p. 312.

* * *

Countess Elizabeth Ivanovna Orloff, the wife of Count Vladimir Orloff, was before her marriage a lady-in-waiting to the Empress Catherine II. In 1767, while the court was in Tsarskoe Selo, Elizabeth was also there. One morning she was busy dressing in the company of several young friends of hers, among them Countess Elizabeth Cyrillovna Razoumovski.

Their conversation was enlivened by gaiety and laughter. Amused and happy, Elizabeth Ivanovna suddenly happened to look out the window. Her face became troubled; she looked again, seemed astonished, and having looked a third time suddenly jumped out of her armchair and cried out, "My dear father has come! He is coming to the window." They all ran into the garden and looked everywhere, but Stackelberg, her father, was nowhere to be seen.

His loving daughter was no longer bright. Her face was sorrowful. Her friends tried in vain to convince her that the vision was a figment of her imagination. The daughter kept repeating that she saw her father three times, and that at first she herself did not believe her eyes. Nothing could be done to distract her.

At dinner with the empress, the other ladies-in-waiting made fun of their impressionable friend. The empress wished to be told what amused them so much, and Prince I. S. Baryatinski informed her. "Be calm," the empress said. "Your father is not in Petersburg, for he could not come here without my permission. You only seemed to see him. However, I advise you to write down this vision."

A few days later there came news about Stackelberg's death in Riga, the very day and hour when he appeared to his daughter.

From *A Dictionary of the Notables of Russia*, in Russian.

* * *

N. I. Grech tells in her memoirs of the following event. "My uncle, Longinus Ivanovich Grech, soon after he became an officer, went to the army, which was fighting against the Turks. He died in 1772 in Jassy during an epidemic of the plague. His mother had loved him more than her other children, and our family tradition says that he appeared to her at the moment of his death. His mother, who was my grandmother, lay down one day to rest after dinner. Soon she ran out of her bedroom and, all alarmed, asked, 'Where is he?'—'Who?' everyone asked. 'My son, Longinus Ivanovich! I was on the point of falling asleep when I heard something rustling and opened my eyes. I saw him passing the door of my room, and he seemed very careful not to wake me. Where is he? Don't let him hide.' Everyone kept telling her that Longinus Ivanovich had not come and that she had only dreamed of him, and she decided that she had been mistaken; but she wept at this thought. At this moment her son-in-law, Besaque, came into the room. When he heard of what had happened, he became thoughtful, took his notebook from his pocket, and wrote down the day and hour of this occurrence. Two weeks later they received a letter informing them that Longinus Ivanovich had died at that time."

From the *Memoirs* of N. I. Grech, in Russian.

CHAPTER 35

The Departed Take an Interest in Their Survivors

Metropolitan Platon tells of the following event which he himself experienced. "When I was a bishop on the Don, there appeared to me the departed Emperor Nicholas Pavlovich (Nicholas I). This happened toward the end of the forty-day period after his death. I was sitting in my room reading the sermon which a priest was going to deliver the next day, a Sunday. It was around midnight, and my attention was entirely given to my reading. My imagination, consequently, was vacant, and cannot be responsible for what followed. To my right there was a door leading to the room where I received visitors, and this door was open, as always. I was concentrating on reading and correcting some passages in the sermon. Suddenly I felt as if I had been struck in my right side by something quite light but definitely tangible, as if someone had thrown at me a child's rubber ball from the open door. I could not help looking to the right. What do you suppose I saw there?

"I saw standing in the doorway His Majesty the Emperor Nicholas Pavlovich, in all his regalia and all his dignity. He seemed slightly bent toward one side. His eagle-like gaze was directed at me. The apparition was not indistinct, foggy, or at all like a spectre. Not at all; I saw my unforgettable czar as if he were alive, and the smallest details of his appearance seemed tangibly real. How could I help becoming confused and embarrassed?

"I kept looking at my beloved czar, who had appeared to console my sorrow, and he kept looking at me with a piercing, majestic, and at the same time kind gaze. This lasted for quite a while. Involuntarily I asked myself: should I get up and bow? But does one bow to a ghost? On the other hand, must I not bow to a czar?

"I began rising, and in that second the clear and wonderful image of the great among rulers of this earth began little by little changing to a misty ghost and disappearing. It vanished from my sight. I, however, was no longer weeping for the departed czar, and later too when I remembered the unforgettable czar of the Russian empire, my tears were less frequent than before.

"I do not know," the metropolitan added addressing his listeners, "if you will believe me. Do not forget that I am an old man, and that, although I am unworthy, I do serve at the Lord's altar: I have no need to tell lies or to invent stories."

From *New Time*, a Russian periodical, April 1893.

* * *

The well-known author Kelsieff tells the following story about himself. "When I was young I studied at a commercial school. I had rooms near my school, while my father and the rest of the family lived on Vasilevsky Island. My father was a customs official and was provided with an apartment by the government. This apartment was situated near the Exchange, and since my father was occupied by his office, he seldom visited me. One night, however, when I had not yet gone to bed and was staying up alone reading a book, I saw my door open and my father come in. He looked pale and sad. I knew of his concern for me and was therefore not at all surprised to see him come at this late hour. He came up to me and said, 'Vassya, I have come to give you my blessing.... Live an upright life and do not forget God.' Having said this, my father blessed me and disappeared through the same door.

"His visit was not an extraordinary event and therefore made no impression on me. But can you imagine my amazement at what happened later? Only a short time after my father left, I heard people knocking at the door. The door was by this time locked, and I had gone to bed. I opened the door and saw our coachman, who had come for me. He told me that my father had died, and that he was sent for me immediately after my father's death. Indeed, I found out that my father had died no more than an hour ago, at practically the same time when I saw him in my room. It became clear to me that my father came to me after his death in order to give me his parental blessing."

From *Rebus*, 1884, no. 11.

* * *

Our Father of the Holy Mountain writes about an archbishop who suffered from severe attacks of melancholia. He diligently prayed God to help him. One evening as he was so praying, he saw a light appear in his room. It continued spreading until it had enveloped him. Then he saw a woman and, after he had looked closely at her, he recognized that she was his departed mother. "Why are you weeping so bitterly, my son?" she asked. "Do you understand what you are asking of God? It is not difficult for the Lord to fulfill your request, but do you realize of what you will deprive yourself if it is granted? You do not know what you are asking for yourself." She instructed him on the virtue of patience and then became invisible.

From "The Letters of Our Father of the Holy Mountain," letter 218.

* * *

Archimandrite Anthony of the Monastery of St Sergius tells of the following event concerning Metropolitan Philaret. "On September 17, I came to the metropolitan with my usual report on the monastery. After my report, His Eminence, who at the time was at our monastery, said, 'I dreamt last night of a warning concerning the 19th.' I objected: 'Your Eminence, is it permissible to put faith in dreams and to search for meaning in them? And how can one pay attention to so indefinite a warning? In a year there are twelve of these 19th days, one to each month.'

"He listened to me and then said in a definite tone, 'It was not really a dream. My departed father appeared to me and spoke to me. I think I shall from now on take holy communion on the 19th of every month.' I said that this was a good decision.

"Two days later, on the 19th of September, which was a Tuesday, he took holy communion during liturgy at his domestic church. In October he was at Moscow and took holy communion on the 19th, a Thursday, in his domestic church there. November 19 would come on a Sunday.

"Before the 19th of November His Eminence felt well and healthy. He received visitors, zealously attended to business, and occasionally went out. The week before the 19th he received one of his admirers, who at parting told him of the request of a great lady who revered the metropolitan so much that she wished to come to him for his blessing. His Eminence said, 'Let her come, but she should do it before the 19th.' So deeply had he been struck by the idea that something would happen to him on the 19th.

"On Saturday the 18th, His Eminence told his private deacon, the monk Parthenius, that the next day he would celebrate the liturgy in his private domestic church, and that everything should be made ready for it. Parthenius, who was an old man well known for his straightforward and honest character, told the old metropolitan that it might be better to celebrate liturgy on the day of the Presentation: it would be too taxing for His Eminence to serve on both days. But His Eminence said to him: 'You should not concern yourself with this. Tell them that I shall serve tomorrow.' He did as he intended and died later the same day, the 19th."

From *Simple Accounts of Complex Things*, in Russian, by M. Pogodin.

* * *

A lady tells us of the following. "I was still a little girl when I became witness to an unusual occurrence which I shall not forget till my dying day. One evening when I had gone to bed and all candles had been put out, to my great amazement I suddenly saw a priest sitting before the fireplace. The fire had not yet gone out, and he was warming his hands. His build, face, and bearing resembled those of one of my uncles, a protopriest who lived not far from us. I immediately called my sister, who slept in the same room with me. She looked at the fireplace and saw the same thing as I, and she also recognized our uncle.

"An indescribable fear took possession of us, and we began shouting and calling for help. Our father, who was sleeping in the next room, was wakened by our desperate cries, jumped out of bed, and ran to us with a candle. The apparition vanished. The next morning we received a letter telling us that our uncle the protopriest had died the very day and hour when we saw him."

From *Petersburg Leaves*, a Russian periodical, 1883.

* * *

Before the feast of the Holy Trinity, His Eminence Demetrius, the bishop of Tula, dreamed that he was in the Cathedral of Odessa. The archbishop of Odessa, Innocent, was standing on the steps of the altar, holding a paper. He gave the paper to Bishop Demetrius and said, "Father Demetrius, finish." Later it became known that Archbishop Innocent had died before the feast of Trinity, and His Eminence Demetrius was appointed his successor.

From supplement to the "News of the Diocese of Chersonese," 1887.

* * *

In the town of Vladimir-on-Klyazma, near the Golden Gate, a hundred years ago there was the shop of a barber named Pavel Vasilyevich Karoff. He had in Moscow a brother, Sergey Vasilyevich Karoff, also a barber. Sergey died during the fifth week of Lent, after a serious illness. His sister, who lived with him, immediately let her brother Pavel know of Sergey's death. But at that time there were no railroads, the spring thaw had set in, there were no paths visible under the slush, and Pavel Vasilyevich did not find it possible to travel to his brother's funeral.

Easter came. The first day of Easter, around ten o'clock in the evening, Karoff lay on a couch and began musing about this and that. Suddenly the door opened and the dead brother came in. He blessed himself before the icons, approached Pavel, and said, "Christ is risen, Pasha!"

Pavel was terrified, but when Sergey came up to kiss him, Pavel answered, "He is indeed risen!" and kissed him. The dead man sat down beside his brother on the couch. "Our mother greets you; she is in a good way over there," he said. "Aren't you dead, Serezha?" Pavel asked.—"Yes, I am dead."—"How then did you come?"—"They let us." Pavel Karoff took heart. He got up, picked up a pipe, stuffed it with tobacco, and offered it to his brother. Sergey, however, refused by saying, "We do not smoke." Pavel could not believe his eyes. He began quietly to feel Sergey's coat and to estimate its quality. The coat turned out to be made of good stuff, in the accepted fashion. Pavel no longer doubted that his brother Sergey in person was sitting before him. After some more talk Sergey expressed his wish to go home. He went out of Pavel's shop and turned toward the church of St Nicholas Zaryadny, where he disappeared behind the columns at the entrance.

During his conversation with Pavel, Sergey had told him the following. "When I was buried, our sister took all my goods for her own use, but she has not found the most important thing. My chest has a double bottom, and this bottom is fitted so carefully that it cannot be found if one does not know about it. Take the chest for yourself. In the bottom you will find 150 rubles and a note from Prince Golitzyn, who owes me for a year's worth of shaving. He will give the money to you." Thus Pavel Vasilyevich had only to verify what his brother had told him.

The Sunday after Easter he left for Moscow. He came to his sister, who had taken care of Sergey's funeral, and asked her about their brother's last days and about the clothes in which he had been buried. His sister said that she had put Sergey into his coffin wearing such and such a coat, such and such trousers, such and such a shirt; in other words, her description agreed with what Pavel himself had seen his brother wearing. Finally Pavel asked if his brother had ended his life as a Christian, and was told that

Sergey had received holy unction and had confessed and communicated the day before his death.

When she was asked about the property that Sergey had left, she showed Pavel an empty chest. Pavel asked to be given this chest as a keepsake. His sister willingly let him take it. Pavel took the chest to his room at the inn and began to inspect the bottom. Indeed, he discovered that a very thin board was screwed to the top of the real bottom of the chest. When he lifted the board, he found under it exactly 150 rubles and a note for 90 rubles owed by Prince Golitzyn. Pavel Karoff took the note to the prince, and the prince, with no objection whatsoever, gave him 90 rubles.

Pavel told his spiritual father, Gabriel Yastreboff, about this event. Father Gabriel did not know what to make of it. After some time, when Father Gabriel had come to Karoff with holy water, he asked him again to repeat this story. Pavel willingly did so in the presence of the priest's assistants and singers.

Some more time passed, and Pavel fell seriously ill. Before death, he called for his spiritual father. Father Gabriel, who wished to learn if Pavel's story had been true, asked him a third time about it: had his brother Sergey actually appeared to him? Pavel pointed to the holy icons, said that his own death was near, and testified before Father Gabriel that everything he had told him about his brother Sergey was really true. He had no need, he said, to mislead Father Gabriel: he had actually spoken with the dead and kissed him.

From "Contemporary News," in Russian, 1887, no. 80.

* * *

S. S. tells us the following. "About a year and a half before the death of Alexey Petrovich Yermoloff, I came to Moscow to see him. I was his guest for several days. As I was getting ready to return to my place of work, I could not keep back my tears at the thought that I would probably never again see him in this life, for he was already very old, and I could not possibly return to Moscow earlier than in a year. Alexey Petrovich saw my tears and said, 'Come, come, I am not going to die before you come back.' 'God alone knows when we are to die,' I said. 'But I am telling you: I will not die this year.'

"My facial expression probably reflected great surprise, and even fear for the soundness of Alexey Petrovich's mind. My feelings did not escape him. 'I shall prove to you that I am not mad and not given to hallucinations.'

"With these words he led me to his study, unlocked a drawer, took from it a piece of paper, and brought it to me. 'Whose writing is this?' he asked me. 'Yours,' I replied. 'Read, then.' I read a list of all the posts and offices which Alexey Petrovich had held, beginning with the post of lieutenant colonel. There were dates, and also the times and descriptions of all the more or less notable events of his life, which was so rich in events. He followed me with his eyes, and when I was approaching the end of the sheet, he covered the last lines with his hand.

" 'You must not read these,' he said; 'here are written the year, month, and day of my death. Everything that you have read here has been noted down in advance and has come to pass exactly as noted. I shall tell you how it happened. When I was still a lieutenant colonel, I was sent to the town of T. in order to find out the details of some business there. I had to work very much. My apartment consisted of two rooms: the first of these was taken by my secretary and my servant, while I took the second. It was impossible to enter my room except through the first room.

" 'One night I was sitting at my desk writing. Having finished, I lighted a pipe, threw myself back in my chair, and sank into thought. When I lifted my eyes, I saw a man I did not know, an ordinary townsman, to judge by his clothes. I did not have time to ask him who he was and what he needed, when the stranger said, "Take a sheet of paper, a pen, and write." I unconditionally obeyed him, for I felt that I was under the influence of an irresistible power. He dictated to me everything that would happen during my life, and finished the list with the day of my death.

" 'At the last word he disappeared, but I could not find out how and where he had vanished. Several minutes passed before I came to my senses. My first thought was that I had served as the object of a joke. I jumped up and ran into the first room, which the stranger would not have been able to avoid. There I saw my secretary writing by the light of a cheap candle, while my servant was sleeping on the floor, near the entrance door, which turned out to be locked with a key. I asked who it was that had just gone out. My secretary was surprised and said that no one had passed through the room.

" 'I have never told anyone of this,' said Alexey Petrovich at the end of his story. 'I knew in advance that some people would think I had invented all this, while others would regard me as a man given to hallucinations. To me, however, my story is factual, and its visible and obvious proof is this sheet of paper. I hope that now you will not doubt that we shall meet again.'

"Indeed, a year later we met again. After his death, I found the mysterious manuscript among his papers and discovered from it that Alexey Petrovich Yermoloff died the same day and hour which had been predicted to him about fifty years before."

From "Russian Antiquities," in Russian, May 1875.

* * *

In the 1830s there were serving at Sebastopol two officers, both excellent seamen, P. and T. They were great friends. Once when T. was getting ready for an expedition, he came to his comrade and said, "I am going to sea. Anything may happen. Give me your word of honor that you will do what I shall ask you to." "Can you doubt me?" P. asked, "tell me what you wish."—"If I should die, marry my widow and be a father to my son."—"Dear me, what are you saying? Are you in your senses? Your trip is a minor one. You will come back; besides, you are an excellent swimmer."

"There is no need to talk about that. I ask you to give me your word."— "Be it so, if it will calm you." The friends parted. Several months passed. One night P. dreamed of T., who was saying to him, "You must keep your promise and get married." When he woke up, he thought it had been only a dream. Meanwhile, no one heard anything about the expedition. After a while P. once more dreamed of his friend, who was reminding him of his promise, and soon after the admiralty was notified that T. had drowned.

From *Simple Accounts of Complex Things*, in Russian, by M. Pogodin.

* * *

Blessed Augustine tells the following: When he was in Milan he knew of a young man who was constantly being persecuted by a creditor of his father. The young man's father was dead, and had paid his debt before he died, but the son had no written proof of this transaction. The father, however, appeared to his son and pointed out to him where he had put away the written note. The son found it and was freed from much trouble.

From the works of A. Calmet.

* * *

In the village of Studenka, in the Dubensk district of the government of Volyn, there lived a well-to-do peasant, Oliynik by name. He was a healthy man of sturdy build. In November 1868, when he was around fifty years old, he fell seriously ill and died within two weeks. He left behind his wife and a son Anton, who was about twenty years old.

One night six weeks after his death, his wife woke in her bed on top of the oven and heard someone weeping. There was no one in the house except her and her son. She listened closely and discovered that the person who was weeping was her husband. She lighted a splinter and indeed saw her husband, who was standing near his sleeping son and weeping. Although the woman was very frightened, she gathered her courage and said, "Why have you come, Simon? I don't suppose you were a magician while you were alive?"

"I had to come to you, and so I have come. Don't speak nonsense, woman, about things which you do not know."—"Why then are you weeping over your son?"—"I am weeping because you do not look after him."—"How so?"—"Quite simply: Anton is in love with a Catholic and is about to marry her."—"Simon, this cannot be."—"What do you mean, it cannot be? I know everything. Woman, do not argue with me. Speak to your son: you are his mother and he may listen to you. But if you do not find the time to convince him, I'll take him to myself ten days from now."

The woman began howling with fear and grief. Her son woke, and the apparition vanished. The mother began questioning her son: was he really in love? He began to deny it, but later he confessed being in love with Adelka, the daughter of the supervisor of a neighboring estate, whose parents would never allow her to marry a peasant, and particularly an Orthodox. Thus Anton and his girl decided secretly to flee to Galicia and there to be wedded by a Uniate priest. They were to flee in ten days.

When the fateful day had come, Anton quietly left the house early in the morning, while his mother was still asleep. His betrothed was already waiting for him in her vegetable patch. He took from the stable his best horse, an animal he had not ridden much before. Suddenly the horse kicked him in his right side, Anton lost consciousness, and that evening he was dead.

From the book *Appearances of the Departed from the Other World, from Antiquity to Our Own Time,* in Russian, by Priest D. Bulgakovsky.

* * *

A physician tells the following. "Not long ago I was treating one of the most outstanding citizens of our city. During my visit to him the patient told me of the following occurrence. A doctor in Philadephia had once spent a busy day visiting patients and was sitting in his study. When the clock had struck half past eight, he thought that the time had come to put an end to his working hours and to rest. He got up out of his armchair to lock the door, but at that moment the door opened and a girl came into the room. She was thin and pale, and her head was covered with a large scarf. 'Doctor, please visit my mother,' she said, 'she is very ill.' The doctor asked the little one to name herself and her mother, and to give him their address. She gave him clear directions and he went to his desk to write down her words. The desk was standing at the other end of the room. While he was writing he had the thought of going to visit the sick woman right away, together with the girl, but when he turned around to tell her this, she was no longer in the room. He quickly opened the door, went out of the house, looked in all directions, but the girl was nowhere to be seen. Very surprised at her sudden disappearance, he quickly picked up his hat and cane and went to visit the sick woman. It was not difficult to find the house pointed out by the girl. He was taken to the patient. 'I am a physician,' he said. 'Did you send for me?'

"'No, I did not,' the woman replied. The doctor thought that he had the wrong address. He checked his notebook and asked her name. It agreed with the name in his book. 'Have you a daughter?' He described and named the girl he had seen. The woman did not answer momentarily. Her eyes filled with tears. 'I had a daughter by that name,' she said, 'but she died an hour and a half ago.'—'She died? Where did she die?' asked the doctor.—'Here,' said the mother.—'Where is her body?'—'In the next room.' The woman's elder daughter took the doctor to that room and he recognized the dead child to be the little girl who had come to call him to her sick mother.

"'Well, doctor,' my patient added, 'what do you think of this? This happening seems to me quite miraculous!'—'But I regard it as quite natural,' I said. 'Do you think that it was the girl's body that had appeared to the doctor?'—'Of course not,' said my patient. 'It can only have been her spirit.' To this I agreed."

From *Appearances of the Departed from the Other World, from Antiquity to Our Own Times*, in Russian, by Priest D. Bulgakovsky.

* * *

Here is an account taken from the memoirs of a statesman, as it has been printed in one of the most widely circulating lay journals with a markedly scientific bent. It is communicated to us by Nicanor, the bishop of Chersonese and Odessa.

The author of the memoirs speaks about his father or his grandfather—I forget which of the two—who received an appointment but died on his way to the appointed place of service.

The sorrow of his helpless family was so deep that his wife, broken by grief, lay in bed unable to get up, and the ladies of the town took it upon themselves to care for her day and night. One night they heard the front door open. The dead man came in wearing the clothes in which he had been taken ill. He passed the servant, who was not asleep and who distinctly saw him. Then he opened the door to the next room and went by the lady who was taking care of his wife. She was lying on the floor in order to rest for a while. She rose slightly and looked intently at him. The dead man sat on a chair near the bed where his wife lay, unable to sleep. His face was deeply sorrowful. His wife rose and stretched out her arms to him with the words, "What is it, my friend?" The dead man uttered several horrible words and then left the same way he had come—through doors locked for the night. They all got up to look at the doors and discovered that they were no longer locked.

From "The Wanderer," September 1887.

* * *

O. D-tsky tells the following. "About twenty versts from our estate there was in the government of Volyn the large village of Vishnevets. The village priest was a great friend of my father's. When the priest's wife died, he was left alone with his sixteen-year-old daughter. He asked my father to let my sister Stepanida visit his daughter a short while in order to make it easier for the orphaned girl to become adjusted to her mother's death. Two weeks passed, but Stepanida did not return. Therefore my father went to Vishnevets to see his friend, the widowed Father G., and to bring my sister home. He took me with him. I was then about ten years old. This was in June 1860.

"We came to Vishnevets around ten o'clock in the evening and did not find the priest home. The girls, however, were there. I decided to run around in the garden, but I was afraid of going deep into the garden. Instead I sat down on a little bench near the house. Suddenly I saw a lady dressed in black who was walking along a path. When she approached me she smiled at me and then went into the priest's house, up the steps which led directly from the house into the garden. This was around eleven o'clock.

"A few minutes later, I ran to the other steps, where my father and the girls were sitting. 'A lady has entered the house by the garden steps,' I said. My sister and her friend exchanged glances at my words and seemed alarmed. My father asked them what had happened and why they were alarmed. They replied that, to judge by my description of the lady and her dress, she was the priest's departed wife, who came into the house every day and was visible to everyone. My father did not believe stories of this kind and laughed at the girls.

"The priest was late in coming home, and we decided to have tea without him. We all sat down in the sitting room, while my sister Stepanida busied herself preparing tea in the next room, where we were able to see her. Suddenly my sister shrieked and dropped a teapot full of boiling water. When my father asked what was the matter, she said that the priest's wife had just gone by.

"We went to bed in the priest's absence. My father and I were to sleep in one room (it was next to the priest's study), while the two girls were put up in another room. Around two o'clock in the morning I became awake without knowing why. I heard voices in the study. A man's voice asked, 'Why did you come so late today?'—'I was here earlier and saw our guests. I wished to embrace the little boy in the garden but he ran away from me; then I thought to thank Stepanida for her friendship to our daughter, but she was so frightened when I passed her that she dropped a teapot and alarmed everyone in the house, and I had to disappear.'

" 'Why did you not prepare her?'—'We are strictly forbidden to appear to those who are afraid of us. Otherwise we may forfeit the opportunity to have other meetings with the living.' When I heard these words I was terribly frightened, for I understood that this was a conversation between the priest and his departed wife. In one moment I jumped into my father's bed and discovered him still awake. He told me not to disturb him: he was eager to overhear the conversation between a living and a departed being.

"The next morning during breakfast my father turned the conversation to last night's visitor and expressed some doubts concerning the reality of what he had heard: he would rather suspect anything else, he said. 'You may believe me or not,' said Father G. 'but being an honest man and a servant of the holy altar, I am telling you that I am in spiritual communication with many of the departed, my wife among them. They frequently ask me to pray for them, and when I fulfill their pleas they personally thank me. As for my departed wife, she visits my house almost every day and often expresses her interest for everything that is happening here, as if she were still alive. But whenever I ask her about the conditions of life beyond, she always avoids direct answers and declares that the departed are forbidden to answer all the questions put to them by the living, and particularly their idle questions.'"

From *Appearances of the Departed from the Other World, from Antiquity to Our Own Times*t, in Russian, by Priest D. Bulgakovsky.

CHAPTER 36

More Accounts of Appearances of the Departed

At the beginning of the nineteenth century, there lived in one of our provincial towns a man named N., an elderly retired official known for his kindheartedness and genuine piety. He was a great friend of V., who had been his companion in childhood, and later his colleague. They were of the same age and had similar convictions. When V. died, his friend diligently prayed to God to rest V.'s soul, and from time to time gave alms for his friend's salvation. He often thought about his friend's destiny.

On the fortieth day after V.'s death, his friend was sitting in his room. He heard the door creak, lifted his eyes, and saw his friend V. coming into the room. "I thank you, my friend," the spirit said, "for your diligent prayers and almsgiving, which have helped me much. With God's help I am saved from hell, and my abode is peaceful." N. was listening to the marvelous visitor. He experienced a feeling of horrified amazement and did not dare to interrupt the spirit. "Farewell, my friend, until we meet in eternity," said his visitor. "I hope that we shall meet soon and shall dwell together, but meanwhile you must labor for your eternal salvation." Having said these words, he disappeared behind the door.

N., who had always been pious, exerted himself even more in his good deeds and devotions, leaving all his earthly cares to his children. Two years after his vision, he died quietly and peacefully while he was kneeling at prayer.

From *Salubrious Reflections*, 1868.

* * *

Metropolitan Platon tells the following. "I myself have experienced the appearance of a spirit, and I must say that this departed soul appeared to me more clearly and distinctly than I see you who listen to me now. This happened in the thirties, when I was the inspector of the Theological Academy in St Petersburg. Among our students there was one named Ivan Krylov. He was a graduate of the seminary in Orel, and had been a student of mine there. He was quite a good student, his conduct was good, and he had a pleasant appearance.

"Once, he came to me and asked for permission to go to the school hospital. I thought that he was suffering from exhaustion and decided to let him enter the hospital; there they would feed him better and he would get well. He might even write the term paper there. Some time passed, but I heard nothing about him. Neither did the doctor tell me anything. One day, however, as I was lying on my sofa reading a book, I suddenly saw Krylov standing before me and looking directly at me. I saw his face as distinctly as I see you, but his body was less distinct, as if covered by a cloud or by mist. I looked at him and shivered. The ghost rushed toward the window and disappeared. I was still thinking about the meaning of it all when someone knocked at my door. The janitor of the school hospital came in and said, 'The student by the name of Krylov has died.'—'How long ago?' I asked, completely surprised.—'It must be about five minutes; I immediately came to notify you.'

"Can you explain this mystery?" the bishop ended, addressing all who had listened to his account. Everyone kept quiet. "All this," said the bishop, "undoubtedly proves to us some mysterious connection between us and the souls of the departed."

From "News of the Diocese of Mogilev," in Russian, 1883.

* * *

There lived in a certain village a widely honored couple: the village priest Father G. and his wife. They were very old and had lived their whole life in total harmony. For his pious life, Father G. was respected throughout the countryside. He seemed to represent in his person the good old times; he was hospitable, friendly, and kind. But there is an end even to the best life. One day Father G. fell ill, no longer got up, and finally, fortified by the Christian mysteries, quietly and peacefully went into eternity, having left behind the companion of his life, who was bitterly weeping for him. A year passed after his death. The day before the anniversary, when he was to be remembered in a *panikhida*, the old woman lay down to rest after various tasks. She dreamed of her departed husband. She seemed to run to him joyfully and ask how he was and where he was. The husband said, "Although I do not have to answer you, answer I shall. During our life together I had no secrets from you and will not conceal from you now that, through God's grace, I am not in hell. Soon you, too, will follow me. Prepare for death in three weeks."

The departed slowly went away, as if he were reluctant to part with her. The old woman awoke and began to tell everyone about her happiness in having seen her departed husband. Indeed, in three weeks she died in peace.

From *Salubrious Reflections*, 1868, pt. 1.

* * *

St John of Damascus tells of a holy monk who had a disciple. This disciple led a negligent and carefree life. In this his state he was surprised by death. The old man prayed and wept for his disciple, and the merciful Lord finally showed him his disciple surrounded by fire up to his neck. The old man continued toiling and praying for the sins of the departed disciple, and God revealed to him the young man standing in fire up to his waist. After more and still more efforts on the part of the monk, God revealed him his disciple completely set free from suffering.

From "Sermon on Those Who Have Died in the Faith," *Christian Reading*, in Russian, pt. 26, 1827.

* * *

At the end of the eighteenth century, there lived Z., the owner of an estate. He was not yet old. He had a very numerous family, but his means were quite limited, and he was his family's only support.

It so happened that Z. suddenly fell desperately ill and seemed close to death. Physicians gave up their attempts to save him. Z.'s wife, almost dead with grief, was weeping for her husband as if he had already died, for she could not imagine how she would manage with her crowd of little children. When Z. saw this, he began mentally to plead to God for a continuation of his life until he could help his elder sons become independent, so that they might take care of their younger brothers and sisters. After this prayer, he went to sleep and slept for a long while. When he woke up, he instantly called his wife and joyfully told her that he had seen in a dream the archpriest of Byelgorod, Father Josaphath Gorlenko, whom he had known but who by then was dead. The priest told Z. that, through God's mercy, Z. would be granted twenty more years for the sake of his innocent little ones. But in twenty years, on exactly this day of the year, the Lord would call him.

After he had told his wife of this dream, Z. asked her to write it all down into their prayer book. She did so. Z. now began improving, to the surprise of his family and the physicians, who had given him up. Soon he was completely well.

In exactly twenty years Z. died in the arms of his sons and daughters, all of whom had been well established in life and provided for. He died with the prayer of thanksgiving on his lips. His prayer book with the account of his strange dream is still preserved by his descendants as a family treasure.

From *Salubrious Reflections*, 1868.

* * *

Countess G. Ch-ova tells the following. "My parents loved each other so deeply that one of them survived the other by only a very short time. Soon after their death there came the yearly local holiday at the church connected with our estate. All my sisters and I were already married, but we all gathered to our parents' estate for this holiday in order to pray for our dear departed. This was a summer holiday. We all had good voices and usually sang in the church choir.

"After dinner on the day before the holiday, we were sitting in the large drawing room. A glass door was leading to the terrace, and from the terrace one could go into the garden. My sisters were getting ready to sing the next day at the liturgy in memory of our parents. I was not quite well and therefore did not take part in the singing. I was sitting at the end of the room opposite the glass door, talking to my cousin.

"My sisters were singing extraordinarily well. As I listened to them, I thought: if our parents were alive, they would be pleased to hear them. As I was looking at my cousin, who was saying something to me, I suddenly, for no particular reason, looked at the door to the terrace and ... I saw my mother standing in the door. She was wearing a simple white dress and a white cap edged with a ruffle. Those were the clothes in which she had been buried. She was intently looking at me. Unable to believe my eyes, I thought that I was imagining her. I turned down my eyes, but when I raised them a minute later, I saw her quietly approaching me.

"I got up and went to meet her. As soon as I began moving, she began drawing back to the door, moving backward with her face toward me. I drew closer to her, but she continued drawing back while looking at me all the time. Thus she went from the terrace into the garden, and I followed her. She stopped on a garden walk. I stopped also and wished to take her by the hand. I said, 'I shall go with you.' But she distinctly said to me, 'Do not touch me; your time has not come.' Then she said a few more words which I cannot repeat. She smiled, her face grew light with some sort of blessed radiance, and she began quietly rising up from the ground, higher and higher, while she herself became airy and light. Finally she disappeared.

From "Contemporary News," in Russian, 1874, no. 19.

* * *

When Queen Ulrica of Sweden died in her castle, she was put into a coffin, and some members of her own guard were placed in the anteroom for a sad vigil. At noon there came into the anteroom Countess Steinbock, whom the queen had loved. She said she came from Stockholm, the capital city. The captain of the guardsmen led her to the queen's body. She stayed there a very long time, so that finally the captain opened the door to see what was the matter. He grew rigid with horror. The other officers rushed to him, and through the open door they clearly saw the queen sitting in her coffin and embracing the countess.

What they saw seemed swimming in the air, but soon this vision changed into a dense fog. When the fog parted, the queen's body was discovered still lying in her coffin, but Countess Steinbock could nowhere be discovered, although the whole castle was searched. A courier was immediately sent to Stockholm. When he came back he brought the reply that Countess Steinbock had not left the capital: she had died at the time when the guardsmen saw her in the queen's embrace. A report was written of these events, and all who had been witness to them signed the report.

From "Journal of History and Statistics," in Russian, 1815.

* * *

In the small town of Theophypol there lived for a long time a widow, A-va, an elderly woman widely respected for her extraordinary piety. She was a particular friend of another old woman, D-a, who had been a companion of her youth. But after some time these inseparable friends quarreled so seriously that A-va, who was suddenly taken ill, told her relatives not to let D-a come to her funeral, should she die. The priest O-sky, who was called late at night to A-va's bedside, found out about the old woman's implacable enmity toward her former friend and attempted to convince the invalid to forgive D-a in her soul; he would not give her the Holy Mysteries before she forgave her friend. The ill woman obeyed her spiritual father. The same night, D-a, who knew nothing about A-va's sudden illness, woke from a deep sleep. She felt that someone was in the room, and heard A-va's voice beseeching her forgiveness. She lighted a candle but saw no one in her room. Soon she went back to sleep. Suddenly, however, D-a heard her daughter, a girl of about fourteen, who was crying, "Mama, come here, A-va is walking about the room. There she is! She is gone! Come, look!" D-a lighted the candle once more and once more saw no one. The clock pointed to three o'clock at night. The mother and the daughter felt A-va's presence. The next day D-a was told that A-va had died at exactly three o'clock in the night.

After A-va had been buried, Priest O-sky, according to the dead woman's directions, brought witnesses with him to her house and made up a list of all her property. He picked out the better things, packed them into trunks, and had them taken to the church building to be stored there until the arrival of A-va's son, who was soon to graduate from the Academy of Fine Arts. Various little boxes and sacks were thrown into the corner, to be removed as unnecessary and worthless refuse. Two days after A-va's death, her niece came to the priest. She was frightened and agitated. "Today my aunt A-va has come to me," she said, "and told me, Father, to tell you that you have not treated her son's property as you should have: you have thrown into the corner that which she has gathered with sweat and blood for her son."

They went into A-va's house and began looking through the little boxes. Among some discarded pieces of fabric they found 500 rubles. Several days later (on the sixth day after her death), Av-a appeared to the priest. She seemed quite real, was eager to thank him, and said, "Be not afraid of your illness. There is something else which you should fear more." She thereupon warned him of some circumstances which later proved to be dangerous. The priest himself testified that her warning was helpful to him.

From "News of the Diocese of the Chersonese," 1886.

* * *

The annals of England record how the English Queen Sophie, who was born a princess of Brunswick and who died on January 4, 1736, twice after her death appeared to her husband, George I, and asked him to break his lawless connection with Horatia, into which he had entered while the queen was still alive. When the queen came the second time, she picked up the king's lace collar, which was lying on his bed, tied a knot in it, and threw it on the king's breast, saying "No mortal will untie it." The next day Horatia tried to untie the knot but could not. She was angered and threw the collar into the fire. The king seized it out of the fireplace, but the collar fell on Horatia's dress, which quickly caught on fire. Horatia died of burns, and George repented of his love affair. He began spending much time in prayer, founded a hospital, did much good in the queen's name, and died two months after her last appearance.

From Schalberg, *On Immortality*, p. 42.

* * *

St Spyridon, the bishop of Trimithus, had a daughter, Irene, who was as pious as her father. One of their relatives gave Irene a precious ornament to keep safe for him. In order to keep it safe all the better, she buried it in the ground. After a short while she died.

When the man who had given her the ornament returned and did not find her alive, he demanded that Spyridon should return his ornament to him. The old man, who sympathized with his relative's loss of property, went to his daughter's grave and pleaded with tears that she should reveal to him where she had hidden the precious ornament entrusted to her. The girl appeared to her father, pointed out to him where she had hidden the ornament, and then vanished.

From *How Our Dead Live* by the Hieromonk Mitrophanes.

* * *

The Count and Countess P. had a wealthy estate in the province of Pskov. It had been left to them after the death of the count's uncle. When they first came to their new estate, they were warned that almost every day since the old count's death the house was being visited by a ghost. These tales did not alarm the count and countess. They were skeptics where stories of ghosts were concerned. Quite calmly they settled in the "unquiet" house.

Their bedroom had two doors. One led to a long corridor, the other to a row of uninhabited rooms, the last of which also connected with the same long corridor. Soon after the first of these doors was locked with a key and the candle was put out, the countess heard something rustle near the door. She listened closely and discovered that someone was trying to open the door. The countess drew her husband's attention to this. They lighted a candle and clearly saw the door handle moving as if someone were pressing on it from the other side. Carrying the candle, the count went through the second door, passed the uninhabited rooms, and entered the corridor. He saw someone standing at the first door to his bedroom. When he drew near, he recognized his uncle. The dead man was dressed as he used to dress during his life. The count forgot that his uncle had died and exclaimed, "How is it that you are here, Uncle?" The ghost gave him a sad look and disappeared, and only then did the count again realize that his uncle had died.

From *Rebus*, 1886, no. 15.

* * *

Once when the holy monk Akakios was praying, he fell into ecstasy and saw a marvelous man who took him by the hand and brought him to a field which seemed limitless and contained many beautiful buildings which seemed uninhabited. Surprised, Akakios asked his guide, "Why are they empty?"—"These places are prepared for those Christians who pay taxes to the Turks and fulfill other duties put upon them, and suffer all this for Christ's sake, thanking God the while." When the vision was over, Akakios called his disciples and bade them pay their taxes to the Turks. "And we must have sympathy with others who pay taxes to them," he said.

From *The Patericon of Mt Athos*, April 12.

* * *

Remember, O Christian, that the heavenly King will call you too! He will call you when you do not expect Him, and everything that happens to all men at death will happen to you, too. Therefore be prudent and wise, and prepare yourself betimes for that hour by repentance and penitence. The hour of death is horrible not only to sinners but also to the righteous, who have always remembered God, repented, and wept for their sins. Remember death. If you do, all the luxury and vanity of this world will be vile to you. You will seek tears and suffering rather than gaiety and comfort.

Part V

PREPARING OURSELVES FOR DEATH

CHAPTER 37

~~~

A Moral Conclusion to Be Drawn from the Previous Accounts

We now clearly see that the hour of our death is hidden from us and we may die suddenly. This is as it should be and as we deserve, but we can be rid of our fear of death. In order not to fear it, we must be faithful and wise servants of the Lord, such as were Abraham and Isaac and other holy men. Then we shall die "in good old age... and full of years" (Gen 25:8), not suddenly and violently. Our death will be joyful and full of expectation of beatitude among the righteous. Let us be wise and faithful servants like Jacob and Joseph, and then we shall know in advance the hour of our death and each of us will say: "Behold, I am dying" (Gen 48:21). We shall see our children around us and leave this life blessing them and praying for them (Gen 49:26). We shall tell them how we wish to be buried and shall then fall asleep and rest in peace and joy eternal.

Let us, then, be faithful and wise servants of the Lord: faithful, for we shall keep and preserve our Orthodox faith like the apple of our eye until our very last breath; wise, for we shall remove ourselves from every sin and observe all justice. Thus we shall fear neither death nor eternal punishment. When the hour of our death will find us ready, our Lord will join us to the assembly of the blessed and righteous, for He has said, "Blessed is that servant whom his master, when he comes, will find so doing" (Matt 24:46).

Since few men can say of themselves that they are ready to enter the future life at any moment, let us at least have firm hope in the all-merciful God, Who will save us because of His unspeakable love for mankind, as well as for the sake of the priceless sacrifice of our Lord Jesus Christ. God will save us as He will see fit.

Yet let us not forget the trials that our soul will undergo when after our death it passes through the air. Let us remember how Holy Scripture confirms this when it calls the air the express realm of the evil spirits: "For we do not wrestle against flesh and blood, but against principalities, against powers, against the rulers of the darkness of this age, against spiritual hosts of wickedness in the heavenly places" (Eph 6:12).

Again, it should be remembered that if the evil spirits take a great interest in our actions and attempt in any way possible to harm us here on earth, then of course they will not leave us unmolested at a time so opportune for their efforts, when our souls pass through their own realm. The teaching on the trials to be undergone by departed souls is expressed in some of the church prayers and also in the writings of many fathers of the Church, who express it on the basis of Holy Scripture. One of our prayers (it follows the Fourth Kathisma in the Church Psalter) says, "For I must pass a fearful and menacing place after I have parted with my body, and a dark and cruel multitude of demons seeks me there." There are similar prayers elsewhere.

St John Chrysostom says in his sermon on remembrance of the departed that, after it has parted with its body, the soul has great need of help and protection by angels, who conduct it safely through the midst of the chieftains and powers and invisible rulers of the air. St Ephraim of Syria in many of his works speaks of the trials of the air, thus proving that this teaching was universally believed in his time. We can be certain that the souls of the departed, both the righteous and the sinful, are subject to personal judgment after they have risen to heaven. In accordance with their deeds, there and then they receive a judgment which settles their fate until the universal resurrection: "For he who sows to his flesh will of the flesh reap corruption, but he who sows to the Spirit will of the Spirit reap everlasting life" (Gal 6:8). The souls of the righteous, who have lived their lives in holiness and observance of what pleases God, are carried by angels to heavenly dwellings and enjoy there a blessedness which will be augmented after the last judgment. The sinners, who have been guilty of vice and have died unrepentant, are cast down into hell and tormented there.

From Abbot Anthony, *Eternal Mysteries Beyond the Grave*, in Russian, as well as other sources.

CHAPTER 38

What the Holy Scripture and the Fathers of the Church Teach About the Location of Paradise

Holy Scripture states that the earthly Paradise created by God was situated in the East: "The Lord God planted a garden eastward in Eden" (Gen 2:8). It is commonly held that the celestial Paradise is also to the East of the earth. Thus blessed Theodora said that after her spirit parted from her body, angels led her eastward on their way to the heavenly dwellings. God's great St Symeon the Stylite saw Paradise in the East (*Lives of the Saints* for May 24). So did St Euphrosyne of Suzdal in her marvelous vision. Thus the East has a great significance in the Christian Church. Our temples are built so that the altar will face the East, our dead are buried with their faces turned eastward, and the Orthodox Christians pray facing East. The Orthodox Church does not however, spend effort searching for the precise location of Paradise within the universe. In her prayers, particularly the prayers for Holy Saturday and the day of the resurrection, she expresses the opinion that Paradise is in heaven.

Many saints of the new covenant were granted a vision of Paradise, and to them it looked like a garden. Yet we must keep in mind that the matter and nature of Paradise are spiritual, just as its inhabitants are spiritual beings, and thus Paradise is really inaccessible to our feelings, which have become coarse after our deep fall into sin.

During the burial of the Mother of God, St John the Apostle carried a branch brought to earth from Paradise by the Archangel Gabriel.

St Macarius the Great writes that those who inherit Paradise meet after death, are conducted into gardens and dwellings especially prepared for them, and are clothed in precious raiment (*Conversation 16*).

St Gregory of Sinai writes that Paradise is the lowest heaven. Its trees are perpetually covered with flowers and fruit, and a river flows perpetually through Paradise, irrigating and dividing it into four parts. Moses also tells about this river in his narrative: "Now a river went out of Eden to water the garden, and from there it parted and became four riverheads" (Gen 2:10).

All fathers and teachers of the Church represent Paradise as a garden of marvelous, indescribable beauty, the nature of which in no way corresponds to the nature of our crude senses. Yet although unapproachable to some, Paradise has, through the assistance of the Holy Spirit, been revealed to others. The Apostle Paul was once taken into Paradise, and so was the pious Abbot Blasius, as well as the monk of his monastery, Euphrosinus, whose story has already been told in this book. This story indicates that Paradise indeed exists: both Euphrosinus's and Blasius's souls were taken to Paradise, just as the Apostle Paul had been there before them. As the apostle himself tells us, he was "caught up into Paradise, and heard inexpressible words, which it is not lawful for a man to utter" (2 Cor 12:4).

These occurrences show us that death is desirable and not at all terrible to the righteous. Why is this so? Because throughout their life they remembered death and readied themselves for it. They were prepared to meet it at any hour, for they kept in mind the words of the Lord, "Watch therefore, for you know neither the day nor the hour in which the Son of Man is coming" (Matt 25:13).

CHAPTER 39

What the Holy Scripture and the
Fathers of the Church Tell Us
About the Location of Hell

The souls of departed sinners, after they have been judged by God, are cast down into hell and undergo torments there. Thus it is clear that hell and these places of torment must have a particular location in the universe. Where is this place, destined forever for unrepentant sinners? This question and other questions, similar to it, such as "Where is the Throne of God?" and "Where are the limits of the universe?" have occupied mankind from the creation of the world to our own time, and all the efforts of man's intelligence have been and continue to be used to answer them. The word of God leaves such questions unanswered and gives no definite definition of the locations of heaven and hell. Scripture limits itself to hints. Any descriptions of these places which are contained in Scripture are represented in accordance with what may be understood by the limited experience of our senses; thus these descriptions are at least partly figurative. Such as they are, they say that hell is situated inside the earth: it is a place devoid of joy, far removed from the living and hidden inside the depths of the earth. The words of God the Creator "unto dust shalt thou return" have penetrated deep into man's consciousness, and the peoples of all places and times have thought that hell is inside the earth. St John Chrysostom says that hell is outside our world, while Augustine teaches that it is impossible to know where hell is.

The teachings of the Orthodox Church on hell may be summarized as follows. Hell is the place where the unrepentant sinners will be after their death. This place is mentioned in Holy Scripture and is characterized as dark, dismal, foul, and deep. Sinners will perpetually remain in this place, far from everyone except those who are similar to them in that they, too, have fallen away from God, such as other sinful men and evil spirits. They will find in hell an unpassable abyss, deep darkness, and a fire that does not give light yet burns, as well as a poisonous worm that will devour them without ever being full. The precise nature of the worm we cannot know, yet it exists. Finally, unrepentant sinners are to expect eternal removal from God, the source of light and blessedness; eternal loss of the heavenly kingdom; incessant pangs of conscience; repentance about life spent in vain—a repentance that will be too late to benefit them; bitterness; shame; and a sense of unworthiness.

Let the endless mercy of God save us from this horrible fate!

CHAPTER 40

The Future Punishment of Sinners

The word of God represents the future state of the righteous as joyous, bright, and peaceful. The destiny of sinners, however, is spoken of as dismal and terrible. They will endure in this state forever after the last judgment.

"These will go away into everlasting punishment," says our Savior about the sinners (Matt 25:46). The place where the sinners will be punished is called in the Holy Scriptures by various names: hell fire (Matt 5:29), Hades (Luke 16:23, Acts 2:27) outer darkness (Matt 22:13, 25:30), the prison of spirits (1 Pet 3:19), the abyss (Luke 8:31), the place under the earth (Phil 2:10), the furnace of fire (Matt 13:50), and other similar names. All these words express one thought: there is a place for those souls that have departed in sin, and this is "a place of condemnation and of God's anger" (*Orthodox Catechism*, Part I, reply to question 68). Scripture gives no definite indication as to the precise location of hell, and those who are curious to find it out will do best to remember the words of St Chrysostom, who says, "You ask where hell is, but why should you know it? You must know that hell exists, not where it is hidden.... Let us attempt to find out not where it is but how to escape it" (St John Chrysostom, "Sermon 31 on the Epistle to the Romans").

The torments of sinners in their future life will consist of knowledge that they are excluded from all participation in the heavenly kingdom and all the blessings of heaven, which the righteous will inherit; and that they are "cast out into outer darkness" (Matt 8:12). St Chrysostom speaks about their torments as follows: "The realization that they have lost such blessings will cause the sinners to experience so great a sorrow, torment, and sense of confinement that, aside from any other suffering which hell may contain, this spiritual torment by itself can tear apart and sicken a soul...."

Communion with God is the greatest good of which the sinners will be deprived in the future life. Their greatest punishment will be their removal from God as well as God's curse on them. The righteous Judge will say to them, "Depart from Me, you cursed" (Matt 25:41) and "I tell you I do not know you, where you are from. Depart from Me, all you workers of iniquity" (Luke 13:27; cf. Matt 7:21). St Chrysostom says, "For him who has feeling and reason there can be no worse hell than removal from God" (St John Chrysostom, "Sermon 5 on the Epistle to the Romans"). Elsewhere he reasons thus: "Hell and its torture are insufferable, but even if we should imagine a thousand hells, they would be meaningless in comparison with the misfortune of losing the blessed glory promised to the righteous, of being cast out by Christ, and of hearing from Him, 'I know you not!' ... For it is better to be struck by lightning innumerable times than to see the gentle countenance of the Lord turning away from us and His bright Eye unable to look at us" ("Sermon 23 on the Gospel according to St Matthew"). This removal from the source of light and life will be most tormenting punishment for the rejected. They will be forever removed from Him in Whom alone they might have found satisfaction for their souls, which have been created according to God's image and thus always hunger for God.

In addition to these inexpressible spiritual torments there will also be in hell physical suffering, no less inexpressible in its horror.... Removed from the source of spiritual light, sinners will also be deprived of natural, physical light. As our Savior Himself says, they will be cast "into outer darkness" (Matt 22:13). The nature of this darkness is mysterious. No ray of light, which is so necessary and comforting to all living, will be able to reach there. St Ephraim of Syria says, "He who has sinned on earth and has offended God will be thrown into the outer darkness, where no ray of light penetrates" (St Ephraim of Syria, "On the Fear of God and the Last Judgment"). It is difficult to imagine how hard this loss of light will be to bear, and how oppressed will be sinners by the impenetrable darkness which will surround them from all sides. Yet in this deep darkness there will burn a fire no less mysterious, "a fire that gives no light," as St Basil the Great puts it, "which has power to burn but no power to light" (St Basil the Great, "Sermon on Psalm 33," 12). The condemned will be thrown into this fire. During the last judgment the righteous Judge will say to those who will stand on His left, "Depart from Me, you cursed, into the everlasting fire" (Matt 25:41). St John the Apostle says, "Anyone not found written in the Book of Life was cast into the lake of fire" (Rev 20:15). The word of God generally represents the torments of hell as sojourn in the eternal fire or in a lake of fire, so that *hell* and *fire eternal* are terms which in Scripture mean practically the same. It is difficult to imagine what the unquenchable fire will be like, and how sinners will eternally be tormented, burn, and yet not be consumed in it. Even though the fire of hell will be a real fire, it will be different from fire as we know it. St John of Damascus says, "Sinners will be given over to fire eternal, not a material fire such as we have, but a fire whose nature is known to God alone" (St John of Damascus, *Detailed Exposition of the Orthodox Faith*, 4. 27). As we have seen, other fathers of the Church speak of it as devoid of power to give light, yet able to burn all the same (St Basil, "Sermon on Psalm 33"). The fire of hell will be more subtle, more spiritual if we may say so, than our fire, and will be able to burn but not to consume and annihilate. St John Chrysostom says, "When you hear of this fire, do not think that it is like fire here on earth, which grasps, burns, and changes what it has burned. That fire will embrace and then continue forever to burn without ever ceasing" (St John Chrysostom, "To Theodore Fallen"). Although more subtle, the fire of hell will be incomparably more horrible than fire on earth.

The torment caused by the fire of hell will be yet augmented by the incessant torment caused by the worm of hell. When our Savior spoke about the future torments of sinners, He said, "Their worm does not die" (Mark 9:46). We do not know what this worm may be, but there can be no doubt of its reality and the horrible physical anguish caused by it to sinners. St Basil the Great in his discussion of the sufferings of hell says that in the fire of hell there will be "some kind of poisonous and flesh-consuming worm which will devour greedily, never be full, and by its devouring cause insufferable sickness" (St Basil the Great, "Sermon on Psalm 33," 12).

The terrible spiritual and physical suffering of sinners will be yet increased by the society in which they will be confined. Removed completely from God and God's saints, sinners will see all around them other sinners, condemned to a like destiny, and also evil demons with whom they will be forced to sojourn; and the other sinners, as well as the demons, will inflict on one another the groans of their own comfortless sorrow and the curses of their unrepentant wickedness (Matt 25:41).

In consequence of all this suffering, hell will be filled with the sound of weeping and the gnashing of teeth: "There will be weeping and gnashing of teeth," says the Savior (Matt 8:12). The sinners will weep not only because of their insufferable pain but also because they will be conscious of the eternal loss of their souls. They will gnash their teeth because of their realization that they have perished and are unable to escape. Applicable to them are the words of the apostle, who says, "In those days men will seek death and will not find it; they will desire to die, and death will flee from them" (Rev 9:6). Intense will be the torments of hell!

Yet not all sinners will endure equal suffering. The apostle says, "Each one will receive his own reward according to his own labor" (1 Cor 3:8). In accordance with the Scriptures, the holy fathers and teachers of the Church have taught about various degrees of punishment for sinners. St John Chrysostom says, "He who has received more instruction will have to endure greater punishment for his misdeeds. The better informed and the more powerful we are, the more severely will we be punished for our sins" (St John Chrysostom, "Sermon 5 on the Epistle to the Romans").

However, all sinners will suffer without end. The word of God definitely and decisively says that their suffering will be eternal and unending, and the Savior Himself has declared that after the universal judgment He will say to sinners, "Depart from Me, you cursed, into the everlasting fire ... and these shall go away into everlasting punishment" (Matt 25:41, 46). St John the Apostle says that "The smoke of their torment ascends forever and ever; and they have no rest day nor night" (Rev 14:11). The Fifth Ecumenical Church Council has definitely condemned the heresy of Origen, who taught that evil spirits and sinful men will suffer in hell until a definite time has elapsed, and after that will again be reinstated in their first, innocent state (His Eminence Macarius, *Orthodox Dogmatic Theology*, vol. 5, 296). To this time, on the Sunday of Orthodoxy, the Holy Church proclaims that all who deny "eternal punishment for sins" are "anathemized," that is, separated from the Church.

Thus, we see that the word of God gives us enough information on the future life, and the holy fathers of the Church do much to enlighten us on the meaning of Scripture. It must be admitted that much concerning the future life still remains unclear and impossible to understand, but we must keep in mind that our senses as well as our intelligence are insufficient for understanding the whole depth of the eternal life that will open to us after our death, while our speech has not enough power to express the height of blessedness and the horrors of punishments prepared for us. What the word of God reveals to us about the future life is quite sufficient. More "it is not lawful for a man to utter" (2 Cor 12:4). It is improper to reason, guess, and conjecture too much about the future life. It is best to feel in one's heart that the future life, life eternal with its eternal beatitude and eternal torments, really exists. Such is the perpetual infallible belief of the infallible Church, which is expressed in the majestic words: "I believe ... in the resurrection of the dead and the life of the age to come."

From S. S-ki *Future Life Beyond the Grave*, in Russian, 1892.

CHAPTER 41

An Answer to the Eternal Question: Shall We Live After Death? An Attack on Atheism and the Doctrine That Death Is Final

O death, death! How impenetrable is the mystery with which you surround mankind! Each of us might ask death, "Who are you, where do you come from, why have you come into the world and exist among men? Is your power eternal? What will happen to us beyond the grave, and what awaits us in your ever-silent kingdom, surrounded with the deepest mystery?"

Such questions about the dark mystery of death have occupied and disturbed the great minds of all nations from the most ancient times to our day. Even now these questions have not been solved in terms of non-Christian philosophies, which are not founded on the great and divine teaching about an all-powerful, omnipresent, ever-living, deathless God, Who has created man according to His deathless image, having breathed into his body a deathless soul resembling God.

Thus the questions about a future life for man still remain unsolved, but not to Christians. If such questions cannot be answered by Christians, then it is only by those among them who call themselves Christians but are not such in effect. As for those who are Christians in the real sense of the word and who in the simplicity of their hearts and in deep humility unconditionally believe in the existence of an ever-living God (and if God exists, man, too, must be deathless)—such Christians never have found these questions disturbing. Nor will such questions exist for them in the future, for Holy Scripture says that the answers to them will be hidden from the wise but revealed to those who are as simple as children. That is, the Lord of the universe reveals its mysteries to those who, with awe and reverence in their hearts, believe in His eternal and most holy truth. A Russian proverb says, "God lives in simple hearts."

How could Christians disbelieve in life eternal when the Savior Himself, our eternal heavenly teacher, Jesus Christ, has announced that the soul is immortal and has affirmed it in His divine testament? After this revelation, how can we Christians dare to deny the future life of the human soul after the death of the body, and the passing of the soul from perishable bodies and from the transient perishable world to another world, imperishable but invisible to us while we are alive—a world of spirits, in which there reigns eternal, imperishable life, in which no one dies and no one is born, but everyone endures as he is?

Those who are in love with their own learning (or what they consider to be learning) can give us no proof that there is no future life, although they attempt to deny it on the basis of their false doctrines. Yet they cannot give us a factual and undeniably true answer. There are also those who are misled by no false doctrine, but they simply cannot resist doubts about a conscious life after death, although they feel guilty about such doubts. They are moral cowards who yield to temptation even while they know that they are wrong in doing so.

All such people, both those who become doubters because of their pride and those who do so because of weakness, are dreadfully mistaken. The first kind are led astray by their exploration of the natural sciences: instead of deriving from science real and incontestable facts, they make deductions which have no firm basis. The second kind are, as it were, dragged along by the first. They are completely unclear as to what they know or do not know: unable to give any proof for their convictions, they follow the first kind of doubters merely because they are too vain to seem behind the times. They think that they follow the recent developments in science, but actually they are only followers of fashionable heresies. Because they are pitifully foolish, they take a particular pride in showing off before those who still believe in the sacred Christian dogmas.

Unbelievers only seem to base themselves on science, but actually science has little to do with what they declare. What science has ever denied an immortal and omnipotent God? History reveals to us the belief—universal among all peoples and at all times, and uncontroverted by the sciences explored by these peoples—that there exists an eternal God. With striking uniformity, all nations have always, even in the most ancient times, admitted and for the most part still admit that there is one ever-deathless and invisible ruler of the universe, a God Who has created all things visible and invisible, and among them man, whose soul is immortal and in this like God.

Scepticism and denial contradict themselves when they point to science, for we see from the history of science how the most educated men and the most renowned scientists have always unconditionally acknowledged that

God exists and is eternal and deathless. Once the existence of God is admitted, the eternal existence of the soul must also not be denied.

Let those who deny the future life try first to deny God. If they take upon themselves to do so, let them give us positive and incontrovertible proofs that He does not exist. They will be unable to give us such positive proofs, unless they provide us with falsified data; and this they will hardly dare, for they would instantly be exposed by the science which they profess. In speaking of God, they can only voice some suppositions and not a jot more.

Only those who have a reputation for learning but really lack intelligence can dare to deny the existence of God. They may boast of their devotion to science and have diplomas as proof of it, but actually they are not intelligent. They resemble the biblical fool who said in his heart "There is no God," and no sooner had he said it than his words were carried away by the wind, and no trace of his denial was left.

We have already reminded the reader that God has created man according to His image and His likeness and has breathed His immortal spirit into man. If God has put into man a soul taken from His own ever deathless Spirit, how can man's soul be mortal? Its being comes from the deathless.

Pride denies everything that seems unintelligible and stands outside the limits of the natural laws to which the unconscious nature is subject. Yet the past and present destinies of nations cannot be fully understood unless recourse is taken to belief that one omniscient, all-righteous, and all-holy Lord of the universe rules all. Before our very eyes the holy and most perfect truth of heaven often destroys the most subtle and cunning devices of men when they have been planned very well but for an evil end.

Unbelievers have their own views of such events. With all their powers they attempt to convince us that God takes no part in guiding man's destiny. Instead, they ascribe everything to the fortuitous outcome of natural laws. But if unreasoning nature guides all, let them answer this question: how can these unseen and essentially unintelligible as well as unintelligent powers act so reasonably and with such clarity as to put up obstacles to the evil intentions of the most powerful men of this world?

Who but God sends terrible and just punishment inevitably and unexpectedly, like lightning, upon conscienceless and evilly criminal people? Can blind and unreasoning nature act so purposefully? If it can, then it has already left the confines of natural law and has become supernatural, has acquired consciousness and absolutely unreachable power and limitless authority to punish justly and perform the highest, most perfect, and therefore conscious and reasonable, acts of justice. How can unconscious and blind nature do so? This would be more than a miracle, and doubters have no faith in miracles.

Here, O reader, we see the sad inconsistency of the doubters' thought and their false teachings. The near-sighted skeptics have become insane under the influence of fashionable philosophy and have in their madness passed the limits of reason. They claim to believe in the blind forces of nature alone and to worship only her as their god, but they fail to see that in this way they go toward creating a wild and destructive anarchy not only in the realm of religion but also on the sacred hearth of family, society, and state.

Such are the sad and pitiful results to which people arrive in their godless blindness. O unfortunate, perditious times of insane unbelief! How can anyone fail to see that the powers of nature have been subjugated by man and enslaved to serve him almost completely, and that far from ruling man they are almost completely ruled by him? Before the eyes of all of us, man, the lord of nature, draws from the depths of the earth nature's life-giving powers in all their forms. The surface of the earth is cultivated by man and serves his wishes, and so do the plants and animals. This power over nature has been given to man from the first days of creation because of all of creation he is the highest creature. He has a heavenly intelligence united with a deathless soul, which the deathless Creator Himself has blown into man from His own life-giving Spirit. Created according to the image of God and in His likeness, man rules nature.

Thus there can be no doubt that man will always live after his death, for that which is deathless cannot perish. Man's body alone is mortal, for it has been created from mortal and perishable parts, while his soul has received its being from Him Who always lives. Thus, according to the will of its Creator, it must always exist, as does He.

If the all-merciful and all-wise God has given to man a high spiritual intelligence, which can open the heavens and arrive with mathematical exactness at the time and direction of the motions of the heavenly bodies, then it is easy to understand that man can have received such an intelligence only from an all-powerful, all-perfect, and omnipresent God, and not from unconscious and blind nature. How could nature give man so divine a reason when she herself has no reason at all?

Nature has become man's slave and has no feeling, no intelligence, and no realization of its own being. According to some weak-minded philosophers, however, nature directs the destinies of nations, commands the highest powers of the universe and the most just laws in it, and determines the limits within which the universe rests in its unfathomable and marvelous order. How could unreasoning and unreasonable nature rule the whole universe? We know that beyond the confines of our solar system in the limitless expanse of the universe there are many other worlds, not yet known to us or to the philosophers, and their nature may be quite dissimilar from nature as we know it. What shall we say now? Are there several Natures then, each different from the others? How many of them are there?

If we follow those who take nature to be their god, shall we then not arrive at a multiplicity of gods (polytheism), such as was expressed in Greek mythology? Or shall we arrive at unconditional atheism, such as the philosophers Hobbes and Spinoza have tried to teach, and after them the atheists of more recent times? Is there no guiding principle behind the universe at all? Let God save the weak among us from this sickness of disbelief!

We must believe in eternal God, for only because of His limitless love do we move and live. But if there is an ever-existing and all-powerful God, then there must also be a deathless soul. Holy Scripture says, "God is not the God of the dead, but of the living" (Matt 22:32). Thus God Himself declares that the human soul is immortal.

Faith, which is a feeling of unconditional certainty in regard to the eternal existence of a human being, is deeply rooted in mankind's consciousness. Man's consciousness is synonymous with knowledge that he exists; consequently, it involves his knowledge about his likeness to God, Who is absolute Knowledge and absolute Being. From man's consciousness there follows his faith in the eternal future existence of his being.

Members of all nations, beginning with the most primitive and ending with the most civilized, are certain that they will exist beyond death. Not all the nations have the same concept of future life, but they all have some concept of it.

Faith is a direct knowledge of the truth, without the intervention of reason. Faith is a direct awareness of one's own existence, of one's origin, meaning, and goal. All proofs of the truth given by reason are less convincing than is faith, for they involve comparisons and analogies and thus cannot be as direct and unconditional as faith. Because of faith I know that I exist as body and spirit at the same time, and that there exists not only I but others also. I know about my own self quite unconditionally, without the need for any logical processes. The author R. Wagner says that faith is a gift. Through faith, the spirit gains a new sense organ, a new way of recognizing the truth, aside from the possibilities of reason. The unbeliever has the same attitude to faith as a blind man to light. The unbeliever has no faith in the future and in the realization of any of his expectations.

Man is not only a material creature, as are the animals, but also a spiritual being. He is not only a product of physical birth but also born in spirit. Consequently, he is not only a sentient being but also a spiritual one. These peculiarities determine his situation and his meaning in the world. They prove that man is a spiritual, superterrestrial being, and that life tied to the earth and to the world of the senses cannot be his only goal.

Man never is satisfied with the gifts of nature, as are the animals. He changes them according to his will, and sometimes even senselessly destroys them in order to prove his might and his power over nature. He feels that he is the lord and master of nature. If, like the animals, man were the creature of nature alone, he would be content with nature, as are the animals. To the contrary, he sometimes goes as far as denying the blessings of nature. The goods of the earth, even though they should be most excellent, are insufficient for human happiness. Man cannot find perfect happiness in material goals. He needs ideal goals for his happiness.

Man treats nature like an artist. He freely changes the natural world according to his goals and wishes. He uses the powers of nature and subjugates them to his thoughts and fancies.

Man is inimical to nature and even looks upon it as an enemy. Nature provides him with no easy living. He must take by force all he needs from her. Man is not a child of the great Mother Nature: he is her stepson, and she is his stepmother. Nature provides animals with all they need: strength, clothing, and a mind such as is necessary for them, as well as means of defense. The human child, on the contrary, has no such gifts from nature, for he is born naked and with his reason undeveloped. All he has for his defense is the ability to cry out. Later, however, he assumes power over nature, becomes her lord, and uses her powers for his own purposes.

Not satisfied with nature's own resources, such as the movement of the winds, the currents of water, the power of fire and steam, and the action of chemical agents—man penetrates to other treasures, not so readily provided by nature. He converts deserts into gardens, builds cities and states, invents writing, and measures time and distance. Still not satisfied with all this, he rises into heaven and measures the remoteness of numberless stars, finds the planets, and knows beforehand when comets will appear. Only an eternal and deathless Spirit can raise man so high, and only this Spirit can prepare for man a paradise here on earth, although this paradise is short-lived.

Man's reason and his will are the tools of his happiness and make him the real ruler of the world. Nature serves only as an incentive for man's struggle against her. During this struggle he evinces the entire power of his conscious spirit. Struggle against nature is good for any man, for it reveals and proves to him how powerful he is.

Can it be that after this, man can be intended for only a brief material existence on earth? He would be a riddle or a freak, not a harmonious combination of material and spiritual contradictions. What purpose would there be in struggle against nature during a man's life if the final goal he could achieve would be only a short existence on earth? Man's creations more than anything else prove his spiritual nature.

The creations of man's spirit bear the seal of eternity and are not limited either by time or by distance. The creations of every genius are for all eternity and cannot be eaten away by time. The history of mankind is, properly speaking, the story of the development of his civilization. Everything else, all chance accomplishments of separate egotistical personalities, represent in man's history only passing and insignificant phenomena, even though for a time they may seem powerful and brilliant enough. The conquerors and destroyers of the world have no logical or ethical meaning for history, or else have only a negative meaning similar to that of natural evils such as floods and fires. The content of mankind's history is the perfection of a process of civilization, that is, perfection of knowledge about truth, justice, beauty, and all that relates to these. Everyone who, directly or indirectly, furthers this process and awakens others to it may give them an opportunity to attain to a higher form of civilization. Every such man is of significance to the history of mankind. The benefactors of mankind are all those who further the perfection of all that is best in our civilization and in our humane outlook. They spread good thoughts, enlarge and spread science, and improve morality and the laws—all these are seeds which always bring good fruit to man. It is not earthly but heavenly work to teach and to help truth, order, and happiness spread. Man has been created in God's image (Gen 1:27), and consequently justice, truth, and virtue are akin to his nature.

The human spirit has destroyed the charmed circle within which there endured superstition, ignorance, and perverted beliefs. The human spirit always creates something new and unfamiliar whenever it joins its efforts to previous discoveries and ideals. Thus is the history of the human spirit built. True creations of man's spirit are inspired and reveal to mankind eternal and unchanging truth. Everything good of which man is capable depends on his spirit, given to him by God.

Man's spirit, and especially in its highest potency, has always been a conductor and herald of eternal divine truths. God greatly benefits humankind by letting some people be born with outstanding capacities. These are, so to

speak, sons of God, and by developing their abilities and powers they become
the benefactors of mankind. All men who have done anything great in the
course of history have been certain of God's immediate influence on them.

This brings us to the great question about the immortality of man and
about our second, otherworldly, country. The constancy and perpetuity of
our works on earth assure us that we too shall endure and be eternal. N. B.
Yussoupoff speaks as follows in his well-known book *The Mystery*, in which
he discusses the immortality of the soul.

"It would be presumptuous of me to pose as an authority on theological
problems. I humbly confess that I have studied such problems with my heart,
under the influence of love for Christ, the founder of the highest science and
wisdom. Our generation is immersed in materialism, spread among us by all
kinds of harmful philosophies which have taken root in our minds. Sound
thoughts, however, have not completely perished but have only been put to
sleep by freethinkers. If a new powerful figure, like the Apostle Paul, should
appear, sound thought should become triumphant and be reborn brilliantly
and powerfully.

"In our times, no good attempt, even if it be most humble, should be
rejected, if only it strives to ennoble the soul and to strengthen religion.
Such good attempts prepare the soil for work; they fertilize dry earth and
make it ready to accept the seed of Christian teaching in all its fullness and
perfection.

"Even though evil free thought is dominant in our age and brings upon
us all the punishments and sufferings which we so deserve for our sins, there
can still be found little out-of-the way corners which can be cultivated and
where rare new flowers will bloom—flowers both bright of hue and tender
of fragrance, which can take the place of incense and myrrh in the censer of
the Angel of Prayer and purify our atmosphere polluted by the miasma of
false learning.

"If my writings will get into the hands of a freethinker, he will no doubt
find it possible to counter them with proofs of his disbelief. If, however, he
will pay attention to the feelings which move me to write, he may give some
thought to them and not remain unmoved himself.

"Those who follow Christ will seek in my writings new food for their
souls and an opportunity to bless yet again the name of the Creator of the
universe. Such is my goal. If I should reach it, my soul will be glad and will
render thankful prayer to the Savior of the human race....

"The Christian soul, which during its life on earth was illumined with
the fruitful light of Christ's teachings, forgets all the sufferings and sorrows

endured at parting from its relatives, friends, and others who were dear to it. As it approaches the gates of eternity, it is struck by the majestic picture before it. It sees Christ our Savior, Who has suffered because of our sins and for the sake of our salvation. It is occupied and supported by one thought only: it sees Christ! ...

"If it were not for the divine mysteries, there would be no divine religion, and there would be no faith in heavenly truth. Faith is a feat and a gift from above. It is a feat because it demands that our will repress the doubts of reason. It is a gift of God because divine help is needed for it. Faith would be powerless without heavenly assistance....

"There is only one road to wisdom, to heavenly truth, and to understanding the whole of creation. Eternal Truth, contained in Jesus Christ, has shown us this way. In Jesus Christ, God became man.

"To go along this road means to approach Wisdom. To stand firmly on it means to be wise. He who knows God knows everything; but only he knows God to whom God has revealed Himself as a reward for his upright life. God reveals Himself only to those who fulfill His commandments.

"He who wishes to achieve Wisdom should purify his heart, repent, and fulfill the commandments. Once he does this, the eyes of his soul will open and he will understand mysteries for which a man of this world has no understanding.

"Use your time well and be merciful to all men as the heavenly Father is merciful to all. Use the talent which God has given you. Be watchful, for you do not know when the Lord will come, and let not the word of the Lord leave your lips.

"Willingly follow the good, and do not postpone until tomorrow that which you can do today. Be constant in your actions as well as your words. Flee from things passing and seek the eternal. Raise your eyes to God and hope for help from above, for when man can no longer help, God does.

"Love God with all your might, and love your neighbor as yourself. If you do so, God will keep you like the apple of His eye and will save you from all evil. He will endow you with every good thing, and your soul will have nothing left to wish either for its temporal or for its eternal well-being.

"Make everything that you learn a part of your soul. Frequently repeat to yourself what you have learned and always remember that you must be reborn in God, and that your soul must renew itself by the spirit of Grace. For only by being reborn does a man approach the Divine and become a participant of It (Col 2:11; 1 Pet 1:4). A man who is reborn in his soul walks along the way of new life and seems reborn even externally.

"O man, image of God, how great you are! Created for infinite blessedness, you carry in yourself powers which surprise and astound. The Scripture says, We are the children of God, but what will we be in the future? We know that when He will come, we shall be similar to Him.

"He who approaches God becomes a participant in His power. The gates of approach were locked to us by sin, but the incarnated God has opened them to us and has taught us the great mystery of spiritual rebirth and holiness. This great mystery is at the center of heavenly religion. Here all powers are united and holiness is to be achieved.

"Learn, O reader, to recognize God, Who is infinite Love. He has created us out of love and saved us out of love and hallowed us out of love, and has prepared us for eternity, where we shall no longer be subject to death. Recognition of God is the highest wisdom, and has been recognized as such from antiquity on.

"In order that man might be able to recognize God, God has revealed Himself to man. The Word became flesh and has lived among us. This Word has built His Church on rock, where the gates of hell shall not overcome her. In the center of this Church is all that is great, marvelous, and holy; Wisdom and Truth live there, and light shines in the darkness, and darkness overcomes it not.

"I have told you, dear readers, everything that it is necessary to know about the highest subjects, so that you may understand the marvels of eternal Truth. If you have not understood me, read frequently what I have said here, but above all begin by purifying your will. Work on your souls, prepare them for unity with the Eternal. Step on the practical road of Christian life, and the powers of the Highest will lead you along and bring you to that place where the throne of the eternal God stands in all its brilliant greatness and all-embracing glory. To be near God and His eternal glory is the highest blessedness. Once you are there, your eyes will be opened and the great mystery of your eternal being and your future life will be revealed to you: you will understand your own immortality."

Compiled by I. Archangelsky from various sources.

PART VI

FINAL WORDS ON IMMORTALITY

CHAPTER 42

More About Proofs of Man's Immortality and of the Preservation of His Own Identity After Death

After all that has been said above, every Christian should realize as an absolute truth the immortality of the human soul after the death of the body. The ancients have believed in this truth, and the Savior Himself has confirmed it before the Sadducees, who did not believe in the future life. We have seen that it is quite possible for departed souls to return to this earth and to appear to those who live here. There is nothing unlikely in the idea that such appearances of the departed take place if God so allows or bids. The Jewish contemporaries of the Savior universally believed in appearances of the departed. Jesus Christ Himself taught that the spirits have no flesh and bones, whereas after resurrection He possessed His real body and thus was not a departed spirit: "But they were terrified and frightened, and supposed they had seen a spirit. And he said to them, 'Why are you troubled? And why do doubts arise in your hearts? Behold My hands and My feet, that it is I Myself. Handle me and see, for a spirit does not have flesh and bones as you see I have'" (Luke 24:37–39). On other occasions also, the apostles did not doubt the possibility of apparitions of the departed, as when they saw the Savior walking toward them across the waters of the Sea of Galilee and thought they saw a ghost (Mark 6:49), or when the rich man of the parable was tormented in hell and he asked Abraham to send Lazarus to earth to warn his brothers of the horrible condition into which he himself had fallen (Luke 16:27–28). This is a sign of belief that the souls of the departed can return into the world, appear to people, and talk to them. Again, if souls were mortal, how could Moses and Elijah appear on Mt Tabor during Jesus Christ's transfiguration? They had died several centuries previously, yet at that time they appeared and conversed with Christ (Luke 9:30). We read also that after the Savior's death, many saints who had died long ago rose and appeared to many people in Jerusalem (Matt 27:52–53).

Several years after his death, the high priest Onias appeared to Judah Maccabee. His hands were raised in prayer for God's people. Together with him there appeared also the Prophet Jeremiah, who had died long ago. Onias said to Judah, "This is Jeremiah, the prophet of God, a man who loves his brothers and prays fervently for the people and the holy city." Stretching forth his right hand, Jeremiah gave a sword of gold to Judas, and as he presented it to him, he addressed him as follows: "Take this sacred sword, a gift from God, by which you will strike down your enemies" (see 2 Macc 15:14–16).

Of course, the souls of the departed can appear among us not of their own volition but only in accordance with God's commands and permission. God commands or permits them to appear only for some worthy purpose. While he was in prison the night before his death, St John Chrysostom saw the holy martyr Basiliscus, who said to him, "Despair not, brother John, for tomorrow we shall be together." Some other events of the early centuries of Christianity are equally noteworthy. In the year 415, the remains of St Stephen, the first Christian martyr, were discovered in the following strange way. A priest of Jerusalem, Lucius by name, usually spent the night in the church baptistery in order to watch over the church vessels. He saw in a dream Gamaliel, the teacher of the Apostle Paul before the latter's conversion, who told him that his own body and that of the First Martyr St Stephen were buried in Cathargamala, a suburb of Dilagabis. This vision occurred three times. John, the Patriarch of Jerusalem, who at that time was at a council at Diospolis, went to the indicated spot, opened the holy remains, and transferred them to Jerusalem, where many miracles occurred as a result. Still another notable Christian saint, the holy martyr Potalina, who had been put to death in Alexandria, appeared later to very many persons and converted many of them to Christianity. Among them was a warrior named Basil, who had defended her from the violent mob while she was going to her death. To him she appeared several times, and once put a crown on his head. Following her directions, he accepted holy baptism and the crown of martyrdom.

As for the question about the kind of bodies in which departed souls may appear, we are unable to answer it. Neither the word of God nor our experience nor our reason (for how can it be independent from Scripture and from experience?) can tell us anything about the form in which beings purely spiritual can appear to mortal eyes. We can only believe that, in accord with God's will, departed souls can appear to us, but the manner and means by which they become known to us are unknown.

St Gregory the Great says that the principal purpose for which departed souls come to earth is that of pleading with us to offer for their repose our prayers and the bloodless sacrifice. Experience also shows that, indeed, the departed come to ask for prayer, as well as to persuade the living to turn to virtue and please God. During their appearances they frequently inform the living about the conditions of life beyond this life, ask for assistance, and warn the living about the misfortunes which await sinners after death. They tell about hell, about good and evil angels, about the severity of God's judgment over sinners, and about God's mercy to the righteous.

We must remark that the departed souls usually appear to the living during their sleep. It is apparently God's will that during their communication with the living they should appear to the spiritual eye without the means of an actual bodily shell.

Among the facts concerning the return and the appearance of the dead to the living there obviously belong the facts relating to the resurrection of the dead. Facts of this kind abound in Holy Scripture and in the history of the Church. The most certain, most important, and most striking of these facts is that of the resurrection of our Savior. Only second to it in importance is the resurrection of Lazarus, which is also beyond all doubt. Lazarus was brought to life by Jesus Christ a full four days after his death, when his body had already begun to decay: this was an actual resurrection after actual death. There are many other similar events recorded in the books of the Old and the New Testaments, all of them not subject to doubt: the prophet Elisha resurrected the son of the Shunammite widow, a dead man came to life when his body came into contact with this prophet's body, Christ resurrected the son of the widow of Nain, and so on.

The history of the Christian Church also offers many instances of the resurrection of the dead. We know, for instance, from the life of St Macarius of Egypt how a man accused of murder, while fleeing from his pursuers, was seized near St Macarius's cell. This man was quite innocent of murder but had been falsely suspected of it. He began swearing that he was innocent, but the crowd that had gathered all around unanimously decided that he was guilty. When Macarius heard the noise he came out to the people, found out what was the matter, and asked where the murdered man had been buried. Then he took the whole crowd with him to the dead man's grave. When he had arrived there, he knelt and, weeping, prayed to God. Then he said to the people, "The Lord will now reveal whether this man is the murderer." He called the victim in a loud voice by his name and said to him, "I bid you by your faith in Jesus Christ: tell us if it was this man, accused by the people, who has murdered you?" The dead man replied loudly from below the ground, "He is not my murderer." The people were astounded, and horrified fell to the ground. Then they all fell to the feet of the holy man and began beseeching him that he should bid the dead man reveal who the murderer was, but St Macarius replied, "I cannot take this upon myself. It is enough for me to save the innocent from punishment, but it is none of my concern to deliver into the hands of justice a man who is guilty."

From I. Archangelsky, *A Beam of Light on Eternal Mysteries*, in Russian, Moscow, 1892–1893.

CHAPTER 43

After His Death, Man Preserves His Identity and Leads a Fully Spiritual Life

Now that we have fully set forth and proved logically that God exists, is eternal, and is unlimited in His omnipresence, let us examine the question about His most righteous judgment over people who are wicked and evil in their hearts and who by their intentional and conscious actions trample on God's great and holy covenant of love toward one's brethren, other human beings.

Men of evil will cause oppression and destruction, and sorrow and unhappiness, both in their families and in all of society. In particular are they responsible for great misery among the orphans and the helpless. Such people pursue gain and knowingly and intentionally trespass divine laws of mercy. They build their happiness on the unhappiness of others. Can it be that those who are so vicious will go unpunished and continue in their low pleasures founded on the oppression of others? Does not the most holy, most high, and all-seeing eye of heavenly God, filled with pure truth, see them? Where would this most high truth be if it were deaf to the outcry of those who suffer innocently and are in sorrow? Indeed, Holy Scripture says that the blood of the innocent who have been killed, tortured, and subjected to suffering cries out to the throne of the All-High.

Yes, my readers, if we were to deny our future life after death, that is, our absolute existence in all eternity after we die, such denial on our part would be like denial of God Himself. You have seen that the human soul is indeed immortal: God, Who is absolute in His love and His power, is eternal righteousness and highest holiness. Thus He is just in rendering to each according to his deeds, and every one of us will receive his due, if not in this life, then in that other one. Of this there can be no doubt.

Each of us knows that God has given us in this life our reason, which enables us to recognize ourselves for what we are and to realize our full freedom. We know what we are doing, and whether what we are doing is good or bad. When a man of evil heart does what is wicked, he does so not because of some strange fancy or because he does not know what is right. He does so because he wishes to live well (as he thinks) at the expense of others. He well knows that he is depriving others of what belongs to them but takes recourse to the most subtle deceit and the most despicable schemes, and disregards his conscience, which cries out in his rough heart. In accordance with God's will, which we cannot fully understand, many such men die in their prosperity and receive no punishment in this world.

How, then, can we reject the idea of our future life at the end of our life on earth? We see how men of evil will are intoxicated with happiness which they have built on the unhappiness of others. They enjoy what they have taken away from others, and cast their fellow men into the abyss of horrible unhappiness and deadly, unbearable sorrow. Yet in accordance with God's destinies, they do not receive their judgment in this life and remain unpunished. We cannot leave unanswered the question how God can endure such people. How can the all-high and most just God allow them to remain unpunished? There must be a future life and a future judgment and meting out of rewards and punishments. Otherwise, eternal laws of justice could not exist, yet we feel that they do exist.

Now we see how inane are the teachings of those who deny the future life. According to their teachings, one may be as monstrous in his actions as he pleases, for the all-seeing and just God leaves many evildoers unpunished in this life, while there is no punishment for them in the future life because no future life exists. But how can our sound common sense admit of such wildly absurd nonsense?

The great mathematician Gauss has said, "O man, man, you are undoubtedly immortal, even if you may not think so and may not wish to be such. Beware of forgetting your immortality, for your forgetfulness may become a deadly poison to your life after death. No matter how long a man may live, even if he should remain alive for millions of years, he is destined to receive his punishment for his evil deeds, and a long life for him is only like some additional days given to a criminal before his execution." It is unnatural, lawless, and criminal to deny heavenly truth, which unconditionally affirms man's future existence after his death. Such a denial goes contrary to man's sound sense and to the eternally holy truth of God. He who denies the future life opposes God Himself!

From I. Archangelsky, *A Beam of Light on Eternal Mysteries*, in Russian, Moscow, 1892–1893.

PART VII

COMMENTS ON CHRISTIANITY, ENDTIMES, STRUGGLES, AND REWARDS

CHAPTER 44

On the Holiness of the Christian Religion

Modern man sways between faith and disbelief, and religion is a stumbling block to him. Some say that religion was invented by the priests of Chaldea and Egypt, who did all they could to support it among the people for the sake of their own gain; others declare that politics created religion; still others, who have not yet lost faith in God their Creator, state outright that religion has its origin in God Himself.

There was no dominant caste of priests among the patriarchs of the Old Testament. They and their tribes lived in freedom and yet they were full of deep feeling of religious veneration for Jehovah. The words of Holy Scripture tell us how elevated was the faith of the great men of the Old Testament: Abraham, Isaac, and Jacob. Abraham is exemplary in his denial of himself for the sake of his faith. He decided to sacrifice his favorite child, a boy in the full bloom of boyhood. This was his own son, still a tender child, born to him of his favorite wife Sarah, and yet Abraham consented to lead him to death as sacrifice to Jehovah. My readers, if you are honest people, you will understand that our will, our manliness, and our powers of denial cannot move us to an action as great as that of Abraham. He too, would not dare to do this if he had not been moved by the divine force of highest faith. Because his faith was higher than we can understand, Abraham was deeply obedient and without questions fulfilled the dreadful bidding of his God. Is there still room for doubt that religion has originated with God Himself? If we assume that it did not, let the doubters tell us where so mighty a faith comes from? Let this be our reply to those who assume that religion has been created by greedy priests.

How about those who think that religion is a creature of politics? Political life is as ancient as the caste of priests, but religion is more ancient than either. It is as old as the day when our almighty God determined in his all-good counsel to create the first man, our ancestor Adam, and then his wife Eve. Anyone can understand that in the first days of man's existence on earth

there were neither priests nor politics, but the beginnings of religious obser-
vances can already be seen in the sacrifice of Abel to God the Creator of
the world.

It would seem that these few lines should be sufficient to end all dispute
concerning religion, and that there should be no need for large tomes and
long treatises to be written in its cause. But we hope for the reader's conde-
scension and shall treat of this matter somewhat more fully, for the question
of religion is of concern not only to individual persons and not only to particular countries, but also to the whole of mankind. Especially is this true, when
there are many who spread false and harmful teachings whose purpose is to
destroy religious beliefs or, rather, the most holy feelings of man. Therefore,
we should like to examine this most important topic more fully and hope
by such a treatment to benefit those who are weak and therefore waver in
their faith.

If religion has not been created by the greediness of priests or the selfish
aims of politics, where does it come from? An indirect answer to this question may be found in the observation that religious faith can be found among
all the peoples of this earth, both the primitive and the civilized, and everywhere it appears as an independent force born in the depths of man's spiritual
life. Who but God can be its origin?

Let the unbelievers, swelling with pride and self-praise, lie to themselves
while they deny everything: divine religion, the highest law of spiritual feeling, and moral sense. They will not convince us, for they are miserable in our
eyes. Aside from bare and weak proofs, they can offer nothing. Yet we feel
sorry for those who are easy to influence and fall into the destructive nets of
the unbelievers. As for us who believe in God, let us kneel with deep reverence before the great wisdom of our eternal God, the Creator of the universe.
We shall believe to the end of ages that the feeling of religious belief has been
put into us by the Creator Himself.

Religion is the chief support of morality. It has a beneficent influence on
the condition of the man who nurtures it in his breast, as well as on the prosperity of mankind in general. A state cannot endure without religion, for it
is religion that keeps intact all the ties that unite mankind. Religion not only
makes man human—that is, makes him a moral being who has the desire
and strength to act to the contrary of the harmful influence of his passions—
but also communicates light to his reason, which without religion wanders in
the darkness of uncertainty, and peace to his heart, which finds its true rest
only in faith in a provident God. The heart finds in religion comfort for sorrow, hope in death, and a door to life eternal.

True worshippers of divine Truth have always realized that wisdom is to be found not in externals but in what is inside our own souls. They have always fashioned their hearts and subjected and set aright their wills in accordance with guidance from above, and the simplicity of their hearts has made them temples of God. The light of religion, which fell on them, revealed to them great truths and has ever been the leader and guardian of the heavenly symbols of religion. For such men, actions and faith were one. They were and are still worthy of the name of Christian.

Any kind of wisdom and any true love of our neighbor issue from the Holy Spirit through our Lord Jesus Christ. This is the essence of religion. The principal problems of true wisdom are recognition of God, enlightenment of reason, and setting the will straight; but these aims cannot be realized outside of the Christian religion. Human reason is prone to making mistakes, but in Christian religion it will find a source of light, for truth rests only there. If we wish to be wise we must call God to our assistance, and He will enlighten us and give us the wisdom to understand the holy words of true religion.

True divine religion resides in Christianity only. It rests on the teachings of Christ, His apostles, and the first fathers of the Church. Yet human pride, instead of following the teachings given to man by God, began disputing about the truth and seeking it in human reason instead of looking for it in God. Thus man fell into many mistakes.

Man's heart became evil because of his pride, and the farther it removed itself from God the greater became the reason's conviction that it was getting close to truth or even was in possession of it. Hence the destructive teachings of unbelievers, whose hearts are ungodly and shameless, and who spread all sorts of contradictory doctrines and persecute those who are unwilling to follow their false teachings. Pure Christianity has frequently gotten lost in inimical disputes; the hearts of the so-called Christians have become sensual; they have sought power, honor, and riches; and the spirit of destructive unbelief has made misuse of religion and fashioned it as a weapon for its own selfish goals. Thus was born the Inquisition in the Catholic countries and other horrors of a similar nature elsewhere.

Such were the results when men left the simple teachings of faith and forgot that the kingdom of God consists of simple faith in the truths of religion. Our Lord God Jesus Christ has given us clear directions regarding this. He did not seek as His followers learned men or the readers of books. Instead, He chose simple fishermen to spread His wisdom. But these simple men put to shame the greatest and most learned philosophers. They performed miracles, because the Spirit of God, the first and only beginning of all wisdom, rested upon them.

Whence was their knowledge? Where did they take their power? Was it not from some higher power? If so, why does man search for knowledge based on his reason alone? Will he not go astray? Unless God will cast His heavenly light upon him, a man will never reach the holy truths of God with the help of his reason alone.

A celebrated scientist of our times has said that reason is a magician that leads us into a thousand errors. We see that the heavenly light alone can bring us to understand truth. The wisest men of ancient times saw this light in the prophecies of the Old Testament. Christ has revealed us His light in its full glory. There will come a time when a great part of men will see this truth in its full majesty, but first heresies will taint half the world, and men will become unhappy because of their passions. Their tardy repentance will be useless, as the holy seer of mysteries says in his apocalypse.

Contemporary philosophers seek through their false reasoning to cast religion aside and wish to find human happiness in cold reason alone. They do great harm to those who cannot think for themselves, for they cast them into grief and depression. Such men do not admit of a higher order and soon come to reject order on earth as well. They resist authorities such as governments and churches, instead of keeping to the divine eternal truths of religion, in which they could find peace, love, order, and prosperity for their families. Instead of recognizing how law and the necessary order rest on religious principles, they spread anarchical destruction and passion. The results of this are lawlessness and general hate. Brothers will soon kill one another and the days of sorrow, predicted long ago, will come upon us. Such are the fruits of new philosophers, our contemporaries, who preach vile teachings and reject faith in God.

Few of us recognize that the disorder of our times has been caused by those of us who have left the way of order. Instead of approaching this sacred principle, they seek to overcome the evil of man's tainted heart by force or by various subtle devices. Thus they oppose passions with other passions and multiply wickedness without thinking that mistakes can be corrected only by truth and vices only by virtues. The world has gone astray and is being punished through its own actions. All this comes of the teachings of contemporary philosophers, who deny God and man's immortality beyond the death of his body. Yet we trust that there will nonetheless remain millions of people who will not in all eternity lose their deep and warm faith in God our Creator and in the mysterious but true laws of the almighty eternal Truth.

God is an almighty Spirit that animates all that lives. Man's spirit lives only through the power of God's Spirit. When God's holy light falls upon man, he sees, and when His flame burns in him, man is active in the deeds of love. In this world he is like a child who exercises himself for his adult life. Eternity will follow our life and will be its fulfillment.

Divine truth is preserved in the heavenly Christian religion and is a source of life for all thinking men. In the depths of Christian religion there is preserved a light which enlightens everyone who seeks the truth with a pure heart and desires to recognize what man is and what he should be. Real philosophy feels a need for the assistance of religion. Led by it, philosophy bravely treads the path between religious faith and disbelief. Religion gives it the thread which leads reason out of the labyrinth of passions into the temple of truth. Religion is for the soul that which light is for the eyes. Without either, man is in darkness. His heart, like his eye, can open or close itself to the light, according to his wish.

God gives man wisdom and reveals to him the mystery of recognizing God Himself, but only if man with a pure heart asks God for help in recognizing the truth. Through God, man is able to comprehend anything normally beyond him, but he must always regard himself as merely a tool of Him Who alone is great and mighty and rules all. God does not forbid reasonable inquiry and study of His creation. Sound Christian philosophy is united with an honest good will and true religion.

We must never forget that while we live on earth we consist of body and soul and that, according to God's will, the body is necessary to us for our life here. The soul must rule the body, and the body must serve the soul: this is the law of both philosophy and religion. Yet the soul must treat the body like its true servant rather than a slave whom it would like to destroy. God has given the body to the soul as a fellow worker. While a man is alive, the soul acts on the body and the body affects the soul, and these interactions have their own laws which must not be disturbed.

A man is wise if he follows the moral laws of religion. Religion contains within itself the highest order, and thus it comes from God, not from men. He who disrupts religion disturbs the equilibrium of things and their harmony. He destroys family ties and the organization and fellowship of society, and creates confusion, uncertainty, and lawlessness.

Evil is the result of deviation from the way of order. All heavenly truths rest upon and form the center of Christian religion. They are invisible to the eyes of the learned men of the contemporary world, yet they exist. The highest mysteries have their own language, which cannot be understood by a man who stands outside the sanctuary. The learned theologian Innocent I wrote to a bishop, "Christianity contains in its depths things great and important which have not been described and cannot be described." These mysteries of Christianity are like a book closed with seven seals, which does not open to any soul except the one that searches for the highest truths and lets itself be guided by the high powers given by the Giver of all that is good.

Historical theology proves that only in Christian religion can heavenly truth and divine righteousness be sought. It is surprising that, disregarding the strength of the proofs offered by Christianity (of these we have listed only a small part), there still exists great resistance to Christian beliefs. Yet the dark powers of hell will be blown apart by the wind like ashes and will finally disappear before the strength of divine, holy, eternal Truth!

From I. Archangelsky, *A Beam of Light on Eternal Mysteries*, in Russian, Moscow, 1892–1893.

CHAPTER 45

A Last Word on the Divine Origin of the Christian Religion

"Rejoice, highly favored one, the Lord is with you; blessed art you among women!" (Luke 1:28). Such were the words with which the holy Archangel Gabriel greeted the Ever-Virgin Mary as he foretold Her joy at the birth of Her Son, the Redeemer and Savior of the world. This good news must bring the most lively and true joy into the soul of every Christian, for it is news about the Son of God, Who was willing to descend to earth in order to prepare everything necessary for our salvation and thus make possible eternal blessedness in heaven for us who are exiles from Paradise. Thus the Archangel's address to the Ever-Blessed Virgin Mary must be regarded by us, too, as an invitation to take joy in the promised salvation. Not in vain does the holy Church call on heaven and earth and the whole of creation to rejoice on the great and luminous feast day of the Annunciation.

Indeed, my Christian brethren, we need only cast a cursory glance at those fruits which the Christian religion has brought and still continues to bring, and we shall be convinced that the Christian must regard himself as immeasurably happy and rejoice with a great spiritual joy because he belongs to Christ's Church.

As soon as the Christian faith began spreading, it brought to this world countless benefits, although the world did not understand it and at first cruelly persecuted it. When under Constantine the Great, Christianity became law in the Roman Empire, the state forbade the gladiatorial combats, which were essentially murders that took place for the sake of amusing a crowd that lost all its sense of human dignity. The immoral theater performances also stopped. Possibilities for divorce became to some extent limited, whereas formerly divorces were granted on the least significant pretexts. Some horrible methods of executing the death penalty were forbidden. Public immorality and shamelessness were universally forbidden by law under threat of the most severe penalty. Christianity, which aimed to develop all the natural resources of man, without distinguishing his familial descent and social position, began preaching the possibility and even the necessity of the infinite perfectability of the human spirit in all the realms open to it, and especially in the realm of morality and spiritual development. Thus Christianity opened to all a wide door to mental development and, consequently, to true education.

Was it not the Christian faith that destroyed the wall that separated the rich from the poor, the nobly born from the lowly, and said the great word on the obliteration of class distinctions, "Ye are all one in Christ Jesus" (Gal 3:28)? Christianity announced to all, rich and poor, educated and uneducated, that we all are the children of one God, the members of one body, the inheritors of one and the same heavenly kingdom. Christianity not only gives us hope of a life after death but also, powerfully and lovingly, does all it can for us in this life. Before Christianity, poverty was regarded as disgrace, and the work of a man's own hands humbled and shamed him. But since the incarnate Son of God Himself and the greatest among the Christian apostles spent their lives in poverty and gained livelihood by the labor of their own hands, poverty and labor can never disgrace us. The Apostle Paul himself told all Christians: "We urge you, brethren ... that you also aspire to lead a quiet life, to mind your own business, and to work with your own hands" (1 Thess 4:10–11).

Was it not the Christian religion that announced and gave realization to the noblest kind of love: the love of every human being for all other human beings? Pagan antiquity is notable for its heartlessness toward the poor and the weak. Even the great Greek philosopher Plato was of the opinion that the sick should not be fed since they can no longer be useful. The ancient Hebrews limited the law of love to members of their nation and their religion. But under the cross of Christ, Christians stretched out their hands toward one another like brothers. Under the cross they forgot differences of class, property, and education. The works of mercy and selfless love are the best and most precious ornaments of the Christian religion. Christians have always founded hospitals and homes for the old, for orphans, widows, and strangers. While feeding the hungry, giving drink to the thirsty, clothing the naked, and visiting the poor and the imprisoned, they were performing the works of mercy toward Jesus Christ Himself. The pagans were surprised at their efforts and said, "See how Christians love one another!" Even a great hater of Christians, the Emperor Julian Apostate, was forced to admit that "these Galileans feed not only their own sick but ours also." This merciful love has left its good fruit throughout the history of the Christian Church.

Christianity did more than look after the poor and the unfortunate, the sick and the weak. Even if it had done nothing more, we still should be most grateful to it for the prevention and cure of so many misfortunes. But Christianity has done much more. It has laid the foundation for our home and family life, and has shed its beneficent light over all. Christianity has hallowed marriage, for the union of husband and wife assumed its true meaning only when it became a symbol of the union between Christ and His Church. While polygamy prevailed among many pagans, Christianity has once and for all condemned it. By doing so it has hallowed marriage ties as unbreakable, for the union of Christ and His Church is also unbreakable. Husband and wife are one flesh, and "what God has joined together, let not man separate" (Matt 19:6). As is obvious in our own times, any attacks on the unbreakable nature of marriage are usually connected with attacks on the Christian Church herself. Women owe many of their rights to Christianity. In many parts of the world, the wives of even well-educated pagans lived in a condition of slavery and oppression. Jesus Christ removed these chains from women. Unashamed of calling one of them His Mother, he raised all women to an elevated position. He announced salvation and freedom from sin to both men and women. The Christian woman should be the joy and glory of her husband, the faithful mother of his children, the treasure of his home, and the nurse of the entire household in all misfortunes. The pagan Libanius, the teacher of St John Chrysostom, exclaimed, "What wives these Christians have!"

Thus, Christianity built home and family life on a firm foundation and shed its light over them. Moreover, the spirit of the Gospel penetrated the life of states and governments. Of course, Jesus Christ descended on earth not in order to establish good governmental systems but in order to save poor sinners. He definitely declined all the political hopes of His contemporaries, saying that His kingdom was not of this world and persuading people to give what is Caesar's unto Caesar and what is God's unto God. The apostles did likewise. Nonetheless, Christianity had a great and powerful influence on the political life of nations. Christianity sees a government not as the invention of man but as a form of divine order. It sees rulers and governments as God's servants, appointed to punish the evil and reward the good, "that we may lead a quiet and peaceable life in all godliness and reverencee" (1 Tim 2:2). Christianity persuades princes and rulers to rule in the name of God, to be true servants of God in ruling for the good of the ruled, and not to be forgetful of their Lord and heavenly Judge, to Whom all rulers must be accountable. On the other hand, it is the duty of the subjects to obey their rulers and to pray for them.

Christianity has also had a beneficent influence on the mutual relations of various peoples and nations. We know how haughty the Hebrews, God's chosen people, were toward all pagans. We also know how the Romans and Greeks despised all the other nations and called them barbarians. Only Christianity obliterated the distinctions between the various nations. The Apostle Paul was able to say, "There is neither Jew nor Greek, there is neither slave nor free, there is neither male nor female; for you are all one in Christ Jesus" (Gal 3:28). It must be admitted that even now many such distinctions remain in force, but Christianity must not bear the blame: it is the fault of nations and their rulers, who do not wish to follow up opportunities for peace and love. The plough, the trades, the arts, science—all these always follow the cross. If we look at the map of the world, we shall discover that the most advanced nations are the Christian nations.

Yet all the benefits of Christianity which we have enumerated above are as nothing when compared to that immeasurably great good which lies in the remission of sins and in eternal blessed life beyond death, on the condition of faith, good deeds, and obedience to the Church. All the benefits of Christianity lose their impressiveness when compared to this priceless treasure, as candles lose their brilliance in the daytime, when the bright sun is shining. In Christ Jesus we have remission of sins, salvation, life, and eternal blessedness with God. Rejoice, my Christian brethren, in remembering that God the Father has sent His only Son, our Lord Jesus Christ, into the world for the salvation of sinful men; that Christ the Savior has revealed to us His Father's will in founding on earth His Church, the home of salvation, and establishing in the Church the soul-saving mysteries, which are our ever-accessible repositories of grace; and left in the Church His divine teachings.

Rejoice in remembering that Christ our Savior has accepted us into His holy Church, has washed us free of the sin of our progenitors in the mystery of baptism, has put on us the inexpressible seal of the Holy Spirit, feeds us with His divine Body and Blood, cleanses our sins in the sacrament of penance, and gives us other gifts of His grace as well, all of which help us on our road toward salvation. Rejoice in the knowledge that the merciful Lord accepts all who repent, and us sinners among them: He rejects no one who comes to Him with real repentance and sorrow for his sins. Great is His kindness and limitless His love of men! Rejoice, my brethren, in thinking that together with this short life there will also end all our earthly sorrows, needs, and suffering, which merciful providence sends for our spiritual good.

Beyond the limits of our earthly life, the Lord our Savior has prepared an eternally blessed life for all who love Him.

"Rejoice in the Lord always. Again I will say, rejoice! ... and the peace of God, which surpasses all understanding, will guard your hearts and minds through Christ Jesus" (Phil 4:4, 7).

From a sermon of the protopriest Gregory Dyachenko.

* * *

A professor of theology, the protopriest Sergievsky, says, "The supernatural quality of Christianity and its divine origin are clearly discernible to an eye skilled in distinguishing natural historical events from those that cannot be explained by natural causes. It is sufficient to examine Christianity at its first appearance in order to draw definite conclusions about its being something quite apart from all other phenomena. Nothing like it has ever existed. Nothing like it could ever be the natural result of the simple causes belonging to this earth."

Christianity is at the center of all truth. Only the Christian religion reveals the eternal truths and the divine order behind all things. To those who are initiated into the sacred Christian mysteries, Christianity explains the causes of all being, for it alone leads to a recognition of God and His eternal laws. God is One, truth is one, and there is but one way to God, the way of Christianity.

All cognition of God and the Truth flows out of religion. All the truths that are outside the reach of science have been preached since the first day of creation and will continue to be announced until the last. The physical laws of nature are only the traces or reflections of the laws belonging to the world of spirit and reason. From the great truths recognized in time, we must ascend to the eternal truths. Even the ancients believed in this great mystery. All religions, past and present, always contained some sparks of truth. In Christianity, these sparks made their way through their rough covering and finally burst into a pure flame. Man is capable of cognition of God and of rising to the religion of justice and then to the religion of grace.

The greatest mystery within the confines of creation is man, his redemption and immortality. Yet these holy and true mysteries were not revealed to mankind until the time of grace, that is, during the sojourn on earth of the heavenly teacher. All the great truths of religion lead man to recognition of the whole. As Christian philosophy becomes fully revealed, we come fully to understand truth. The famous philosopher Bacon says that "only bad philosophers and superficial scientists reject religion." Those who deeply penetrate the holy precinct of religion come to honor religion unconditionally and believe in its heavenly origin.

From I. Archangelsky, *A Beam of Light on Eternal Mysteries*, in Russian, Moscow, 1892–1893.

CHAPTER 46

The End of the World, the Resurrection of the Dead, and the Last Judgment

The word of God reveals to us some signs of the approaching end of the world and the glorious second coming of Christ. Physical nature will then be characterized by famine, earthquakes, epidemics, and other particularly terrible manifestations of the powers of nature, as well as various signs in the sky (Matt 24:7). The moral nature of men will be characterized by suffering and exhaustion resulting from fearful expectation of something terrible to happen (Matt 24:21). Yet at the same time people will experience a strange carelessness about their own destiny, like a deep sleep at the dead of night (Matt 24:37–39). Faith will become so scarce among men that when the Son of Man will come again, he will scarcely find any on earth (Luke 18:8). Mutual relations among men will continue changing for the worse: love will slacken and grow cold (Matt 24:12); hate and treachery will increase (Matt 24:10); and there will be cruel enmity even among close relatives (Mark 13:12); and there will be terrible wars among whole nations and countries (Matt 24:6–7).

Mankind, however, will be unable to see its disastrous moral condition. On the contrary, men will proclaim that they have reached prosperity, will grow unable to see that they are doing well only as far as the temporal goods of this earth are concerned, and will have forgotten the Christian's desire to prosper in matters spiritual, which are important if one is mindful of eternity and of God (1 Thess 5:2–8). Although men will be immoral, the Gospel will not yet have been preached to all the nations (Matt 24:14). Finally, there will appear the forerunners of the antichrist, numerous false messiahs and teachers not appointed by God, who will, however, speak in God's name (Matt 24:24). After them the antichrist himself will come. According to the testimony of the holy Apostle Paul, Christ will not come before the antichrist will have appeared (2 Thess 2:1–4). The antichrist will come for a short time only (Rev 12:12), but during this short time his kingdom will spread throughout the earth (Rev 13:8). Then the Lord Jesus Christ will break and destroy the antichrist and make him perish by the mere breath of His mouth and the view of His glory as God and Savior (2 Thess 2:8; Tit 2:13).

When the kingdom of the antichrist will have ceased, the eternal kingdom of the Lord Jesus Christ will begin. He, the Son of God—Who was incarnated for the salvation of mankind, lived on earth and died, was resurrected and has risen into heaven—will once again appear from heaven in the same way in which the holy apostles saw Him rising there (Acts 1:11). He will come with great glory and power, as He Himself predicted: "Then the sign of the Son of Man will appear in heaven, and then all the tribes of the earth will mourn, and they will see the Son of Man coming on the clouds of heaven with power and great glory" (Matt 24:30). His coming will be sudden, like the lightning which comes from the east and shines to the west (Matt 24:27). It will also be unexpected for all: the apostle says that "the day of the Lord will come as a thief in the night" (2 Pet 3:10).

As soon as the Lord Jesus Christ comes in glory, He will resurrect the dead (1 Thess 4:16). The resurrection of the dead is proven by the precedent of the resurrection of Christ the Savior Himself. The holy Apostle Paul says, "Now Christ is risen from the dead, and has become the firstfruits of those who have fallen asleep" (1 Cor 15:20). The Christian faith makes a close connection between the truth of the resurrection of the dead and the truth of the resurrection of Christ. There can be no doubt about either. To the doubter, the Apostle Paul gives advice to look at nature, which provides a visible sign of resurrection to us: "But someone will say, 'How are the dead raised up? And with what body do they come?' Foolish one, what you sow is not made alive unless it dies. And what you sow, you do not sow that body that shall be, but mere grain—perhaps wheat or some other grain. But God gives it a body as He pleases, and to each seed its own body" (1 Cor 15:35–38). A simple seed is thrown in the ground, but it is not destroyed. Instead, it prepares for a new birth, assumes a new body, and thus brings full fruit. If nature, which with time must end and disappear, contains such miracles testifying of resurrection, then our bodies, too, can rise. They rise in order to live again; being worn out, they are buried in the earth in order to become new bodies and bring new fruit. The Lord Jesus Christ Himself has proven the resurrection of the dead. He resurrected the daughter of Jairus, the ruler of the synagogue, and also resurrected before the eyes of all His friend Lazarus, who had died and been buried for three days. Lazarus was resurrected by only a word: "Lazarus, come forth!" (John 11:43). At the time of Christ's crucifixion and death there came to life a great number of the dead, who "coming out of the graves after His resurrection, they went into the holy city and appeared unto many" (Matt 27:53).

Thus, when the Lord will come in His glory, the dead will all arise. There will be heard the terrible sound of the trumpet of the archangel, announcing to all the coming of the Lord (1 Thess 4:16); the dead will hear the voice of the Son of God and, having heard it, will come to life (John 5:25). By the action of the almighty God, all the bodies of the dead will arise, assume a new guise, and be united with their souls. Those who will not yet have died by the time of the general resurrection will not die at all but be changed. The apostle says, "We shall not all sleep, but we shall all be changed" (1 Cor 15:51); that is, the bodies of such men will suddenly assume a new and different appearance and become like the bodies of the resurrected dead.

After the resurrection of the dead, the visible heaven and earth will also end. While speaking of His second coming, Jesus Christ said, "Heaven and earth will pass away" (Matt 24:35). The psalmist King David says that heaven and earth will perish: "They shall perish, but Thou shalt endure; yea, they shall all wax old as doth a garment, and as a vesture shalt Thou change them, and they shall be changed" (Ps 101:27). God will change and renew all of creation by means of fire, just as the earth was renewed at the time of the flood by means of water. The apostle says, "By the word of God the heavens were of old, and the earth standing out of the water and in the water, by which the world that then existed perished, being flooded with water. But the heavens and the earth which are now preserved by the same word, are reserved for fire until the day of judgment and perdition of ungodly men.... The heavens will pass away with a great noise, and the elements will melt with fervent heat; both the earth also and the works that are in it will be burned up" (2 Pet 3:5–7, 10). The end of the world will consist only of the destruction of the material world as it is now, not in its ultimate annihilation. The Apostle Peter also says, "Nevertheless we, according to His promise, look for new heavens and a new earth in which righteousness dwells" (2 Pet 3:13). And the prophet Isaiah speaks of God as saying, "For behold, I create new heavens and a new earth; and the former shall not be remembered or come to mind" (Isa 65:17). This world will change into a better new world suited to men whose bodies have been renewed.

The coming of the Son of God will be majestic. He will appear in all His glory, as the King of heaven and earth, not alone but surrounded by a throng of angels and saints, who will witness His terrible judgment. The coming of the Lord will be terrible. He will appear as an awesome Judge, as a severe retributor of His laws, in order to reward some and punish the others. "When the Son of Man comes in His glory, and all the holy angels with Him, then He will sit on the throne of His glory. All the nations will be gathered before Him, and He will separate them one from another.... and then He will reward each according to his works" (Matt 25:31–32; 16:27). His judgment will be solemn and open, for the Judge will appear in all His glory together with all the holy angels and will judge in full view of the entire world, the heaven, the earth, and the underworld. St Ephraim of Syria says, "He will call on heaven and earth to be at His judgment; and both high and low will stand before Him and tremble. And the hosts of heaven and the armies of the underworld will tremble before the Judge Who does not forgive, and Who will come accompanied by terror and death." All men, living and dead, good and evil, not only Christians, but also those who do not believe in Christ, will appear at the judgment.

The apostle says, "He has appointed a day on which He will judge the world in righteousness" (Acts 17:31). This judgment will be universal and will concern all the deeds of men, both good and wicked, which will have been committed throughout every man's life (2 Cor 5:10; Rom 2:6), all their words (Matt 12:36–37), and all their thoughts, intentions, and even the most hidden desires (1 Cor 4:5). "Everyone will see standing before him his own deeds," says St Ephraim of Syria, "his deeds, both good and evil, whatever deeds he has committed." Elsewhere he says that during this judgment no desire of one's heart will remain undiscovered. Even the shameless word that was whispered in secret will on that day be discovered before the just Judge. St John Chrysostom says, "Even the least deeds, both good and evil, will be subject to strict inquiry. We shall be punished for an indiscreet glance, shall be held responsible for an idle word said in jest, for calumny, for evil desires, for drinking; while among our good deeds not even a cup of cold water given to the thirsty, not even a gentle word, not even a sigh of penance will be forgotten, but all will be rewarded." Thus all will be judged according to their merits, and the judgment will be severe, terrible, and fair, for it will be in accord with God's truth, and everything in it will be true. This will be "the day of wrath and revelation of the righteous judgment of God" (Rom 2:5).

St Gregory the Theologian says, "This Judgment will be the only, the final, and the terrible one, and more just than terrible." This terrible judgment of God will be the ultimate and last judgment, for it will decide the fate of each of the judged for all infinity. Here are the words of Christ Himself about it: "Then the King will say to those on His right hand, 'Come, you blessed of My Father, inherit the kingdom prepared for you from the foundation of the world'.... Then will He also say to those on the left hand,

'Depart from me, you cursed, into the everlasting fire prepared for the devil and his angels.... And these will go away into everlasting punishment, but the righteous into eternal life" (Matt 25:34, 41, 46). After this last verdict of the just Judge the future life will begin, that life in which we trust and which we expect when, in the words of the Creed, we say: "I expect ... the future life."

From the *Full Christian Catechism* of Metropolitan Philaret, and from other sources.

CHAPTER 47

The Blessed Condition of the Righteous
in the Future Life

A great reward is prepared for the righteous in the future life (Matt 5:12). They will be brought to the most perfect and beautiful place, which Holy Scripture calls Paradise (Luke 23:43), heaven (Matt 6:9), the kingdom of God (Luke 13:28–29), the heavenly Father's house (John 14:2), and the city of the living God and the heavenly Jerusalem (Heb 12:22). According to the teaching of the Orthodox Church, "no matter which of these names one apply to this place, one will not sin: only let him know that the departed righteous dwell in God's grace in the Heavenly Kingdom or, as the church songs proclaim, in Heaven" (*The Orthodox Confession of the Catholic and Apostolic Eastern Church*, pt. 1, reply to question 67).

The blessed condition of the righteous in their blessed dwelling, Paradise, is given various names by Holy Scripture: eternal life (John 3:15), rest (Heb 4:9–10), an inheritance incorruptible that does not fade away (1 Pet 1:4), a joy that no one will take away, a full joy (John 16:22, 24), and many similar names. To sum up, the condition of the righteous in the future life may be called blessedness (Matt 5:3–12).

The greatest and highest source of this blessedness will be communion with God and the possibility of seeing Him. "God is the source of our blessedness," says the blessed Augustine. "He is the goal of all our aspirations. While we are searching for Him ... we aspire to Him in our love in order to reach Him and find rest. We are blessed only insofar as we progress toward this goal. We have no other good except union with God" (Augustine, *The City of God*, 60, 3). The Prophet Isaiah prophesies that the Lord Himself will be eternal light for the righteous. The Lord says, "As one whom his mother comforts, so I will comfort you; and you shall be comforted in Jerusalem" (Isa 66:13). In the New Testament, Jesus Christ Himself promises that the pure in heart will see God (Matt 5:8). The holy Apostle John the Theologian says that "our fellowship is with the Father and with His Son Jesus Christ"

(1 John 1:3), and that the blessed kingdom of glory will be "the tabernacle of God ... with men, and He will dwell with them, and they shall be His people, and God Himself shall be with them and be their God" (Rev 21:3).

We thus see on the evidence of Holy Scripture that all who love Christ will be united with Him forever in the eternal kingdom of God. This union with Him will undoubtedly be the highest and most perfect degree of their blessedness. If the saints love Him not yet having seen Him and, believing, "rejoice with joy inexpressible and full of glory" (1 Pet 1:8), how much greater will their joy be when they will see the never-setting Sun of Truth in all His beauty and greatness! Of course they will see the human nature of Christ the Savior by means of the bodily sense of vision, while His divine nature together with that of God the Father and the Holy Spirit will be perceived spiritually, insofar as this is possible for a limited being like man. The close communion of the saved souls with God will consist not only in their spiritual union with Him through the most intense love, but, according to the words of the holy Apostle Peter, it will also consist in partaking of the divine nature (2 Pet 1:4), which in this world is possible only through the most holy sacrament of communion, while in the never-ending day of God's kingdom such a communion will be more true and real, so that God, in the words of the holy Apostle Paul, will be "all in all" (1 Cor 15:28). As St John the Theologian says, He will be the spring that gives water to the thirsty, the light that illuminates the just, and the tree of life that feeds them (Rev 21:6, 22–23). So close a communion with God, inexpressible and unintelligible to us now, will be the highest good of all the good things that are prepared for the righteous by the endless love of our Savior and which they will enjoy in the blessed kingdom of glory. "What a glory, what a joy there will be," says St Cyprian, "for those who are found worthy of seeing God and who, together with Christ, our Lord God ... will taste the joy of salvation and light eternal!" (St Cyprian of Carthage, Epistle 4).

In having perpetual communion with God and in seeing Him all the time, blessed souls will find a full and unceasing source of happiness. They will be happy in a consciousness of high perfection in themselves and of close agreement between their spiritual and physical powers. By their very nature, the blessed will have a perfect intelligence, a perfect will, and perfect senses. All parts of their being will be in perfect harmony. Thus they will reach the perfect development in them of the image and likeness of God, which man had when he was created by God (Gen 1:26–27).

St Gregory the Theologian says that, as he understands it, future blessedness "is the most perfect cognition of the Father, the Son, and the Holy

Spirit" (St Gregory the Theologian, "Against the Arians"). In cognition of God we shall find also cognition of all that has been created by Him. Our failure to understand the seeming imperfections of the world will then be resolved, and the great plans of God concerning the whole creation, not only man, will be revealed. The world of spirits will then stand before man in the purest light; he will clearly see many other beings, and will recognize their qualities and purposes and their place in the order of creation. In the future life, according to St Ephraim of Syria, "the unknown treasures of wisdom and knowledge are opened" (St Ephraim of Syria, "On the Second Coming of the Lord"). In the future life, the real activity of the human intelligence will only begin, and in it man will find an unceasing source of blessedness.

The moral condition of the inhabitants of the kingdom of glory will also be excellent and perfect. Being free of all impurity and sin, there will be no temptations to sinful actions and to deviation from the law of God, and sin will no longer exist (1 Cor 15:56–57). Nothing impure will enter Paradise (Rev 21:27). The righteous will be filled with the righteousness for which they only thirsted here on earth (Matt 5:6), and the love which, according to the apostle, never fails (1 Cor 13:8) will then reveal itself most perfectly to them and give their will an unswerving direction to the good, so that they will never be in danger of swaying from this direction. Consciousness of all this will fill the hearts of the righteous with greatest satisfaction. Their conscience will be bright and pure, as was the conscience of the first man before the fall, and no recollection of the past will disturb their joy and serenity, for the prophet records the words of God: "The former troubles are forgotten, and ... they are hid from My eyes. For behold, I create new heavens and a new earth; and the former shall not be remembered or come to mind" (Isa 65:16–17). In their love for God, the righteous will, with all their soul, direct themselves to the source of all that is exalted, good, and beautiful, they will desire and do only that which pleases God and thus will continuously approach Him in holiness and come into the closest spiritual union with Him, the kind of union for which Christ prayed to His Father before He left this world (John 17:21–23).

The hearts of the righteous, which thirsted for happiness here on earth, will be fully satisfied there. They all will enjoy the blessedness of cognition of God (1 Pet 1:8). Through their love they will be found worthy of the closest communion with God Himself, the source of happiness. As the apostle says, "God is love; and he who abides in love abides in God, and God in him" (1 John 4:16). How great this blessedness of the heart will be, we can neither feel nor understand now, and even less can we express it in words. St John Chrysostom says, "What words can describe what will be then? Communion with Christ will result in sweetness and joy indescribable. It is impossible to say what pleasure the soul experiences after it has regained its nobility and has come to the condition which allows it to see its Lord; it not only finds pleasure in the possession of good things but also is certain that these good things will never end. Thus this joy can neither be fully described in words nor understood by reason" (St John Chrysostom, "To Theodore Fallen").

Set free from the destructive action of the powers of nature, the bodies of the righteous will be free from illness and death: "There shall be no more death, nor sorrow, nor crying. There shall be no more pain, for the former things have passed away" (Rev 21:4). The imperishable body will not make the holy soul heavy in its aspirations, will not prevent the soul from fulfilling what it may desire, but will be the best and most effective instrument for realizing and fulfilling the pious and exalted desires of the soul. The body will be like a beautiful palace in which the soul will be totally occupied with the exalted aspirations of its godlike nature.

The blessedness of the denizens of Paradise will be yet deeper because they all will always be in perpetual communion with one another. Scripture says, "Many will come from the east and west, and sit down with Abraham, Isaac, and Jacob, in the kingdom of heaven" (Matt 8:11). We see then that every blessed inhabitant of the kingdom of glory will enter into communion with those with whom he was united on earth by the close spiritual bonds of pure love, kinship, and friendship. It is particularly wonderful that there he will see and recognize all the saints of God: the first men, the patriarchs, the prophets, the apostles, the martyrs, the confessors, the fathers of the church, the hermits, and all the righteous, and will communicate with them. No doubt the saints will also be in communion with the angels and all the pure spirits. The holy Apostle Paul says, "You have come to Mount Zion and to the city of the living God, the heavenly Jerusalem, to an innumerable company of angels, to the general assembly and church of the firstborn who are registered in heaven" (Heb 12:22–23). St John Chrysostom says about future blessedness, "What is most important of all is the unceasing pleasure in communion with Christ, with the angels, the archangels, and the heavenly powers.... There will be no confusion, no struggle, for the unanimity among the saints will be total, since they will all think alike" (St John Chrysostom, "To Theodore Fallen"). About this state of blessedness, St Ephraim of Syria says, "There are multitudes of angels, the triumph of the firstborn, the thrones of the apostles, the first seats of the prophets, the scepters of the patriarchs, the crowns of the martyrs, praise of the righteous: there rewards are reserved and something is prepared for each principality, power, and rank" (St Ephraim of Syria,

"About the Second Coming of the Lord"). The righteous will, moreover, be closely united by their common activity, which will correspond to their blessed condition and will consist of contemplation of God and His endless perfections, in presence and worship before the throne of God (Rev 19:4), in serving God and fulfilling His will (Rev 7–15), and finally in ceaseless praise given to God (Rev 5:9–13).

All the saved will, in accordance with the Lord's promise, enter the blessed kingdom of Jesus Christ, but not all of them will enjoy there an equal state of blessedness. Each will be blessed according to the measure of his labors and accomplishments on earth. The apostle says, "Each one will receive his own reward according to his own labor" (1 Cor 3:8). Some souls will occupy a higher level of spiritual perfection and holiness, others a lower one, but all will be satisfied and blessed. Even the lowest degree of future blessedness will far transcend all that we here can express, understand, and feel.

The blessedness prepared for the righteous in their new life will be eternal. The word of God so clearly assures us of this that a real Christian can have no doubt of it. The holy Apostle Paul says that the dwelling of the just in heaven will be eternal (2 Cor 5:1), and the holy Apostle John reveals that the just will "reign forever and ever" (Rev 22:5). St John Chrysostom says, "Our best condition lies in the hereafter, and we must act always in such a way that we may shine forth there, rejoice with the angels, and stand before the Heavenly King always, to all the endless ages. Our soul is created immortal so that the body too may be immortal and that we may enjoy endless good" (St John Chrysostom, "Sermon 31 on the Gospel of John"). St Ephraim of Syria speaks of the future good in exalted language and describes it as endless and eternal. "There," he says, "will be a great gift, an incomparable joy, unfailing rejoicing, unceasing singing, never silent praise, endless thanksgiving, incessant theology, kingdom without end, riches uncountable, limitless ages, an abyss of generosity, an ocean of mercy and love..." (St Ephraim of Syria, "On the Second Coming of the Lord").

Thus the righteous will receive the inheritance of eternal life and will there enjoy all goods in the full measure of their perfection. All the sources of true and pure joys that we can only imagine will there form one ceaseless stream of blessedness which will flow through the entire eternity and nourish the heart and the spirit.

From S. S-ki *Future Life Beyond the Grave*, in Russian, 1892.

CHAPTER 48

About the Eternal Blessedness of the Saints

We quote here the words of one of our most illustrious preachers, Alexander the Bishop of Mojaisk, about the eternal blessedness of the saints. "No matter who you may be, my reader—whether a young man or an elderly one, whether rich or poor—I entreat you not only to read what I am saying but to give some serious thought to my words. I entreat you to do so in the name of the Savior, Who will at some unknown time in the future call you before His divine judgment and announce to you your eternal destiny. Recognize that God in Christ is the only source of your happiness and put all your hope in Him. Let us pray that the everlasting God, the source of peace for all the saints, may purify our earthbound hearts and lift them up from the earth, so that our love for Him and our joy in Him may contain our whole life! O Lord, let us be determined in our journey toward Thee, so that Thy promise of repose with Thee may apply to us and we may not lose it because of our unfaithfulness and indolence!

"Through Adam's fall we not only upset our relationship with God and lost our close communion with Him but also lost all spiritual cognition of our Creator and all inner inclination to such happiness.

"O Lord, help me recognize that which I must announce to others! Reveal Thy glory and show us our common inheritance! Reveal it to us not as Balaam was shown the rich tents of Jacob and Israel, having yet no portion in them. No, rather reveal our inheritance to us as to the merchant of the parable, who after hearing about the precious pearl, found no rest until he had bought it and made it his own; and as to the holy First Martyr Stephen, who contemplated the open heaven, which he was soon to enter, and the brilliant glory in which he was to participate.

"What is the essence of the saints' blessedness? The saints are completely free from all evil, are most closely united with God, the source of the highest good, and all their bodily and spiritual powers are harmoniously active in their union with God.

"First, heavenly repose completely excludes all evil. Heaven contains nothing impure or defiled (Rev 21:27). All such things remain outside, while in heaven neither sorrow nor sadness is known.

"Second, in the heavenly kingdom the saints are united with God, the source of the highest good. My reader, be not surprised at the confusion which I experience in trying to tell you about this union. It is inexpressible. If human beings or angels could at all express similar happiness, they would not be able to call it anything except union with God. What an inexpressible joy is opened to the believer in the words of Jesus Christ: 'Father, I desire that they also whom You gave Me may be with Me where I am, that they may behold My glory which You have given Me' (John 17:24). Be firm, O Christian: the time is approaching when you will be as close to God as you now desire. You will dwell with Him; you will be an inheritor of His kingdom; you will be together with Him Who is One with the Father, as He Himself has said in His prayer for you, 'That they all may be one, as You, Father, are in Me, and I in You; that they also may be one in Us, that the world may believe that You sent Me. And the glory which You gave Me I have given them, that they may be one just as We are one: I in them, and You in Me; that they may be made perfect in one, and that the world may know that You have sent Me, and have loved them as You have loved Me' (John 17:21–23).

"Third, the blessedness of the saints is distinguished by harmonious activity of all their human powers, both bodily and spiritual. All these powers are active in union with God. Our bodies will be so changed in the kingdom of God that they will no longer consist of this flesh and this blood, which do not inherit the kingdom of God. Instead, we shall have spiritual bodies: 'But someone man will say, "How are the dead raised up? And with what body do they come?" ... But God gives it a body as He pleases him....' (1 Cor 15:35, 38). No doubt, just as here God helps the development of our concepts and of our ability to assimilate ideas, so there, too, He will help the good qualities of our reason grow, and will direct all our powers. What a great happiness it is to the glorified body to be always present before the throne of God and the Lamb and ceaselessly to repeat, 'Worthy is the Lamb who was slain to receive power and riches and wisdom, and strength and honor and glory and blessing! ... Blessing and honor and glory and power to Him who sits on the throne, and to the Lamb, forever and ever' (Rev 5:12–13).

"O Christian! You will then be filled with love, but no matter how much you may love God, His love will always be greater than yours. As the arms of the Son of God were spread out on the cross, so His heart will be open to all in the midst of the heavenly glory. He Whose love is greater than yours will love you always. He loved you when you were still His enemy and a sinner; will He not love you indefinitely when you will have become His son and perfect in holiness? He shed tears over Jerusalem not long before its destruction; how greatly will he rejoice in the glory of the New Jerusalem! O Christian! Come to understand this great truth: you will always be in the embrace of a love without beginning or end, the same love which brought the Son of God down from heaven to earth, from the earth to the cross, from the cross into the tomb, from the tomb into glory; the love which brought Him to suffer weariness, hunger, temptation, contempt, blows, slaps, spitting, crucifixion, and wounds; the love that fasted, prayed, taught, healed, wept, shed His blood, and died. This love will always be with you!

"And remember, O Christian, for your comfort, that when you will be united with God by your faith, neither sin nor the earth nor hell will remove you from Him. Christ will unite with you more closely than a brother; He in Whom there is no change, is superior to all your enemies: 'Neither death nor life, nor angels nor principalities nor powers, nor things present nor things to come, nor height nor depth, nor any other created thing, shall be able to separate us from the love of God which is in Christ Jesus our Lord' (Rom 8:38–39).

"Your joy will not belong to you only: it will be shared, as love, too, is shared. Heaven rejoices in your conversion; will it not rejoice when you will be glorified? Will not the angels greet you and rejoice in your coming? Our happiness is the end and the ultimate goal of Christ's service, His suffering, and His death. He will be glorified in His saints and beloved by all the faithful and will be satisfied in beholding the fruits of His service to mankind.

"While you are waiting for that wonderful condition to come, be attentive in all your ways, be incessantly watchful, commend yourself to divine providence, and prepare for yourself in this life the token and the measure of future joy."

From Bishop Alexander of Mojaisk, in I. Archangelsky, *A Beam of Light on Eternal Mysteries*, in Russian, Moscow, 1892–1893.

* * *

The blessedness of the saints will first of all consist of their communion with God, and consequently in their direct cognition of Him and contemplation of Him. This is clearly expressed by the apostle when he says, "For now we see in a mirror, dimly, but then face to face. Now I know in part, but then I shall know just as I also am known" (1 Cor 13:12). Hence it is natural that saved souls will possess an inner feeling of their blessed condition and that all their desires will be directed to God, the source of all that is good, and will find their satisfaction in Him: a full satisfaction for the mind that ever thirsts and longs for the truth. The apostle says, "When that which is perfect has come, then that which is in part shall be done away" (1 Cor 13:10). Consequently, faith will no longer be necessary and will be done away, for it will be replaced by direct cognition of God. Man's will, which always seeks the good, can be satisfied there, for the more the blessed spirits will contemplate and recognize God's perfection, the more they will be strengthened in their love for Him and burn with this love, which, according to the apostle, "never fails" (1 Cor 13:8). They will continue perfecting themselves in becoming like Him, as the Apostle John says, "Beloved, now are we children of God; and it has not yet been revealed what we shall be, but we know that when He is revealed, we shall be like Him, for we shall see Him as He is" (1 John 3:2). Their hearts will be fully satisfied, while now our hearts can only wish for happiness and thirst for it. Then, however, satisfaction will be possible because of contemplation of divine qualities, and as a result, our love for God will increase even more. Already in ancient times did David express this longing and a hope that it would find satisfaction: "But as for me, in righteousness shall I appear before Thy face; when Thy glory is revealed, I shall be satisfied" (Ps 16:15). The Savior also prayed for this when He addressed God the Father, "As You, Father, are in Me, and I in You; that they also may be one in Us.... I in them, and You in Me; that they may be made perfect in one" (John 17:21, 23).

This inner feeling of blessedness will increase because of communion with the saints and with God's angels. Nothing will disturb their mutual love and there will be no love of honors or of gain, and no envy; their spiritual ties will be the closest possible. Tertullian thus describes this condition: "Our mutual ties will become closer, just as life itself will be better. After resurrection we shall live in spiritual communion. When we shall be near God, we shall also be near one another, for in God we all shall be as one." The Savior Himself also points to this communion when He says, "Many shall come from east and west, and sit down with Abraham, Isaac, and Jacob in the kingdom of heaven" (Matt 8:11). The Apostle Paul says, "You have come to Mount Zion and to the city of the living God, the heavenly Jerusalem, to an innumerable company of angels, to the general assembly and church of the firstborn who are registered in heaven" (Heb 12:22–23).

This elevated, blessed condition of the righteous spirits will correspond to their bodily condition. The place which they will inhabit is called "a new heaven and a new earth" (Rev 21:1) and will be totally unlike our present habitations, for there will be in that new place none of the evils which here frequently harm our bodies. Quite the contrary, the habitations of the righteous there will be as good as Paradise was for the first men. They will be removed from all the needs of our present life. The Apostle John says, "They shall neither hunger anymore nor thirst anymore; the sun shall not strike them, nor any heat.... And God will wipe away every tear from their eyes; there shall be no more death, nor sorrow, nor crying. There shall be no more pain" (Rev 7:16, 21:4).

As the book of Revelation describes it, the activity of the righteous will consist of contemplation of God and His infinite perfections, in standing before God's throne and bowing to Him Who sits on it, in serving God and fulfilling His will, in endless praise to God and in singing a perpetual song to Him: Alleluia.

* * *

The most righteous judgment of God will take place after man will once more have become complete after his resurrection. Thus all the parts of man will be judged: soul, spirit, and body. After the judgment, the eternal existence of the perfect and complete man will begin. We see an image of this complete man in our resurrected Lord Jesus Christ, Who had His flesh and bones once again. Our perishable body will after the resurrection consist of such a flesh and such bones as are possessed by the New Adam, our Lord Jesus Christ.

In the heavenly kingdom there is no sun, no moon, and no stars. It is illuminated by the glory of God (Rev 21:11), and its only, all-illuminating light will be the Lord Jesus Christ. The sun does not parch there; there are no frosts, no storms, no bad weather, no hunger, no thirst, no darkness, no sorrow, no oppression, no groans, no sighs, no temptation, no fear, no despair, no parting with one's dearest, no death. In the heavenly kingdom there will be one eternal, everlasting day lighted up by the Lord God Himself; the earth and heaven will be new and will form the kingdom of undying blessed life, which will be supported by the waters of life and by the tree of life (Rev 22:1–2). The tree of life is the Lord Jesus Christ, while the water of life is the unending fullness of the priceless and countless gifts of the Holy Spirit. With such powerful assistance, the souls of the blessed will be found worthy of seeing God, and in seeing Him will lie all their blessedness both internal and external. The kingdom of grace will have ended and the kingdom of glory begun, in which the righteous will inherit the kingdom prepared for them from the creation of the world (Matt 25:34), where human reason will no longer be subject to mistakes and faults but will contemplate the eternal truths and rejoice in recognizing them. Man's will also will not swerve aside onto the paths of vice but will feel the highest sweetness in absolute obedience to God's will. The desires of man's heart will be completely satisfied by the contemplation of divine glory. Vision will rejoice in seeing the face of our Savior Jesus Christ as He is (1 John 3:2; 1 Cor 13:12); hearing will ceaselessly be delighted by the songs of the angel choirs; the sense of smell will be filled with an inexpressibly pleasant fragrance; and the sense of taste will also be full of sweetness. Thus everyone who is found worthy of the kingdom of Heaven will be constantly and thoroughly satisfied with his condition.

Both the soul and the body of the righteous will be blessed, for after the resurrection man will be possessed of both his natures, spiritual and bodily, yet the body will be new and different from what it is now. As on earth man took part in all his actions with his spirit, his soul, and his body, so after death too, punishments and rewards will be extended to the spirit, the soul, and the body. According to the Apostle Paul, everyone will receive recompense for his actions, good and bad. The bodily senses will find their reward in two ways: first, they will be delighted by the beauty of the heavenly kingdom, which will be such that, as the Apostle Paul testifies, no one has ever heard or seen anything like it; and second, they will be delighted by the company of the holy angels and the holy souls of men.

That the blessedness of the departed righteous will be eternal can be seen from the teachings and writings of all the holy fathers and teachers of the Church: Theophilus of Antioch, Ephraim of Syria, Hilarion, John Chrysostom, Clement of Alexandria, Cyprian, Ambrose, Gregory the Theologian, Basil the Great, and many others.

Not even the most highly developed reason can conceive of life in the heavenly kingdom in all its fullness. Here on earth the faithful can only see some indications of what is to come; and as the dawn precedes the day, those who are enlightened by the grace of Christ realize that even the most true, the best, and the most beautiful on earth is a barely discernible shadow of the future blessedness, the true nature of which can only partly and only sometimes be glimpsed here on earth. Even the Apostle Paul, who himself had been taken up to the third heaven, has been unable fully to describe the blessedness prepared for the righteous. He merely said that he was taken up and heard words such as man cannot speak. His words indicate only that the blessedness of the righteous and the beauties of Paradise cannot be expressed even by those who have seen them. Even if it were possible to express such things in words of human speech, men on earth would be unable to understand the description, just as children frequently are unable to understand what they are told.

Yes, my reader, God's chosen testify to the great blessedness of the saints and the righteous in heaven, who to all eternity together with the cherubim and the seraphim praise eternal God their ruler. May the soul of each of us rise to a feeling of awe and praise the greatness of God!

Collect yourself, my spirit! Collect all your powers in order to praise the eternal Father and Creator! Tear apart the ties that keep you to earth and the insignificant attractions of the earth. Remove yourself from those creatures that take away from you your greatest beatitude, union with your Creator. Stay away from the temptations of the senses, belong all to yourself, control yourself, and, as an enlightened Christian, experience deeply and humbly His greatness. Contemplate it and marvel and bow before Him.

My eternal and unfathomable God, unintelligible Being! My Creator! I approach You with holy awe. Forgive my finite spirit its daring and yet powerless aspiration toward You and You holy place. No human wisdom is able to reach You. The spirit of Your creatures lacks strength to touch upon the realms where You dwell. You have absolute power over all Your creatures. You have created us not to test Your but to bow before You and to recognize You in the miracles of Your being. You alone can recognize Your depths; You alone can comprehend Your infinity. Eternal power of great, holy truth! I feel You, no matter how deep below You I stand; I recognize Your autonomous Being and the beginning of all creation from You. I feel Your omnipotence and my own insignificance. Who am I to approach You and to talk to You, God! Creator, let righteous feelings always prevail in my soul. They alone bring me, unworthy as I am, to contemplate God, they alone bring the creature up from the dust to the throne of the Creator. Eternal, uncreated! How shall I call You? I am dust and nothing; what name shall I give You?

Can an earthly tongue pronounce Your holy name? Can a soul chained to earth ascend to You without Your help? No! In vain, in vain do I collect my strength; You have no name, Being of beings! God of kings, worlds, and the universe! Lord of lords! Unspeakable is Your name and incomprehensible is Your Being!

O You Whose Spirit fills the universe, Whose power manifests itself in all its wonders, Whose uncreated beauty shines forth through the immeasurable—how inexpressible is Your greatness! You, unlimited in Your actions, bring the worlds out of nonbeing into being. Trembling, the chaos heard Your voice and brought forth creatures appointed to exist. Changes followed changes; countless worlds and suns shone forth at Your voice in the darkness of the limitless abyss, and You appointed their way to millions of planets. Your will manifested itself in order, beauty, and the incomprehensible miracles of all the kingdoms of creation. The sun has lighted up the darkness, and the worlds began flowing along their bright paths. The entire new creation has become a mirror of Your eternal divinity, a revelation of Your omnipresent power (Rom 1:20).

God! I find Your greatness in all Your works! It is indelibly imprinted on the prime matter of all that has been created, its traces are noticeable in all that exists, down to the least significant things, up to the extreme limits of the universe, all-powerful in Your beginnings, almighty in completing them! You are God in what is great and what is small. You are in all (1 Cor 12:6, 15:28). Unfathomable in Your Being; omnipresent but hidden from all eyes; unseen, but attested to by all Your creatures! My exalted soul feels You in its depths, inseparable from itself.

Source of spirits! What am I before You? How a mortal loses all his strength at the thought of Your omnipresence, Your limitless power and Your glory! O eternal, You Who created and supported me and supports me even now, what would my life be without Your help, where would I be if the all-powerful spark of Your glory did not inspire me (Isa 42:5)? What would this world be without You—this world, filled with Your marvels? Whenever You wish, the suns that have been set on flame by Your will yet blacken; whenever You order, creation will not be able to stand without You and will turn to chaos again. Eternal God; Who can find the limits of Your power? Who can comprehend Your eternity? Who can measure Your infinity? All-merciful and all-good Creator! How glorious You are amid the whole wonderful web of Your creatures (Ps 103)! You established laws for nature, and nature must follow them and cannot break them, and behind these mysterious laws You have hidden a great purpose to which You destined Your creation. By Your power, the universe lives and moves, and Your wisdom makes it beautiful and lends it a harmonious order. You, omnipresent one, has most wisely established all the millions of Your creations. You call on winter, and the earth grows old, and the meadows are covered with glistening snow. You call on spring, and the dead fields blossom with new life, and a more powerful influence of the mild light of the sun dresses them in beauty. You bless the renewed fields with fruitfulness and give fruition to the plants of the earth, for it obeys You (Jer 5:24). You have given crimson color to the rose, the color of innocence to the lily, and their health-giving balsam to other plants. You, all-powerful, give many varied beauties and miraculous powers to the exhalations that rise from the earth. The voice of thunder announces to the peoples Your greatness, and the destructiveness of the lightning tells of Your terrible yet merciful power.

All-holy God of Sabaoth (Isa 51:15)! Who is Your equal? Whose spirit reaches the altitude of Your thoughts? Who can comprehend the limitlessness of Your marvels? Who can oppose his power to Your actions (Dan 4)? You, the Only God of all! You keep up the heavens and turn the earth around its axis for thousands of years. You established the limits of the sea and bound the rivers within their banks. You command the storm and shake the foundations of the mountains. You excite the powers of nature and turn them into the tools of Your goodness and of Your justice. All the nations from the East to the West and all the creatures that live under the sky know You by Your works. Holy and powerful, almighty and immortal God! Heaven and earth are full of Your Spirit, all the creatures feel Your blessed existence, Your glory blinds the seraphim and the archangels, countless myriads of spirits tremble around Your holy place, and eternally rejoicing praise Your name. God of all the worlds! You are always glorious in Your immense power, unfathomable in Your wisdom, infinite in Your ever-present goodness. Let everything that breathes bow before Your throne, tremble at the thought of You, and fall down before You! Merciful God of us all! Accept mercifully the thankful praise of Your servants! For You are the beginning and the end of all our hopes, joys, and comforts. You are holy and eternal.

From I. Archangelsky, *A Beam of Light on Eternal Mysteries*, in Russian, Moscow, 1892–1893, and various other sources.

PART VIII

CONCLUSION

CHAPTER 49

A Defense of Christian Faith Against Disbelief

Our times can in all truth be called the times of disbelief: from all directions all sorts of teachings inimical to Christian religion come to us, and also in our midst there unceasingly come about all manner of fantastic ideas contrary to the spirit of Christian faith. These ideas are usually born among the so-called educated. Contemporary disbelief utilizes for its own ends the liberty that it finds throughout the civilized world. It engages faith in a decisive battle and uses all its efforts and rejects no means in order to uproot faith from the hearts of men.

The press proves to be a suitable tool for this purpose in the hands of unbelievers. No misconceptions of human reason are too monstrous to be released by it. How much blasphemy, how much mockery of all sorts, how many words of ridicule, both crass and subtle, are directed against the holiest and most heartfelt feelings of the faithful! These attacks against our faith, both obvious and concealed, can be found in almost all kinds of contemporary secular literature: in novels and stories, in works historical, scientific, and philosophical. "Down with faith; there is no God!"—such is the slogan displayed on the military standards of the armies of faithless fanatics who with feverish zeal devote themselves, as they say, to the cause of education and the good of mankind. In reality, it would have been better if they had expended their zeal on some cause other than their ostensible one.

The spirit of falsehood has captured contemporary scientists at the moment when they began to trust nothing but man's reason, and began to deify it and to trust the sinful freedom of man's will. They began to understand free will in terms of liberty to do any kind of evil: liberty not to know and not to honor God, liberty not to obey God's laws, liberty for any kind of protest, liberty to give vent to one's passions, and liberty not to accept Christian teachings. All the intellectuals subscribe to such views and corrupt the simple, less well-educated people.

Learned professors and teachers in their pride have directed the natural sciences not toward the praise of God but toward the mockery of His holy Name. They have found out that the earth is one of the smallest of the planets and have consequently concluded that mankind could not have been worthy of the Creator's attention, and that He did not descend to earth, live there, suffer, and die for mankind. They even teach their students that such Christian beliefs are fantasies. They do not believe in God's goodness and in His truth, most marvelous, joyful, and life-giving. They perish because of their disbelief and the wickedness of all kinds that results from it.

How many Christians are there who say, "I believe in God," but do not reveal their belief in their actions! How many lips remain closed when it becomes necessary to defend publicly the glory of God and of His saints, whom the sons of this world blaspheme! We keep silent whenever there is an opportunity to talk about God or to put a stop to some kind of unruliness or some presumptuous remark.

Considering that the struggle of disbelief against faith has reached in our times its greatest intensity, we may regard the warning of the great Apostle Paul to be written directly to us: "Do not be carried about with various and strange doctrines. For it is good that the heart be established by grace, not with foods which have not profited those who have been occupied with them" (Heb 13:9).

It is no longer surprising to observe in contemporary society a cold, indifferent, even contemptuous attitude toward everything that reminds us of religion. Questions of a higher order, namely, those dealing with morality, and answers given to them by our contemporaries, frequently reveal an unclear, confused grasp of even the most elementary rudiments of the Christian outlook. The basic commandments of the Gospel become subverted and interpreted in a way grossly inconsistent with Christian doctrine. The highest demands of Christian morality are rejected as utopian, a dream never to be fulfilled and inapplicable to life. A whole series of concepts, whose content should wake men to moral energy and transform their spiritual selves, are reinterpreted in a way which does not at all suit these concepts, and seems to derive from them some basic meaning or other.

At the same time we see revealed a broad realm of new phenomena of extreme importance. A whole new way of life is being developed, foreign to any direct influence of religion, yet universally acknowledged to be natural and reasonable. Its supporters categorically assert that the religion of Jesus Christ has had its day, has said all it had to say. They declare that the morals of the Gospel were useful only for the simple fishermen of Galilee, while the contemporary educated man needs different guidelines. These guidelines, they say, can be given to him only by science. Science, they say, is a lighthouse before the brightness of which the light of religion grows dim and must go out completely.

Yet look with an unprejudiced eye at the religion of the New Testament during the last nineteen centuries. You will be surprised to see how much it has done for mankind. What an ineradicable trace has it left upon our civilization, our customs, manners, laws, sciences, and arts! How much has it changed mankind for the better! It has ennobled man and put into his life much warmth and love. Millions have derived from it strength to live in the name of goodness and truth, have put on its altar their best feelings and thoughts, and found in its service their greatest joy.

Can this faith now have lost its life-giving strength? Can the spring which used to satisfy the spiritual thirst of hundreds of generations have suddenly gone dry? Can an encyclopedia take the place of the Gospel? Does science have the strength to replace religion as the guide of man into the bright distance of the future? This is a serious question, impossible to be solved lightly. A mistake can lead to catastrophe.

The history of Christianity is almost 2,000 years long. We can embrace and measure the internal, constant process of its development, as well as the degree of its mighty influence upon the conscience and the life of mankind. We should be able to see that Christianity is as yet far from having expressed the entire content of its thought. It is far from having said all it has to say.

In order to make the kingdom of God on earth a reality, mankind must still continue for a long time to work diligently at improving the moral condition of its heart. The Gospel has awakened many good feelings in man. It has touched in man's heart such strings as he had theretofore not known, has evoked from them sounds of magical beauty and irresistible power. Yet these sounds have not yet united in a mighty chord, a hymn of triumphant love and truth.

If science wants to replace religion, it must take upon itself the responsibilities of religion. If it wants to be preferred to religion, it must give man more mighty means and a quicker path than does religion to the realization of the ultimate ends in his life.

The realm of science is vast; if you wish to say so, it is endless. Its problems are great. It has achieved much for mankind, and will achieve even more. Its very name must be holy for anyone who thinks about it. Still, intelligence is not the only force behind moral progress, and education alone does not make us better human beings. Science broadens our intellectual horizons, increases our power over nature, but it is unable without the cooperation of religion to make man spiritually reborn and to elevate him morally. It is not for science to renew men's hearts and to lead them toward the realization of the kingdom of God on earth.

Science can improve the future of mankind in its own way, but this is not a complete improvement. Science explains the laws of the universe, reveals how we can use the forces contained in matter, and thus gives us enormous power over nature. There was a time when man trembled before every tremendous natural phenomenon, but now he is the master of nature.

Science has converted the sun into a printing machine, has saddled the wave, enchained the free wind, yoked steam to do work, and has made lightning do the postman's work. Diamond drills go through the deep heart of rock and get water in the midst of a hot desert. Gigantic hammers with no effort compress masses of metal. The telegraph, the telephone, and the telescope have abolished distance. Spectral analysis has determined the composition of planets. Millions of factories with a minimal application of muscular strength accomplish work impossible even for the giants of mythology.

If in antiquity men were able to look into the future and see what science has accomplished by now, they would have decided that ours is the Golden Age about which their poets always dreamed. Yet despite all the victories of man's intelligence, the Promised Land continues to elude us like a mirage. In many places there still is deep ignorance, overwork, and abysmal poverty side by side with idleness and luxury.

In spite of its promises to create by its own powers a kingdom of highest truth and equality on earth, science has shown itself powerless in this respect. The age of electricity has as many vices as the ages of greatest barbarity. Instead of uniting under the guidance of God and then struggling against the universal enemy—darkness and injustice—men struggle under the banners of science for nothing except gain. The basic slogan of everyone's life is "Might is right." Man is like Ishmael, about whom the Bible says, "His hand shall be against every man, and every man's hand against him" (Gen 16:12). Everyone struggles and toils on his own behalf and for his own sake only. Thus there is universal enmity, universal distrust, irritability, and anger. Nowhere can we find restfulness, justice, mercy, and love.

Science declares that the severe, merciless law of the struggle for survival moves the world and rules it. "Be firm," say philosophers like Nietzsche. "Give no way to mercy, sympathy, or love. Oppress the weak; climb higher on their corpses. You are children of a higher race. Your ideal is the superman."

A horrible theory! According to it, not the best but the strongest and greediest will triumph. Goodness, love, and truth must step aside and give way to violence, shamelessness, and vice. Those who have behaved like the Nietzschean ideal are Dionysius the tyrant of Syracuse, Herod the Great, Nero, Cesare Borgia, Lenin, and Stalin.

Where, then, is the happiness of all the members of the family of man, a happiness promised by science? Where is the triumph of the highest love and truth? Why does not science, along with material progress, bring an improvement of morals? Why does it not remove evil, root and all? Alas, to do so is not the provenance of science. The origin of evil is of a moral kind, and science can do nothing against moral evil. It can break a rock and compress a glob of metal, but cannot make mild a cruel, hard heart.

Nineteen centuries ago the Gospel proclaimed that the heart is the origin of all thoughts, both evil and good. The divine knower of hearts, Christ the Savior, first showed that man's spirit is the only source of social, political, and every other kind of life, and that the more perfect man will become, the more perfect will be all that he creates. If you wish to change life and the world surrounding you, says Christianity, change yourself first and change your heart. It is possible for a brotherly life filled with love, in short, for the kingdom of God, to exist on earth, but we must look for it not somewhere in our surroundings, not in something external, but inside ourselves, in our hearts. And our hearts cannot be influenced by science but are influenced by religion.

The Gospel tells us about God as perfect Love and absolute Truth, about His attitude to the world and our duties toward Him. It fills our souls with reverent adoration of the Highest Being, wakens in us a desire to become worthy of His love, evokes in us subjection to His commandments as expressing incontrovertible moral law. Christianity alone, in the name of supreme holiness, which is God Himself, ceaselessly motivates man to go on growing morally.

The highest universal ideal of the whole of mankind is revealed in the Gospel. This ideal is the kingdom of God. The way to the kingdom of God is a moral rebirth of man's whole spiritual nature, a development in him of a Christian outlook, and a formation of his will in the spirit of New Testament love and truth. The moving force in this development is religion. Science can in no way find this preeminence of religion humiliating for itself and can have no reasons to quarrel with it. Science has its own sphere of activity, honorable as far as it goes, and its every success is usually a great benefit for mankind.

The realm of religion and the realm of science do not contradict each other at all, once we understand the differences between them. On the contrary, they complement each other. If there are conflicts between the representatives of religion and the representatives of science, such conflicts are due to unfortunate misunderstandings, incapacity to deal with something outside one's competence, and desire to judge a realm of activity foreign to one's own.

Science determines eternal, unshaken laws in accordance with which the whole universe lives. It reveals and subjects to man's reason more and more powers of nature, thus establishing the degree of man's external, physical dependence on the surrounding world. In brief, science searches for the best answers it can find to the question "How does the world operate?" Religion has a different problem. It answers the questions: "How ought a man to live in the world? What should be man's relation to the world and to Him Who is above the world?"

All of mankind has not yet completed its search for the eternal meaning of life. Therefore, it is strange to say that religion has played out its part, and that science alone must be the guiding star and the moving force of future civilizations.

During the nineteen centuries of its existence, Christian religion has made a strong and indelible impression upon a long series of generations, their laws and institutions, and their intellectual and moral upbringing. No matter what are our own religious views, we all are, every minute of our lives, consciously or unconsciously, under the influence of Christianity.

A considerable number of the ideas first announced to the world by Christianity have now become common property. Although the opponents of Christianity will not acknowledge it, they owe to the Gospel almost everything of which they are proud. However, let clouds conceal the sun! Daylight surrounding us is not independent from its origin, even when that origin is hidden. Once the clouds are dispersed, the sky grows bright and shines in all its beauty, and the sun pours forth streams of warmth and light. The day becomes bright and glorious.

When will such a day come? No one can answer this question. Jesus Christ has said that we cannot know this. But although we cannot know the time when He will come, we must always be ready to meet Him. We must be watchful like the master of a house. We must be prepared like the virgins whose lamps are ready for the coming of the bridegroom. We must work with all our strength toward the coming of that hour, as worked the recipients of the talents in the parable.

It is not within our power to save mankind and to change the nature of the world. But it is within our power to correct our own spiritual nature, to perfect our character, and to educate our will in a Christian way. All these actions are within our power and are, moreover, our duty, the personal obligation of each one of us.

All the enemies of divinely revealed teachings, all those who deny the existence of God, must grow silent before the arguments presented by ordinary common sense enlightened by divine revelation. The simple logic of human intelligence should be able to convince them. If they continue in their error despite the incontrovertible proofs of theology, despite proofs taken from the Holy Scriptures, despite the history of mankind from the most ancient times, and despite the belief in a Supreme Being by even the most aboriginal peoples of the world; if they are not convinced of the existence of God and the eternal life of the soul by the greatness, endlessness, and beauty of the material world, the harmony of the created world, and the very eternity of time and space, in which an infinite number of bodies perform their movements, all of them enormous and mysterious; if, finally, they are not convinced of the truthfulness of many of the biblical accounts by the archaeological excavations in ancient Assyria, Babylonia, Chaldea, Palestine, or Egypt, then they should at least on the basis of simple common sense come to the conclusion that, besides the visible world there is also an invisible one, since the chain of causation must have a final cause, namely, God, the basic source of all that is.

If there is in the universe the apparent, the not hidden, then there must be, contrasting with the apparent, also the mysterious, the hidden, the supernatural. If there exists the material, the seen, then there exists also the spiritual, the unseen. The former is the object perceived by our bodily senses; the latter, by our inner, spiritual feeling, our faith. If our bodily senses have objects of perception, then there are similar objects to be at least partially perceived by the inner senses. Thus there exists in the world a whole series of contrasting objects, phenomena, and actions—for instance, good and evil, the infinitely small and the infinitely large, complete inertia and complete activity, light and darkness, and so on.

If my self exists, then there must be others like it, and those who are higher than it (angels). If we and those higher than us exist, then there must exist One incomparably the highest and most perfect of us all and of the whole world, the beginning, the cause, the foundation, and the Creator of all that exists.

This most incomparable, eternal, endless, all-filling, most perfect, most holy, almighty, and all-high Being is God in the Holy Trinity. He is that greatest, incomprehensible cause from Whom everything originated; that living and all-wise, eternal, and almighty power Who upholds all and provides for all. The inquisitive mind of man cannot go farther. Here is the limit beyond which none of the creatures ever has stepped, nor will any ever do so.

If the world which surrounds us is inexpressibly marvelous and lovely, if it is created incredibly wisely and surprises our weak mind with its severe and majestic harmony both as a whole and in its details, in the limitless expanse and in the small things seen only under the microscope; if it is marvelously ruled according to great and eternal laws by an invisible, all-powerful hand, in accordance with a wonderfully strict order and harmony, then there must exist also the most wise and great power Who has created it and supports it even now.

Look at the sky on a silent, clear, starry night. Does not the inexpressibly beautiful vault of heavens, studded with a countless multitude of enormous worlds, speak to you about God and His wondrous greatness and wisdom? It will overwhelm you even more if you look at it through a telescope. Will not your heart tremble at these countless sources of light: the constant stars, the planets, the comets, all of which proceed on their unchanged paths, set in accordance with eternal laws, all of them separated from us by immeasurable, terrifying distances? Do we not then understand the divinely inspired words of the holy prophet and psalmist, "The heavens declare the glory of God, and the firmament showeth His handy-work" (Ps 18:1)? And not only in the great things of this universe do we see the marvels of God's creation— we see them also in the immeasurably small. Look into a microscope and you will see a whole world of creatures in one drop of water. Do we not see everywhere the undoubtable wisdom of God's creation? Can these wonders of wonders have come about of themselves, without a cause, without a Creator? Does anything in the world come about without an external cause, all by itself?

Can those who consciously deny the existence of God and the immortality of the soul be called normal, psychologically balanced people? Hardly. Otherwise, how could we explain the strange contradiction between, on the one hand, their knowledge of the Bible and their acquaintance with weighty theological proofs of God's existence, and on the other hand, their inability and unwillingness to know that great and most perfect truth which has been revealed to the world from the first times of creation, and then continued being revealed in many ways by the Lord of the universe Himself; and finally was clearly and undeniably attested by the Son of God, our Savior, Who assumed flesh and exactly fulfilled all the prophecies and witnessed to the truth of His teachings by countless signs revealed to the Christian world at various times through His divine power? Speaking of the exact fulfillment of prophecies, we may remark that at present we seem to see clearly an exact fulfillment of the scriptural revelation concerning the appearance in the world of many false prophets and false teachers, who deny the truth and teach men not to believe in God (Matt 24:11–24; 1 Tim 4:1–2; 2 Tim 4:3–4; etc.).

Believers need no proofs of the existence of God, the existence of the soul, the supernatural world, and so on. All these they acknowledge with their believing heart, enlightened by the divine teachings and with their uncorrupted reason and will. Nothing in the world will replace for mankind the divine revelation attested by the Bible. The truthfulness of the Bible has been in many respects confirmed also by science. Let the wise of this world understand that the truthfulness of the Bible can be perceived also from the strict simplicity and order of the biblical narrative itself, and from the deep sincerity and conviction which fill the entire content of this holy and divine book.

The burden of proof to deny God's existence is on unbelievers. Let them quite definitely, with scientific exactness, deny the biblical narrative about the creation of the world, the flood, and other events of like nature. How can they explain such strange and mysterious occurrences as when lightning incinerates one man so that he is on flame like a bunch of straw, while another man struck by lightning has his hands burnt to a cinder while his gloves remain untouched? Why can lightning forge together the links of an iron chain but on another occasion can kill a hunter without discharging the gun in his hands? How can it melt the earring in a woman's ear without doing any harm to her skin? How can it undress a man and leave him naked without harming him, but on another occasion burn only his shoes or his hat?

Let unbelievers also attempt to explain scientifically and incontrovertibly all kinds of supernatural events experienced by people in all parts of the world throughout the history of mankind. Let them explain the essence of so-called hypnotism, somnambulism, clairvoyance, and telepathy (that is, mental communication between two people at a distance). How can they explain facts well attested but inexplicable, such as the appearance of a man's double while that man is still alive? What is split personality, and how can it be fully explained? How will they explain the appearance to one or several people of their absent relative or friend at the moment of his death, or the appearance of the shade of someone dead long ago?

How and in what way can skeptics, who deny the supernatural world, explain the existence of houses inhabited by mysteriously invisible beings who, however, clearly reveal their presence: the motion of various objects which no one has set in motion; the raising into air by an invisible hand of very heavy objects; the appearance of a hand in the air; the ringing of a bell or the sounds emitted by a musical instrument; or mysterious knocking due to an invisible hand?

Can the wise of this world say anything at all definite about the fourth dimension? Can they precisely interpret the concepts of space and time? Can they explain why time is shortened in dreams, and what dreams are? In what way will they explain prophetic dreams, premonitions, and second sight? How will they explain the ability of some people to read the thoughts of others?

In addition to the questions already offered, we should like to put before contemporary wise men some other questions, of a different kind, namely, With what do they expect to replace faith in God and in the divinely revealed teachings of divinely inspired faith? Will the Bible be replaced by all sorts of philosophic books, systems of morality concocted by man, materialistic theories, and all sorts of utopias and inventions of human reason denying the truths of divine revelation? Having lost religion and rejected divine laws, will mankind be happier, more perfect, more upright, more humane, and more honest?

With what will they replace the comfort which religion alone gives man in sorrow? If, as these false wise men wish, Christianity should disappear, where will people find a replacement for the fountain of divine faith, from which they have been drawing pure spiritual joys, patience in the midst of toils, obedience to fate, meekness, brotherly love, strength for their struggle against evil, and hope for a better future? Will they be able to get all this from some kind of philosophic teaching, some moralistic pamphlet, or some materialistically scientific theory? The fruits of work over a microscope in a laboratory will not substantially improve man's life.

The mysterious facts and phenomena enumerated above have, for the most part, been acknowledged as insoluble problems by representatives of science. We have borrowed them partly from scientific journals and papers, especially from the essays of Camille Flammarion on psychic problems in the realm of the unseen, and partly from the writings of Butlerov and Aksakov.

Let, then, contemporary skeptics, materialists, deniers, and freethinkers reply to our questions with scientific exactness. Let them reply to us, and then we may acknowledge something solid behind their materialistically scientific theories, their liberal pamphlets full of denial, and their positivistic or rationalistic views and ideas.

Then we shall believe that the scientific conclusions of the materialists have been derived from a reliable source, that the limits of human reason are indeed nonexistent, and that reason, intelligence, and science are the only means and the only way for the cognition of the universe, its phenomena, and its mysteries. However, let us repeat that we shall never get such answers to our questions.

From *The Spiritual World*, Protopriest Grigori Dyachenko, in Russian, 1900, pp. 348–55.

CHAPTER 50

Final Exhortation—Stand Firm

Against the raging floods of faithlessness and disbelief, our most firm and trusty defense is our conviction that the truths preached by Christianity are divinely revealed to man and that the Christian Church is indeed founded by God. Everyone searching for the truth can easily be convinced of the divine nature of Christianity and the Christian Church. He need only attentively examine the following:

1. The marvelous way in which the Old Testament agrees with the New, as all the symbols and prophecies of the Old Testament find their fulfillment in the person of Christ.

2. The amazing greatness of the miracles brought about first by the prophets, then by Christ, and finally by the apostles, and the exactness with which what was foretold by them actually came about.

3. The way in which Christ's teachings and life manifest a true holiness and a divine wisdom.

4. The unusually fast spread of Christianity and its victory over paganism by means as simple as the preaching of simple fishermen, who had no help from those in power.

5. The endurance of the Christian Church despite all the storms raised by the false reasoning of the heretics, the thirst for power on the part of various popes, and the warlike fanaticism of the Muslims.

6. The admirable way of life on the part of true Christians, who attract us as exemplars of virtue, and the miraculous strength of grace dwelling in them.

7. The fact that the truths revealed by Christianity communicate to us information about things such as our reason could in no way whatsoever reach by itself, and moreover, these truths solve successfully all our questions about the Author of our being; the beginning of the world;

the origin of all creatures, including man; the primitive condition of the latter; the conditions necessary for blessedness; the cause of evils falling upon mankind; the meaning of death; the life hereafter; and the end of all visible things.

Everyone acknowledges as obviously true the theories of Copernicus about the movement of the earth around its axis and around the sun, as well as the theories of Newton about gravity, for on the basis of such theories a multitude of phenomena belonging to the physical, visible world are resolved, even though no one can find out by experience that the earth actually moves around its axis and around the sun, and that the force of gravity is such as Newton described it. Why should not everyone similarly acknowledge as undoubtedly true the truths revealed by Christianity? They absolutely agree with one another and together form such a harmony and such a glorious system of explanation of the spiritual world, on the basis of which all our questions are fully and satisfactorily resolved, so that we no longer fail to understand the nature of this world as relating to the life of the spirit.

When a man becomes convinced that the Christian faith is actually founded on divine revelation, and that the Christian Church is founded by God, he will easily subject himself to this faith, subjugate to it his questioning intelligence, and thus achieve a calmness of spirit beyond the calmness to be achieved by reason alone. Then he will approach with reverence the mysteries offered by the Church as salubrious means of purification from the vileness of sin and means for attaining to the grace-giving gifts of the Holy Spirit. After this he will feel in himself the activity of the Spirit, about which Christ talked to Nicodemus, will understand what it means to be born anew, and how God, Who is Love, appears to mortals and converses with them. He will feel in himself that sweetness of God's love whose semblance we all have felt as children when our mothers caressed us, that joy of the soul which is the foretaste of the blessedness of eternal life and which the Apostle Paul called the acquisition of Christ, and for the sake of which he considered everything that is in the world to be dross. For the sake of preserving this blessedness within themselves, the holy fathers left everything they had in the world and closed themselves up in their desert cells and caves and subjected themselves to deprivations of all kinds. Some of them, as we know, witnessed to their experiences in their written works, in which they expressed the most precious psychological observations concerning souls in which such workings of grace took place. Being conscious of all this, a man will be conscious of truth within himself and will calmly observe all the storms raging around the Church and all the floods of faithlessness that direct themselves against her.

Yet such workings of the Spirit, much as they are desired by us, are brief. Our corrupt nature cannot contain God, and our manifold cares in this world, our contacts with the world, and the distractions connected with such contacts make it difficult for us to concentrate. They displace the gifts of grace from our souls. Aside from this, it must also be pointed out that only simple souls, which are in full command of the treasure of humility, can avail themselves of grace more often and for a longer period of time, while others can use even grace for harm rather than for good. Thus many who have experienced the sweetness of grace became proud in spirit and imagined themselves as saints or prophets inspired from above. They became heretics, ruined themselves, and drew after them to destruction many who rashly believed them. Therefore, let us always remember that we receive the gifts of grace not in accordance with our deserts but because of God's grace, and only because of it; and that even where sin abounds, grace too is abounding, as our Lord has briefly but clearly revealed in His parable about the prodigal son: the father runs to meet his son, embraces and kisses him, and orders the best clothes and footgear to be brought for him, a ring to be put on his finger, a well-fed calf to be slaughtered, and a feast to be prepared. Thus the Lord desires to attract the sinner to Himself by the riches of His love. Therefore, once he has felt the grace of the Holy Spirit, man must subdue himself even more and in the gratitude of his heart reverently fall down and bow to the ground before the all-merciful.

Yet even though such minutes of grace are brief, they are of extraordinary importance for us. They signify the descent of the all-high to us, the lowly, the visit of the King of kings and Lord of lords to worthless slaves, the conversation of Wisdom with those who know nothing, the cares of the heavenly Father Who loves His recalcitrant children. Such is the promise of the truth witnessed within us. We must always keep such blessed minutes in our memory, as the seafarer always keeps his eyes upon the guiding stars. We must always keep confirming ourselves in faith under the tutelage of the Church, as a ship that has cast anchor within a safe harbor saves itself from the storm raging out at sea.

* * *

Standing firmly on the rock of faith, the Christian can easily avoid the wily traps of the enemies of Christ and tear their nets like cobwebs. Their nets are for the most part made of all kinds of arguments directed against Christianity. They say, "The concepts of the unity and of the triple character of God are irreconcilable; how can we believe that God is One yet in Three Persons? It is impossible to visualize anything created from nothing; how then did God create the matter of which the universe consists? Geological findings assure us that the earth took shape during countless years; how can we believe that the world was created in six days? According to Christianity, God is just and good; how can we believe that, just because the first human beings ate a forbidden fruit, God subjected not only them but also all their descendants to such a terrible punishment as sickness and death? Why did the Son of God have to become flesh for the salvation of mankind for this punishment, and why did He have to make a sacrifice of Himself? Could not God have been powerful enough to forgive man without such a sacrifice? We see how man and even whole races of man rise from a low, uncivilized, animal-like condition to civilization and science and gradually reach an ever greater perfection and development. Should it not be natural to assume that man, instead of falling from the heights of perfection into an ignorant and animal-like condition, rather reached his present high development after starting from a beastlike state?"

He who is firm in his faith can calmly reply to all this: because our reason is limited and because an infinite multitude of things still remain unattainable to scientific investigation, I may not understand much, but I know that the truths announced to us by religion are in reality announced by God Himself, Who is Truth. Therefore I firmly believe in their immutability and dare not doubt them, the more so because only on the basis of these truths can both my individual life and the life of society be firmly and reasonably built. Only on the basis of these truths can man reach a serenity of mind and a moral perfection, and in them alone can he find the guiding thread to the solution of all his questions about his own existence. The doubters, on the other hand, have destroyed one after another all the scientific systems produced by them. Many have been the social systems invented by them, yet it has been discovered that none of them led to anything good, misfortunes alone resulted from such systems. It has also been discovered that the preachers of freedom were always the first to become cruel persecutors and oppressors of all who did not agree with their ideas. Captivated by liberation from the burden of laws and governments, they and their supporters have always turned into cruel despots, robbers, arsonists, and slaughterers of other men. You who are full of the contagion of disbelief! You do not believe because you do not know Holy Scripture and the power of God.

* * *

It has been revealed to us that the name of our God is, in human speech, this: Father and Son and the Holy Spirit, Trinity One and indivisible. It has been revealed to us that the Son is eternally born of the Father and is One with Him. The Son is in the Father, and the Father is in the Son. The Son is also called in human speech the eternal Word, the Wisdom of the Father. The Holy Spirit, the Life-Giver, eternally issues from the Father and is sent by the Son. All three are one Love, for, although Each of the three has a separate will, this will is one for all three; although Each has His own Being, They are united into One; although They form One, They are not identical.

We cannot understand this, for this is the mystery of God's being. How could we fathom God, when we cannot even fully penetrate into the essence of matter? To assert that the unity of God's Being and the Trinity of Persons in God are irreconcilable, and on this basis to reject the doctrine of the Trinity, announced by God Himself—this is extreme audacity, even madness! The more so because, if we carefully examine our own soul, created by God according to His image and likeness, we shall note a similarly trifold nature. For the likeness and image of God are reflected in our soul as the image of the sun is reflected in a drop of water.

What is the soul? Do we not understand by the soul a reason capable of comprehending itself—that is, comprehending its own existence and its internal, spiritual, condition; to form concepts of objects surrounding us; to establish connections among these objects and of these objects to us; to draw conclusions about causes and effects; to judge accordingly what is good and what is evil; and to choose the goal of its activity and the means for reaching that goal?

How is it that reason becomes acquainted with the external world? Is it not thought which represents to reason all the objects understood by reason and their relationships, and does not thought accomplish this by means of suitable combinations of words? Does not thought encompass all the realms of the universe and, in accordance with the goal indicated by the mind, choose suitable objects and, having found the means, adapt them to the desired goal? Is it not thought which has created all the works of man, beginning with a simple axe and ending with the most amazing machinery, beginning with the most miserable hut and ending with magnificent palaces and temples, beginning with the simple folk proverbs and ending with wise didactic works, most graceful poems, and penetrating philosophic systems? Thought is, however, the same as word, for when we think, even if we do not speak at the time, we still clothe our thought in words.

Is not thought (or word) born of reason? Is not our reason in our words and our words in our reason? Are not reason and word one? Yet reason may make an estimate of words or of thought. How else should it be that a thought rejected by the reason yet often takes possession of us and we abandon ourselves to it, even though it has been rejected by reason, and even make our reason work in order to accomplish that thought? Is it not hence clear that thought is inseparable from reason, yet not one and the same with it?

Still, we may form in thought the most magnificent plans and have them confirmed by our reason, yet they will always remain in our reason unless we put them into actuality. In order that thought should be realized, a separate faculty is needed, namely, will. Will proceeds from reason: when reason decides to realize thought, will moves all our resources to act in accordance with the bidding of reason. It not only marshals our bodily organs but also directs thought and even reason to activity.

Our will can in no way be separated from our reason. Yet we sometimes have a passionate desire for something which reason condemns, and then we do not listen to reason but act in order to attain what we desire: our will directs our reason and our thought to this end. Consequently, will is not only different from reason but is sufficiently independent of it so as to influence both reason and thought and master them.

Can we now recognize the triple nature of our spirit? And yet our spirit is a unit. Do we not see the revelation contained in the words "Then God said, 'Let Us make man in Our image, according to Our likeness....' So God created man in His own image, in the image of God He created him; male and female He created them" (Gen 1:26–27).

If we reject the Trinity and acknowledge only the Oneness of God, how can we understand that God is Love (1 John 4:8)? To whom could His love be directed before the creation of creatures endowed with reason? And how can the blessedness of God be imagined without love? Someone may say His blessedness consisted of the recognition of His own perfections. But such a self-contained pleasure taken in one's own perfections, without love, cannot form absolute blessedness. A concept of God without love and blessedness will be only a very limited concept of the Highest Being. But if we allow that God is triune, we shall understand that He is love and blessed in love, for "In the beginning was the Word, and the Word was with God, and the Word was God" (John 1:1), and "The Father loves the Son" (John 5:20).

The Second Person of the Holy Trinity is, in human speech, called the Son of God, the Wisdom of God, and the Word of God. No doubt, such names are but approximations suitable to human intelligence and expressed in words which carry human associations. Thus with the word Son we connect the concept of birth, that is, the generation of one person from another of the same kind, and when we say that the Son is born, we mean that He has His eternal beginning from the First Person, the Father, Who is of the same kind as He. With the word Wisdom we connect the concept of thought, ever associated with reason and being one with it; and thus the Second Person, the Son, is always in the Father and One with Him. With the Word we connect the concept of thought as expressed through combinations of sounds and signs, and thus the manifestation of God's wisdom in His creation.

* * *

Thinking that God cannot have created the world through His mere word, and thus rejecting the evidence of Holy Scripture, some philosophers prefer to believe that matter is contemporary with God and that God created the world out of this matter. But it is revealed to us that God alone has eternal Being, while the world is created by His word. He said, let there be light, and light appeared. What does "He said" mean? What if it is not the same as "He ordered"? What does "He ordered" mean? Does it not mean that He established the laws in accordance with which there came about such a combination of phenomena that through them God's wisdom and the laws of spiritual life became clear for creatures of reason?

The human word is feeble, yet even it has some duration and some power. We know from experience how lasting and influential it can be, and we call the products of human speech its creations. But even this speech and its creations need no physical matter on which to work in order to last. So much the less should God's word and His creatures need already existing matter.

Other philosophers imagine that the world is the manifestation of God and that, consequently, the world and God are the same. Thus they establish anew the essence of ancient paganism, which grossly adored the sun and the moon, crocodile and cat, onion and garlic, man and all his passions and vices. For if everything is God or His manifestation, then man, too, is God, and the wickedness and the passions of man are manifestations of divinity!

The limits of madness should seem to lie here, yet there are still other philosophers who completely reject the existence of God and regard the world as a kind of self-created machine, which, in accordance with laws which came about by chance, brings into being all the creatures, and even man, without a goal, unconsciously. They deny the existence in the world and in man of anything spiritual—reason, will, or moral laws.

Thus they acknowledge themselves to be madmen and want to make mad the whole human race as well. How can such people exist? Have these wretches completely lost that high gift by which the all-high Creator has distinguished men from all the other creatures of the earth, and has made them similar to Himself? No! They speak well and even write books in order to prove their insane ideas. Consequently, we must assume that they have the gift of speech—the gift of words—characteristic of only those creatures who have reason. How can we explain this contradiction?

The Prophet David gives us a good explanation when he says, "The fool hath said in his heart, There is no God. They are corrupt, and become abominable in their doings; there is none that doeth good, no not one" (Ps 13:1).

We see that the fool said this not in his reason but in his heart, for the desires of his heart moved him to corruption and abominable works, while the commandments of God forbade him such works and demanded that he do good. When once we give way to sinful desires of our heart and decide to follow them, then our reason too—or, rather, our capacity for thought—is used for the justification of our ways. Since such sinful ways cannot be justified while we believe in God, we then force our capacity for thought, against sound common sense itself, to prove that there is no God. And thus our mind toils for the sake of madness. This is the only possible explanation for the above contradiction. Few words can so fully explain something which can be understood by the untutored yet also satisfy the most demanding intelligence as to the primitive condition of man and the cause of his present condition.

In order to show that man has not been created like other creatures, Moses tells us how God, having completed the creation of the world and its creatures, takes counsel with Himself in the Trinity and says, "Let Us make man in our image, after Our likeness; and let them have dominion over the fish of the sea, and over the fowl of the air, and over the cattle, and over all the earth, and over every creeping thing that creepeth upon the earth." Then Moses goes on to say: "The Lord God formed man of the dust of the ground, and breathed into his nostrils the breath of life; and man became a living being. The Lord God planted a garden eastward in Eden, and there He put the man whom He had formed. And out of the ground the Lord God made every tree grow that is pleasant to the sight and good for food. The tree of life was also in the midst of the garden, and the tree of knowledge of good and evil.... Then the Lord God took the man and put him in the garden of Eden to tend and to keep it. And the Lord God commanded the man, saying, 'Of every tree of the garden you may freely eat; but of the tree of the knowledge of good and evil you shall not eat, for in the day that you eat of it you shall surely die.' And the Lord God said, 'It is not good that man should be alone; I will make him a helper comparable to him.' Out of the ground the Lord God formed every beast of the field and every bird of the air, and brought them to Adam to see what he would call them. And whatever Adam called each living creature, that was its name. So Adam gave names to all cattle, to the birds of the air, and to every beast of the field. But for Adam there was not found a helper comparable to him. And the Lord God caused a deep sleep to fall on Adam, and he slept; and He took one of his ribs, and closed up the flesh in its place. Then the rib which the Lord God had taken from man He made into a woman, and He brought her to the man. And Adam said, 'This is now bone of my bones, and flesh of my flesh; she shall be called Woman, because she was taken out of Man'.... Then God blessed them, and God said to them, 'Be fruitful and multiply; fill the earth and subdue it; have dominion over the fish of the sea, over the birds of the air, and over every living thing that moves on the earth.... And they were both naked, the man and his wife, and were not ashamed" (Gen 2:7–9, 2:15–23, 1:28, 2:25).

From this narrative we see that the human body was formed by God with special care, if we may say so, directly from the earth, rather than from some other already living creature, and was endowed with a divine soul—reasoning, intelligent, free; that his wife and all the rest of mankind had their origin in the body of the first man; that man immediately at his creation became the possessor of a natural capacity for being a thinking creature, to such an extent that he was able to give names to all the other creatures; that man not only found the place of his abode full of things necessary for a pleasant life lacking in nothing, but also became the lord of all the living creatures and the possessor of the earth, and consequently was in no danger of being attacked by wild beasts; that the climate of his abode was such that the earth, without any effort on man's part, produced everything in abundance; that the first man and his wife had no need of clothes, for they were innocent like small children and therefore were not ashamed of being naked; that God's grace was with them and blessed them; and that no passion disturbed their hearts, while pure conjugal love united them and crowned their blessedness.

Man was, however, inexperienced, and because of his lack of experience or because of carelessness could have harmed his physical body. Therefore the all-good and wise Creator prepared for man in the place of his abode a tree of life, whose fruits had the medicinal property of completely renewing man's health and thus making him immortal. And since idleness and lassitude could have impaired man's bodily and spiritual powers, God gave him the obligation of caring for his abode, the garden of Eden.

Thus the first human beings were blessed. But they could continue blessed only while God's grace was with them, and this grace could remain with them only while man endured in his love for and obedience to God. To test his obedience, God established the commandment not to eat the fruit of the tree of knowledge of good and evil, with the warning that in the day when man would abandon his obedience to the Creator and eat the forbidden fruit, he would recognize the good of which he would become deprived and the evil which he would acquire. Grace would be taken away from him and he would lose life and die. Thus we discover that the Creator had done for man everything that could be expected of His power, wisdom, and goodness. We see also that God appeared to the first human beings, announced Himself as their Creator and the Creator of the whole world, the Lord of all, the giver of all that is good, the teacher and merciful guide of men, ready to come at their first call and converse with them again and teach them.

* * *

All this should have been quite sufficient to inspire man with gratitude to God and love for Him as his benefactor, and recognition of his duty to subject himself to God as his Lord and to learn to recognize Him. Did the heart of man actually develop gratitude to God, did man actually love his benefactor, did he subjugate his spirit to Him, and did he try to recognize Him? This is a mystery to us, for Moses is silent on this subject. We know, however, that, in order to reveal the justice of His judgments and thus to edify mankind, God allows at times temptations and dangers to beset men and reveal the thoughts of their hearts and the things hidden in their souls. We see in Moses' narrative that a tempter penetrated into the paradisal dwelling of the first human beings.

Moses does not tell us how long the first human beings spent in Paradise before the temptation, but our concept of God's justice does not allow us to think that the temptation took place very soon after the creation, before they had an opportunity to confirm themselves in the blessed direction of their thoughts, wishes, and leanings. We may think that, perhaps, the time spent in Paradise before the temptation may have lasted as long as the time of life of the second Adam, Jesus the Son of the Virgin Mary, from His birth to the time when He was tempted by the devil, that is, approximately thirty years.

The tempter appeared in the shape of a serpent. Moses' narrative concerning this event is brief: "Now the serpent was more cunning than any beast of the field which the Lord God had made. And he said to the woman, 'Has God indeed said, "You shall not eat of every tree of the garden"?' And the woman said to the serpent, 'We may eat of the fruit of the trees of the garden; but of the fruit of the tree which is in the midst of the garden, God has said, "You shall not eat it, nor shall you touch it, lest you die."' Then the serpent said to the woman, 'You will not surely die. For God knows that in the day you eat of it your eyes will be opened, and you will be like God, knowing good and evil.' So when the woman saw that the tree was good for food, and that it was pleasant to the eyes, and a tree desirable to make one wise, she took of its fruit and ate. She also gave to her husband with her, and he ate. Then the eyes of them both were opened, and they knew that they were naked; and they sewed fig leaves together and made themselves coverings. And they heard the sound of the Lord God walking in the garden in the cool of the day, and Adam and his wife hid themselves from the presence of the Lord God among the trees of the garden" (Gen 3:1–8).

Thus sinned our first parents, and for this sin were they deprived of God's grace. Such a deprivation, in itself death, followed the same day when the first parents tasted the forbidden fruit, in strict accordance with God's word. What remained to them was a wretched, tortured existence. With the help of the tree of life, this existence could have been infinitely prolonged, but God's justice found attenuating circumstances for the guilt of the transgressors, and His wisdom found means for restoring those who fell: not only to return them to their former blessed condition but also to reveal at the same time the whole infinitude of His goodness and love. The access to the tree of life was barred, and man was destined to return to the earth from which he had been taken. He was to be mindful of the death of the body in order not to forget the death of the spirit as well. Recognizing himself to be a stranger and a wanderer on earth, he was to be in such a state of mind as not to attach his love to the goods of this earth. He was to subject himself to his Creator and to accept from His hands in all humility the bitter fruit of recognition of good and evil. His life was to be crowned by his humble obedience to the divine will. The remains of his body, harmed by sin, were with time to bring forth a new, spiritual body, as a seed brings forth a plant.

* * *

Clearly, the narrative of Moses and the other prophets have divine truth as their source, for they are simple and clear and can be understood even by children and uneducated adults. The all-too-clever reasoning of the so-called wise, however, issues from the darkness of false hell and is full of dark, obscure words devoid of sense, for their authors wander in darkness.

Divine revelation tells us that man is the immediate creation of the highest and most wise Being, God, and that man appeared on earth with a body perfectly suited to him and a soul endowed with reason, thought, and freedom. Only later, because of his attachment to earthly pleasures, his loss of faith, and dedication to his passions, did he come to resemble the senseless beasts. Yet the so-called wise men regard this revelation as nonsensical. They call it nonrational and strain their minds in order to prove that primitive man was a beastlike animal, like an ape, and only in the course of thousands of years did he gradually perfect himself and gradually, thanks to his own efforts, reach his present bodily and mental condition. Many lengthy books have been written on this subject by men very well known for their learning, while other learned men criticize the former and proceed to prove that their works are obscure and illogical, and that the change from a beastlike animal to man can be neither proven nor explained. And we need pay but a little attention to what is happening before our eyes in order to see for ourselves how a man who has lost faith in God assumes a beastlike condition.

What is the difference between a beast and man? Is it not that a beast has no concept of God, of beauty, of sublimity, of moral duty, of property, and of marriage? Is it not that a beast's entire life is contained in its earthly existence, his only good is the satisfaction of his hunger, and his whole activity consists of search for food? Is it not that a beast has no intelligence, is greedy, and lacks mercy? Is it not that a beast obeys only the needs indicated by its senses or its fear of pain?

All these beastlike qualities can easily be seen in those men who have been corrupted by faithlessness, and especially in many revolutionaries and Communists, nihilists, and anarchists. Thus nihilists took pride in declaring that the concept of God cannot be reconciled with their reason, and that they saw no beauty and no usefulness in the phenomena of nature or in the creations of poetry, sculpture, architecture, painting, and music, or even in the self-sacrifice of which virtue is capable. All such things, they said, are worth nothing. Only that which serves the satisfaction of bodily needs has meaning. They recognized neither the immortality of the soul, nor the freedom of the will, nor moral duty, nor the existence of anything spiritual. Owning property they regarded to be a form of stealing, marriage the invention of barbarity, and government and laws the inventions of the powerful and rich for the oppression of the weak and poor. The madness of the French revolutionaries went so far that they declared human intelligence to be a divinity, put up idols to it, honored it by festivities and special religious rites. They declared that man's existence stops after death and he turns into nothing, and that man's whole happiness consists of the satisfaction of his senses. These detractors of law and government and preachers of universal equality tried themselves to get into power by force and treachery. When they succeeded, as cruel as bloodthirsty animals they destroyed and tore apart all those who seemed to be dangerous to them or of a different mind from them.

When a godless man comes from an ignorant class of people, he is like a beast even in his external appearance: he is uncouth, morose, wild, crass, and bloodthirsty. If he belongs to the educated classes, his external appearance may have little resemblance to a beast, he may be neat, well dressed, polite, and well spoken. Yet he resembles a different kind of animal: the serpent that deceived Eve.

We know how snakes on a warm sunny day like to come out of their holes to a place where the sun shines especially warmly. There they lie enjoying the warmth and letting their poison ripen in their glands. When they see a man approaching, they spring at him, bite him, and let their poison flow into his wound.

The preachers of godlessness also love the light of learning. They study and enrich themselves with knowledge, but seem to absorb together with it also whatever godless thoughts anyone happened to have uttered, along with all the skepticism and doubts that they can find. They develop a predilection for such doubts, regard it their problem to support them and to reject the truths of religion. Thus prejudiced, they take note of every fact that, in their opinion, could possibly serve their purposes and reject with mockery everything that seems to contradict their prejudice. The desire to express themselves well, to let their wit and their knowledge shine, to shock by expressing extreme opinions, to carry away their listeners with their oratorical skill, to gain the reputation of men learned and intelligent, and to acquire more and more admirers and followers—all these desires take possession of them. Every success only increases their self-reliance and pride, and they devote their entire life to spreading their teachings—in other words, contaminating the greatest number possible with their poison.

Like snakes they shine with the brilliance of good education; like snakes they crawl on the ground, attached to their senses and rejecting everything spiritual; like the godless serpent they reject the basic beginnings of all knowledge, namely, faith in God and in the hereafter, and want to reach the heights of knowledge by their intelligence alone and to explain that only from physical matter did the world, and life, and even all the manifestations of the soul arise. Like the serpent they quietly, imperceptibly, treacherously approach us and pour into our ears the poison of their teachings. By means of serpent-like cleverness of speech they either skillfully circumvent those topics which would expose them as liars, or darken our reason by a senseless combination of terms invented by them, as if they were actually saying something wise. On other occasions they pounce on some small detail of Christian teaching, usually as insignificant in itself as a dry twig on a large tree, and display their skill in rhetoric by expressing witty guesses and intentional falsehoods, and intentionally misconstruing the meaning of the words and the sense of Holy Scripture, as well as falsifying actual historical events. They represent everything only in a sense suitable to their message. Where, however, it is impossible to do anything like this, they jump over the subject uncomfortable for them and either keep completely silent about it or say that it is insignificant and does not deserve being talked about. If even this is not possible, they approach such an impediment in the guise of friends, and begin to praise it and, as it were, to embrace it with love, but actually they are twining themselves around their victim like a boa constrictor, with the sole purpose of crushing and swallowing it.

* * *

Oh you deceivers, indeed are you the "most subtle" of beasts, the sons of that tempter who destroyed the first human beings! Through you the ancient dragon gave vent to a whole river of poisonous waters in order to destroy Christ's Church, that marvelous woman of Revelation, crowned with a crown of twelve stars and established with her feet on the moon, who fled into the desert with her newborn infant. Yet she is surrounded with the four gospels as with a wall. You cannot go around this wall and cannot jump over it. Therefore you have approached it like friends and have opened wide your arms as for an embrace. With the works of Strauss, Renan, and their like, you have grasped the wall, have surrounded it like a giant boa, and already are thinking and even boasting that you have destroyed the wall, and that now it only remains to take the Church and cast her into the open jaws of your father the devil.

But you are mistaken. The wall of the Gospel stands unharmed, and the Church is safe behind it. Your waters have drowned only the rash who went too far from the wall, while men of sound sense are unafraid of you:

as they have done in the past, so now too they remain safe behind the wall. Let true scientists reveal your falsehoods and disentangle your rhetoric, tear the nets that you have set up to catch those who easily believe everything they are told, and throw on your heads that mud with which you wanted to besmirch the Man-God and His friends. We need nothing except sound sense in order to understand the miserable madness of your deviousness. You assert that the Gospels were not written by the apostles, eyewitnesses of the deeds of the incarnate Son, but were put together several centuries later on the basis of various legends and fables that had taken shape among the masses of the people. If so, tell us who did this, when, and where? You have dug up the ruins of the Egyptian Thebes, of Nineveh, and Babylon; have discovered the way of reading Egyptian hieroglyphics and Semitic cuneiform; have collected the monuments of ancient life in Egypt, Babylon, Assyria, Phoenicia, Greece, and Rome; have studied in great detail all the surviving creations of their literature and art; and have penetrated the greatest secrets of their life. How is it that you have found no answer to our question?

How is it that none of the countless number of the enemies of Christianity, among whom there have been all kinds of convictions, all kinds of education and geographic and historical background, none has so far been able to discover this answer, even though consistently during more than nineteen centuries, all these men have been applying all their efforts to destroy the Church?

Tell us how it could be that the four Gospels, put together, as you say, by unknown authors several centuries after Christ on the basis of various local tales, did turn up under definite titles—the Gospel according to St Matthew, for instance—in all the Churches founded by the apostles, even though some of these churches were separated from one another by seas and deserts and barbaric nations? The churches in Libya, Scythia, Persia, Spain, and everywhere honored these as the holiest books of all, believing them to express incontrovertible truth and be in complete agreement with the tradition of apostolic preaching.

Tell us also how, if the Gospels were of human origin, it could be that the bishops gathered from all the parts of the civilized world unanimously acknowledged only these four Gospels as being of apostolic authorship, while they rejected all the others, which were indeed of local authorship, such as the Gospels of Nicodemus, James, Thomas, and so on. Although you may be skilled in casting a shadow upon truth in various other situations, you can counter nothing to this argument.

For a man of sound sense, the most important proof of the divinely inspired origin of the Gospels and their authorship by actual eyewitnesses of the Lord become flesh is this: each of the Gospels does full justice to the matter of which it treats, that is, the life, teachings, divine nature, and life-giving death of Jesus Christ. The spirit behind all the gospels is alike. They all are clear, simple, and elevated, and agree with one another. When one of them omits some detail of our Lord's teachings, another Gospel completes the account. If we take various parts of various Gospels, we shall discover that they do not contradict one another but complete one another in such a way that the combination is even more precisely and lively than each of the four taken by themselves.

Thus the four Gospels appear to us as a marvelously harmonious song of the four cherubim supporting the glory of the omnipotent in the Person of the God-Man. In this song we hear now one voice, then another, then three together, then four at once, all of them praising the triune God. Their song resounds in all the parts of the universe. One of the French freethinkers of the eighteenth century, having decided to write a confutation of the Gospels, was astounded in the process of his task and remarked that no human wisdom could possibly put together such a book, even if the thought to invent something resembling the four Gospels had come to a man. One of the greatest modern skeptics, Lord Byron, as was discovered after his death, had written on the flyleaf of his Bible that the mystery of mysteries was contained in this majestic book. Happy, said he, were the mortals given by God the grace to read, understand, revere, and utter in prayer the words of this book! Happy were those who attempted to open the door and enter upon the path! But Byron said, it was better that those who read only in order to doubt and despise should not have been born.

* * *

To the faithless question "Why should the Son of God have become flesh for the salvation of mankind and have sacrificed Himself?" we can answer that love always expresses itself in sacrifices. When I love someone, I give him gifts, thus sacrificing a part of my property; or provide him with some comfort, possibly denying myself, consequently sacrificing my own comfort; or help him in need or in sickness, consequently sacrifice my work or my leisure; or else I may defend him and save his life, incurring danger for myself, and perhaps even sacrifice my life. Sacrifice is always an expression of love. Therefore the sacrifice on the cross took place in all the greatness of God's justice, so that His love for man should appear in all its power and attract to

Him the love of man, captivated as this love was by the senses and the goods of this earth.

* * *

Those who completely reject revelation and miracles say, "God has given man intelligence, and that should be sufficient for man. By his own intelligence he should and can discover everything. There is no need for revelation. God has established the laws in accordance with which everything in the world takes place, and His laws are subject to no change. Hence, no miracles."

But they forget that the experience of thousands of years has revealed the weakness of human intelligence, which easily falls into error, and that, aside from the natural laws, in accordance with which everything in nature happens, there are also the laws of God's truth, which hold true in the moral and spiritual realm. The laws of God's truth are superior to the laws of nature, and thus the latter can and must adjust to the demands of the former.

Would it be consistent with God's truth to leave men involved in the errors of their intelligence and incapable of reaching the goal for which they have been created? In order to reach this goal, men must have a correct concept of their Creator, but they went so far as to adore the forces of nature instead. The law of God's truth demanded that men be shown how God is above the laws of nature and how the laws of nature are themselves the products of His wisdom. Therefore, in God's name, were the waters of the sea separated, rocks produced water, the sky rained manna, a wind brought to the Israelites a flock of birds, Jordan turned back, and fire did them no harm. Because of His inexpressible love for mankind, the Son of God came down to earth in the guise of an ordinary man and revealed to men the path of salvation. God's truth demanded men should clearly see that it was none but the Son of God Who had come into their midst. Consequently, in accordance with His grace, water turned into wine, a small quantity of bread and fish satisfied the hunger of thousands of people, the waves of a lake became firm under His feet, a storm grew quiet at His words, many hopelessly ill people grew healthy, the dead revived, and finally He Himself rose from the dead.

Only if miracles contradicted God's truth, would it be possible to reject them. A rejection of miracles is also a rejection of the Creator, for it makes Him subject to the laws of nature, which after all were created by none but Him, and powerless to direct them in accordance with the higher purposes of His truth. In such a case, why should one pray to the Creator? But everyone who pays attention to his inner state knows that, when misfortunes gather all around us, an instinct moves us to call out to our Creator, and our prayers do not remain unanswered, as can be seen from the history of the Church and the experience of pious people.

* * *

Now let us pay some attention to the history of the Church on Russian soil. We cannot help seeing a particular instance of divine providence in the fact that the Slavs turned to Christ, and the Russian nation formed, precisely at the time when the Roman popes began to give clear indications of their lust for power and to demand that the Eastern churches be subject to them. Thus began their discord with the Eastern patriarchs, and together with it the separation of the Western churches from the Eastern Orthodox Church. As this discord grew and developed, Christianity took root more and more firmly among the Slavs, and the Orthodox Church grew ever stronger. There she found a good soil. Removing her torch from the West, she for a while concealed herself with her infant in this desert from the anger of the dragon, but later she shone forth in all her glory (cf. Rev 12:6).

The conversion of the Russians to Christianity is an extraordinary event. Their Prince Vladimir, being a man of keen intelligence, recognized the falsehood inherent in paganism and the vanity of worldly joys. He searched for the true faith and investigated the religions of the surrounding nations with the help of men chosen by him for their sense. He recognized the faith confessed by the Greeks as the true one and received baptism from their priests. All along, however, he acted in such a way as to be completely independent in his faith from any human influence and not let religion impede the political development of his country. The people subject to him did not refuse to follow the example of their wise prince: they destroyed pagan holy places, did away with idols, followed the decrees of the Church, developed a keen love for her, and, although later hard pressed by, on the one side, Muslims, and on the other, Papists, humbly endured for a destined time the will of providence as a punishment for their sins. All the time the people remained true to Orthodoxy, despite the false but clever blandishments of their enemies and the cruel persecution which followed upon such faithfulness.

Divine providence revealed itself in the fact that at the same time as Constantinople fell under the sword of Islam, and thus the only still independent Orthodox state, namely, the Eastern Roman (or the Byzantine) Empire, ceased existing, the Russian people, who theretofore had been split into small principalities and subjected to the Tartars, became united into a vast, mighty state under the power of the princes of Moscow, then grew into a kingdom, and finally into a great empire. The enemies of this empire were scattered like chaff before the wind; the sciences and the arts, which meanwhile had once more sprung up in the West, took root in Russia also.

Awesome conquerors, to whom other nations had bowed, broke before the might of this new empire, and the Russian emperors became the liberators of the enslaved and oppressed nations, the protectors and hope of all Orthodox Christians, and a terror for those who oppressed them. The glory of Russia resounded throughout the world. At the same time, the true Christian Church, until then concealed from her enemies as in a desert and despised by the rich and the wise of this world because of her poverty and external simplicity, began to reveal herself to the world, clothe herself in the external magnificence suitable to her, and more and more brightly spread everywhere the brilliance of the light of truth inherent in her. Even now after the fall of the Russian empire, Russian Orthodox churches are being built in all parts of the world, and those who hunger and thirst for the truth find in them satisfaction for their needs. Even among the nations which heretofore shunned or despised her does she now find diligent followers.

* * *

The struggle of hell against the Christian Church has not ended. Even though in the process of this struggle the lord of hell, the red dragon, has been able to sweep down from heaven the third part of its stars and has opened his jaws wide to swallow the woman clothed in the sun and crowned with twelve stars—but she has concealed herself in the desert, will remain unharmed, and will appear in all her heavenly beauty and divine majesty.

"So the serpent spewed water out of his mouth water like a flood after the woman, that he might cause her to be carried away of the flood" (Rev 12:15). What flood is this? Is it not godlessness and skepticism, self-will and disbelief, spread by destructive teachers, followers of hell, who carry red banners in their hands, and indeed, have come into the lands of Orthodoxy from the West like a flood? Yet another prophecy of St John must still be fulfilled, namely, "The earth helped the woman, and the earth opened its mouth and swallowed up the flood which the dragon had spewed out of his mouth" (Rev 12:16).

* * *

We possess a treasure more precious than any of the goods of this earth taken all together, namely, the Christian Church, founded by God Himself on earth for the enlightenment of mankind sunk into the depths of ignorance and sin. By the light of her truth, the Church sets man up again as a moral being. We are in possession of a model of heavenly origin according to which all human societies and governments ought to be organized, for then they, too, would reach moral perfection. How beautiful, how good, how very wise is our mother Church! Let us love, honor, and obey her.

* * *

The entire visible world always and everywhere ceaselessly announces to us that there is an all-wise and all-good Creator. It tells us about the foundations and the laws of a real, blessed life, and about love, which unites and supports all. Our sound common sense tells each of us clearly and irrefutably that it is our undeniable duty to love our Creator and obey Him, and that such love and obedience are the basis of a life really blessed. The experience of thousands of years testifies that there is no other path to blessedness, and that the violation of the holy laws of love destroys the foundations of life itself and contaminates our very nature. The Creator Himself has pronounced these laws and indicated this path in our human words spoken and exemplified by men inspired by Him, and especially by His only Son become flesh. The Church founded by Him continues ceaselessly to speak of the path of love.

Since men violated the laws of life by disobeying their Creator and removing themselves from Him, they contaminated their own nature and subjected themselves to the just condemnation of divine justice. The Creator Himself in His goodness and wisdom found means to save the human race from eternal destruction and indicated a new way of changing the judgment of divine truth into mercy which accords with that very truth. God's love found a way to pour itself out upon us in the form of rich benefits: men were not only raised again into their first, lost state but also became brothers in flesh of the only Son of God. Mankind has been given the opportunity of becoming one with His love, as the branches of a vine are one with the vine. We all have become the children of God.

The way to achieve this condition is simple and easily available to each of us. All that is necessary is to love Him Who has loved us to the end—the most sweet Jesus. If we do this, we shall call to life within us the seed of real life, the love of God, Who through Jesus has revealed the whole greatness of His love for us. Once we have recognized our spiritually destitute, fallen condition, we can find our justification in the merits of Jesus Himself, Who has been established by God as His first priest. He will suffer with us, ignorant and erring as we are, for He has already offered Himself as a sacrifice of reconciliation, has taken His seat on the right hand of the throne of glory in the heavens, and remains there forever. We must only feel a sincere repentance for our sins, sincerely desire a life in accordance with God's will, have a holy love for Jesus, Who is rich in love, turn to Him with a firm faith in His sacrifice of atonement, and trustingly turn to the Holy Mysteries and the guidance of the Church. Our sins will be removed, our conscience liberated from its torments, our soul will receive peace from above, our thoughts will become clear, and our strength for good works will increase. The sign of God's love, spiritual joy, will gladden our hearts. In brief, the unction of the Holy Spirit will come and His grace-giving gifts will descend upon us, and we shall become participants in the kingdom of God.

Everything is ready for the wedding feast of the King's Son: the well-fed calf has been slaughtered, the halls are decorated and illuminated, the paths leading to them are smoothed, there are guides set up at all the crossroads, and the Master of the house is calling and waiting for us all.

Yet men do not hasten to the call. Some are immersed in ignorance, superstition, prejudice, cares, vanity, passions, and earthly attachments, so that only with difficulty can they hear the voice of those who announce the truth, and barely see the paths leading to the truth. They are full of indolence, and their minds have become so inactive that they are unwilling even to lift their hands in order to sweep away the cobwebs that have closed their ears and eyes. Others' ears hear well and their eyes see, but some false prophet or one of the so-called fathers and teachers closes their eyes for them and forbids them to hear and to see. They stop their own ears so as not to hear and close their own eyes so as not to see, and when by some chance they see or hear after all, they use all their efforts so as not to understand what they have seen or heard. Some others hear and see and understand, but they are sorry to leave their sinful attachments or to give up their profitable business, and they say that there still is time and that they will repent at some future time. Still others hear and see but are puffed up with their knowledge and proud of their intelligence and therefore despise God's messengers and guides, who seem to them to be too simple and ignorant. They say that their paths are built according to the guidelines of science and that their own knowledge is better than that of these guides. Still others have become so proud that they regard the truths of religion as fables unworthy of the attention of educated men. Their easily influenced followers think that it must be very important to seem educated and consequently are ashamed of not only paying attention to these truths but even of hearing someone speak of them.

Thus some do not hear the call to the wedding feast because they refuse to cleanse their eyes and ears from the accumulated dirt of ignorance; others do not dare to listen because they trust the word of liars more than their own intelligence; others hear but hesitate to go because they prefer the temporal and the secular to that which is eternal and true; others, instead of hastening along, spend precious time continuing along their own path, for they consider themselves above God's messengers; and still others completely refuse the call because they think themselves to be gods. The doors of the hall are being closed now to some of them, and then again to others, and a multitude of those called remain outside in the empty darkness, where there is weeping and gnashing of teeth, where the worm dies not and the fire burns everlastingly. A pity! A multitude of intelligent beings, created for blessedness, of their own will refuse it and choose instead destruction and eternal torments! What foolishness, what senselessness!

From Yakov Tyagunoff, *A Christian View of the World and Man*, in Russian, St Petersburg, 1876.

A Prayer for Mercy

MEDITATION ON THE OMNIPRESENT WISDOM OF GOD
GLORY TO GOD!

Great God, merciful Creator, everlasting light! Enlighten the spirit created by You to know You, the spirit that searches in Thee for its enlightenment and blessedness. Dispel the darkness that surrounds me and conceals Thee from me, Thou Who art everywhere. My God! Send down into my soul one beam only of Thy light, so that a recognition of Thy mysterious ways may bring me near the goal of my journey. For what is the spirit of mortal man when he, apart from Thy light, wanders in the shadow of death (Isa 9:2)?

Such a spirit searches for true being but embraces only a shadow; it holds on to the thoughts of its reason but cannot come to the summit even of earthly wisdom. O hidden God, Whom all creatures seek! How far above all our concepts Thou art, how far above all our feelings! From Thee only the rays of the great light of Truth pour onto all the creatures of earth and heaven! O sun of eternity! Enlighten our pristine darkness and change it into a blessed radiance, so that we may recognize Thy Being. And for this small favor, O God, let Thy name be praised forever! Without it, all Thy ways would be unrecognizable for us. We are indebted to it for our weak comprehension of Thy glory. It confirms our feeble eyes raised to Thee, lights up our path so that we may reach a concept of Thy perfection, brings to life in us a hope of pure enlightenment in the future and a comforting feeling that at some far removed yet definite time we shall see clearly.

O holy, holiest of all, omnipresent and full of mystery! Fill my spirit with that never-perishing wisdom which in the recesses of Thy eternity and in the most removed depths of Thy divinity always finds Thee. Thou art the beginning and the crown of all beings! In vain does the thinker, deceived by his imaginings, seek in Thy creation anything not directed by a benign Will, any miracles without omnipotence, any omnipotence without Wisdom. In vain does he search in the chaos for a chance which could have brought into being worlds of so great a harmony. In vain does he attempt not to acknowledge Thee Who art in heaven, Who art confessed by all the beings, givest life to the least worm and inspires to immorality even him who denies Thee (Wis 13). Autonomous God! Forgive Thy weak servant his pride, which stems from his senses, darkens his reason, prevents light from entering his soul, and raises the teachings of madness to the status of wisdom. Forgive the blind self-assurance which rushes across false and shaking bridges toward wisdom and in the meanwhile destroys the Truth: such a self-assurance is content with the creatures, while it forgets Thee, the Creator of it and of everything else.

What thanksgiving can I offer Thee, O my God? I live because of Thee, for Thou hast formed my soul to recognize Thee. To Thee alone I am indebted for the never-dying light which illumines my path far into eternity. I slept in the eternal night until Thou wakened me to recognize myself and to live forever. Without Thee, O eternal Being, I would have remained eternally confined in my nothingness. Thou gavest me a destiny in Thy universe, Thou didst call me to the state of enlightenment in which I now bow before Thee. Thou Who fillest all, fillest me also with certainty about Thy Being and Thy influence on my changeable existence. O King of all the worlds, all the spirits, and the whole universe! How late have I come to recognize Thee! How late have I begun to enjoy this heavenly light which I find in Thy creation! My nothingness endured for many years without learning how to recognize Thee, adore Thee, and entrust myself to Thee. My existence, my life, all the powers of my being, and my joy in Thy presence—all these are gifts of Thy mercy. Eternal God! The sun takes its light from Thee; the planets exist because of Thee. What is the origin of this sun which sheds its light over me and warms me? Whence if not from Thee, its Creator? Who set on fire these stars which glisten over me in the quiet of midnight and scatter their rays throughout the blue immeasurable expanse? Who supports this moving sphere of the earth, which unchangeably turns around its sun? Autonomous Being! Thou alone supportest the earth with all its creatures; Thou biddest the earth to flow freely and unobstructed in her course, to change according to season and according to weather, and to produce the most varied fruit for the sustenance of the creatures (Gen 1).

Indeed, Thou art the Lord of powers! Thou hast existed forever! Thou art the Lord of Thy creation and wilt always remain the beginning, life, and blessedness of Thy creatures. To me, too, O omnipotence, Thou hast shown a path in this world filled with Thy wonders. Thou hast created me from the dust of the ground (Gen 2:7), having ordered the perishable matter to combine with thoughts of Thee and to be filled with recognition of Thy divinity. Receive my thanksgiving! Receive the words of a worm whose feelings are too weak to express Thy goodness and too limited to express Thy immeasurable Being. Without the gift of life my eyes would see neither the sun nor the glistening stars, which preach of Thee, nor Thy world, filled with order and wisdom. The ravishing songs of the nightingale, the enchanting fragrance of the rose, the bracing odor of the carnation, the delicate spring air, the majestic voice of the thunder—all these wonders of Thy creation would be eternally hidden from me. While millions of beings created by Thy hand would continue recognizing Thee and adoring Thee, I alone would remain speechless and senseless and would not praise Thee; my uncreated nothingness would be unable to bow before Thee. Who am I? What was I before Thou hast created me? Where did I lie hidden before Thou didst call me into being? In Thy autonomous and omnipotent power lies the very basis of my ability to exist (Isa 41:24). From Thee, never-failing source, I flowed into this visible world of innumerable beings; I became a creature in order to recognize Thee, my Creator, and my dependence on Thee. Thou hast created my soul capable of thought and feeling and raised it above innumerable orders of lower beings whom Thy wisdom destined for lower purposes. To thought and feeling, the two essential characteristics of the human soul, Thou hast joined an impression of Thy beauty, a sense for Thy order, a tendency to virtue, a love for all that is heavenly and divine. This created image of Thy uncreated perfection Thou hast clothed in the loveliness perceived by the senses, and Thou hast created us free. Mysterious God, how many purposes do we discover in Thy actions! Even the struggle of the spirit against sensuality has a purpose.

What meaning would there be in virtue if we were attracted to it by our whole being and found no impediments in our desire to be virtuous? Would the freedom of our spirit have any meaning if we were created such that we would be unable to change the existing order? How would we find the blessings of truth and virtue if the pain of our hidden, innermost wounds did not impel us frequently to search for the healing balsam contained in truth and in virtue, for they alone can heal us? How would we find the rule of wisdom if we ourselves did not poison the joys of life whenever we stepped beyond the measure of enjoyment? God, properly worshipped for Thy benefits to Thy creatures! Properly worshipped despite the apparent existence of evil, which exists in accordance with Thy unfathomable will! Thy wisdom has set limits to our natural powers of intelligence, and we are kept on the level appointed to us. The natural weakness of man's intelligence has made all the greater the beneficial illumination of Thy revelations; weakness has multiplied our marvelous abilities for rebirth. O triune, unintelligible God! Confirm my soul in faith and enable it to adore Thy decrees in reverent silence. Teach me how to tremble with awe while I am thinking of the mystery of our rebirth.

Thou hast created the first human beings pure and blameless. Destined to immortality, the first man received from Thee all that could help him please Thee. Thou hast enriched his spirit with understanding and freedom, filled his heart with aspiration for perfection, and thus enabled his heart to hear and recognize the masterful voice of truth. These Thy gifts were to guide him in his actions and help him reach the goal of his desires: beatitude. He, however, fell deeply when, blinded with the superficial glitter of sensuality, he left Thy law (Gen 3:12)! Insidious flattery killed his reason, led him into a labyrinth of wild instincts, and brought destruction upon him and all his descendants (Gen 3). Thus fell he who desired to rise above himself, rose against Thy law, and let his insane curiosity darken Thy bright image in his heart. Woe to the first man, whose proud reason became the victim of error! He ceased pleasing the eyes of his Creator; torment and sorrow flamed up in his heart, initially created for the most tender emotions. He became conscious of the harm which he had inflicted upon himself, and this poison spread and brought pollution upon all his yet unborn descendants. O eternal one, Whose breath is life! Great and most glorious are the works of Thy omnipotence, but even more glorious are the wonders of Thy mercy! Because Thou are good, Thou didst not destroy the worm who dared to disrupt Thy order; in Thy right hand was the flame to burn him up; in Thy hand was lightning to strike him down, and abysses to swallow him. But Thou hast spared the sinner who transgressed Thy beneficial law; Thou art merciful to the helpless creature that harmed himself; Thou didst keep the madman on the edge of the abyss.

Thou Whose eternal eye embraces millions of worlds! Thou hast foreseen everything before it actually happened, and hast allowed it to be. O limitless Being, forgive human weakness, which measures Thee by a created measure and desires to comprehend Thy destinies! In vain are our dim eyes lifted to Thee Who art covered with darkness, as in a secret place (Ps 18:11). Thy appointed decrees are always holy, but no mere mortal will comprehend Thy ways. Thy avenging truth is also a witness to Thy goodness. The first man did not recognize the price of freedom but used Thy goodness for evil; yet in accordance with Thy wisdom, the punishment of our forefather became a salutary lesson for us, his descendants. We all suffer because of his mistake, but we remember that punishment follows inevitably upon the misuse of freedom. With the loss of our first innocence we lost also a part of that perfection to which we were destined in our condition of bliss. But Thou didst not leave us: Thou didst give us enough strength to rise to Thee, holiest of holy, even amidst evil. We are still able to purify our polluted souls with the heavenly flame of grace and to form them in Thy semblance.

Before Thou didst establish the foundations of the earth, before Thou didst set the sun on fire, before the beginning of ages, Thy omnipotence gave birth to the Lawgiver of Gentiles, the Redeemer of the sons of Adam. Adam's children were inclined to sin and did not turn away from it after the destructive deluge sent upon them by Thee; yet even after the deluge, men always remained an object of Thy mercy: Thou hast kept sending to them Thy prophets, whose duty it was to reveal to mankind its blessed future and to announce the coming of the Messiah. Those who walked in Thy light continued humbly and hopefully waiting for the fulfillment of Thy promises, while the pagans tested the reliability of the predictions of the prophets enlightened with Thy spirit. Finally the years of waiting were over: they had been lengthened because of the lack of patience on the part of the believers and because of the contrariety of the unbelievers. One prophecy after another met with fulfillment, and then Thou, O eternal and changeless Truth, didst fulfill them all (Heb 1:1–3).

O my soul, filled with holy reverence, think about the mystery of your redemption! Trembling, adore the Lord rejected by Israel and acknowledged by the Gentiles. He Who is eternal assumed the image of man. The Creator became united with His creatures, walked among them, established their path to perfection, and gave them a part of His own blessedness.

O God, Thou Whose benefits are as countless as the miracles contained by the heavens and all the worlds! It was not enough for Thee to descend into a mortal body, to show to erring human kind its way to heaven, and to hand down to man laws such as are of manifest heavenly origin, as their content, establishment, and purpose clearly reveal. This was not enough for Thee: Thou didst not spare Thyself but hast subjected Thyself to the law given by Thee to the lawless. Thou didst walk the same ways which lead the mistaken creatures to their goals; Thou hast taught by Thy example how the righteous remain pure in the midst of a world filled with error and wickedness. Thou hast taught us to recognize that our brief earthly life is that precious thing for which we can buy real life, namely, eternity. Thy entire life on earth was an unbroken chain of wise and beneficial deeds, heavenly examples which Thou didst hand down to the lawless, who did not recognize Thee in Thy humility, persecuted Thee for Thy truth, and hated Thee for Thy way of life. How these ungrateful creatures failed to know Thee! Thou didst endure in the world for the length of time which was appointed for this purpose from the beginning of time; finally there came that solemn day predicted by the prophets, which had to complete the divine work of reconciliation. Thy sufferings multiplied. Thou wast delivered to Thine enemies, dragged from one judge to another, ridiculed, spat at, martyred, and condemned to death! Neither holiness nor innocence was spared the horrible sentence of death. O Love, unending Love! Thou didst shed Thy blood on the cross for Thy murderers; Thy death was the conciliatory sacrifice for our crimes, the seal of eternal truth that was put on Thy revelation. Thy death shook the earth and darkened the sky. None except those who were culpable of Thy death remained unconvinced. Everyone else recognized the importance of what was happening. The sun, which had been shining, grew dark; day turned into night, the mountains split, the earth shook down to its foundations, and the bodies of the dead rose. These marvelous events and the universal confusion proved the death of the God-Man.

O Being of beings, Thy destinies are unfathomable. O eternal, yet hidden light! Illumine the darkness in which I am immersed! Scatter the cloud which does not admit Thy beams into my soul and prevents it from being illumined. Wandering far from Thee, amid confusion, I am lost in darkness which continuously grows more intense. I have found the truth which I sought and have become convinced of the reality of Thy work of redemption; the fulfilled prophecies have assured me of the coming of the true Messiah, and so the testimony of those who heard His teachings, saw Him, and wondered at His miracles. All this has reassured me.

The sun itself which, contrary to the unchangeable natural laws, lost its light, preached the Divinity in the man Who died on the cross. Everything that followed established more firmly His divinity. His resurrection from the tomb that was watched by those who denied Him; His subsequent appearances to those who did not yet believe; the Spirit of truth that descended on those who confessed Him; the miraculous spreading of His divine teaching and the growth of His holy community which endured unmoved in the midst of all the storms that were set in motion against Christianity—yet Christianity was not destroyed by torture, death, or any other kind of persecution—all this testifies to the divinity of our Savior, and everything confirms the perfection of our blessedness. I find all reasons to be calm and expect the fruit of universal renewal, the marvelous effects of Jesus' death on the creatures for whom He shed His blood. O God Full of mystery, Whose omnipotence is resisted by creatures dependent on Thee, and Whose wisdom remains hidden from us! Thou enlightenest us, yet we sink back into darkness; Thou revealest Thyself to us, but we do not acknowledge Thee; Thou preparest us for blessedness, but we turn away from it; Thou renewest us by the power of Thy law, but we reject it; Thou puttest before us the example of perfection, but we struggle against our sanctification; Thou fillest the world with Thy Spirit, but the world does not admit Thy influence. O God! How many contradictions there are in Thy world, filled with omnipotence and wisdom! Thou didst give us Thy laws, but we, helpless creatures dependent on Thee, break Thy ordinances! Thou willest happiness and blessedness for Thy creatures, but they ceaselessly look for their own destruction. Truth is oppressed by error, while virtue, Thine image, which Thou lovest and which Thou hast promised to defend, becomes the victim of vice; justice becomes the toy of gain; innocence becomes the laughingstock of shamelessness; and piety becomes a disgrace in the eyes of madness! All this Thou seest, eternal lawgiver! All this Thou seest from Thy heaven above, and yet Thy vengeance remains the depths of Thy unfathomable patience. O Lord, Lord of Powers! Thy heaven is still filled with the outcry of the righteous, while Thine earth is watered with the tears of the virtuous! God, Thou reignest and doth not yet allow the powers of nature to destroy the world which rises against Thy holy will! The world is senseless to Thy benefits; the world is blind to Thy omnipotence and justice.

O eternal one! Thy highest love suffers our lawless breaking of Thy holy and most just laws, but Thou wilt not suffer this forever. Thine eyes penetrate the heart and the soul, and Thy truth weighs all our thoughts and deeds. Not long will Thy sun shine on the vain doings of the blind; not long will Thy truth remain unrecognized. Yet for a while Thou wilt still be patient, and years of Thy kindness to us will go by. Yet what meaning do days and years have? What are thousands of years, as the mortals count them, before Thee? Thou wilt come as the Judge of the living and the dead; Thou wilt come in light and glory in order to separate virtue from vice and to take innocence out of the nets of falsehood. This will be a terrible judgment, yet a just one, and will take place before all the nations of the earth.

Then, great God, spare me, be merciful to my soul standing before Thy throne! Then, O Lord of Powers, confirm, the souls of the righteous who have honored Thy will, as it was revealed to us by Thee in Jesus, and unite them to Thee, for Thou art their beginning. Look then at the tears of the repentant sinner who will beg Thee for mercy and blessing! Let Jesus' blood then give satisfaction for the ignorant, for whom He prayed dying. O Judge of the worlds, in Thy hands there repose creation and nothingness, annihilation and eternity. Eternity without beginning and end, how you make my heart shake! Shall I be eternal? Thousands of millions of years will flow by, but I shall still reason and live! And yet more thousands of thousands of millions of years will pass, yet I shall not even approach the end of my existence! O spirit of eternity! O life of my spirit! What number is sufficient to measure my existence when I shall live in Thee, Whose years are eternal! Thou, O eternal one, art my beginning and end! In Thee, in Thee are all my powers, in Thee rests my soul, the creation of Thy omnipotence and the eternal object of Thy wisdom and kindness. Receive, O Father of beings, the offering of Thy creature that sacrifices to Thee its very self! Receive my imperfect thanksgiving for all Thy mercies! I am Thy creature; lead me into Thy eternal kingdom, so that I may never die.

Thou art the eternal Being. Thou art omnipotence united with wisdom and highest love. My soul rises to Thee; the creature, feeling the influence of Thy Goodness (Rom 5 and 8), flies to Thee. In quiet solitude, far from the blinding glitter of luxury, free from the nets in which my heart is frequently caught, I am closer to Thee, O beneficent Being! How near Thou art to the spirit seeking Thee! O source of goodness! Where will mortals find rest for which their hearts sigh? Where will they find sweet fulfillment of their never-dying desires, if not in Thee, the only object of their desires! Thou alone fulfillest those desires which the world can never fulfill!

What is the world, which tires me with its pleasures, if I seek in it only the satisfaction of my wishes? When I think that I am only tasting innocent joys, my heart is really being worn by impetuous passions. Shall I, mad as I am, find my rest in this world and in these joys? This world gives me poison instead of food, inflames my passions instead of sating me, removes me from my center instead of bringing me near it. O Holy Spirit, destroy these contradictions in me! Thou dost repose within me, but I am looking for Thee in things outside me; Thou art autonomous and eternal, while I am searching for Thee in creatures whose existence is a dream and whose life is but a moment. Teach me that wisdom which is able to find Thee, for it does not look for Thee outside itself. Rouse me from the mortal sleep of inactivity to an active recognition of my salvation! Give me Thy eternal Spirit, the Spirit of unchanging truth (John 14:16–17), the life-giving Spirit of Thy revelations (Eph 4:14–15), and grant me to understand myself and to recognize myself for what I am, without the prejudices of self-love. This recognition of myself and of my weaknesses and of my real needs—be it the first step toward my rebirth!

O true goodness! How blind I am without enlightenment from Thee! How weak I am without Thy help (Ps 90:14)! I was pure and innocent when Thy creative power led me out of nothingness, in which I otherwise would have remained forever. As soon as Thou connected my marvelous existence with the destinies of mortals, I lost a part of my innocence; I took part in the pollution and perdition of the children of Adam. But in accordance with Thy endless mercy, Thou didst purify my soul with the power of the triune Name, leading me back to the eternal covenant established between Thee and mankind (Matt 28:18–20). Yet how brief was my reestablished perfection! As soon as the innocent years of my infancy had passed, as soon as I felt in myself the unfolding power of reason and the freedom given by Thee to my spirit, I immediately began to use the gift of reason to evil purposes and to put my reason to shame. I became the enemy of my happiness, an offender against Thine eternal laws; while Thou, God of my salvation, hast always remained unchanged in Thy love and unceasingly kind to me. Thou didst multiply the strength of my body and the days of my life, enlightened my reason, formed my senses, and refined my feelings; while I, senseless I, attempted to overlook Thee in Thy miracles, attempted to deny Thee in Thy creation and to forget Thee in Thy benefits! Thou didst daily bless the bread that I ate; Thou didst establish the paths along which I walked; Thou badest Thy sun shed its light upon me, as upon the righteous; Thou didst touch my heart by the examples of the honest and virtuous deeds of my fellow citizens or else didst strike my callous soul with the terrible thunder of majestic eternity; but I—oh, if I could conceal myself from Thy holy and terrible eyes!—I repressed Thy goodness and truth in my soul and hardened in my madness; I shut my heart to Thy severe truth and gave myself over to the power of shameful deception which rushed me away from my goal, wisdom and virtue, into destruction.

Now, my God, I am beginning to feel the effects of Thy judgment and the righteousness of Thy decrees; in the abyss into which I have stumbled of my own will, in the midst of destruction threatening my noble being, I call to Thee. Lord and Judge of creatures! Terror of the sinner, yet also his only refuge! To Thee do my sighs rise, before Thy throne does my soul fall down in its deep feelings of weakness and deepest repentance. My recognition of my weaknesses and intentional crimes has destroyed all feelings of real joy in me; only innocent souls are capable of such joy. What then remains for the vicious soul, if blessedness and rest are appointed to virtue only? Highest God! Thus is the sinner avenged upon himself for virtue which he has offended and truth upon which he has trampled. Thus are fulfilled the prophecies of his conscience, which predicted to him that he would groan at his errors. Lawgiver of spirits! Why did my rebellious heart so frequently withstand truth which my reason always recognized? Why did I so frequently quench in my breast the divine flame for which I could easily have found food in the lively feeling of Thine omnipresence? Eternal God, immortal Creator of my being! Trembling do I fall down before Thee. God, forgive and be merciful to the trembling sinner! My soul grows sick at the thought of Thy justice: be merciful to Thy creature that asks Thee for mercy and grace! What am I before Thee, King of the worlds, spirits, and the whole universe! My weakness puts an immeasurable distance between Thee and me, the lawless being that has forgotten the dignity of his nature and has resisted his destiny. Life and death, blessedness and condemnation are within Thy most righteous hand. The whole universe, limitless as it is, has received movement and life at one indication from Thee. Thou, Immortal One, hast created me according to Thine image so that I, too, might see to all eternity Thine imperishable glory.

Thou art God, the Highest Being, Thou hast always existed and always will exist. Thy Being is an all-embracing good and limitless mercy. Thou art always and everywhere: in the sea, in the abysses, and in the limitless expanses of heaven.

None of mortals can comprehend Thee Who art always limitless; none born or created can comprehend Him Who was never born or created; only the feelings of deepest love, faith, and truth can lead us to a recognition of Thee through our reason. We are created in order to love Thee, our Creator, and humbly to study Thy ways, but not to test Thine unfathomable wisdom with impious daring. Amen.

O my readers! Must we not always and everywhere raise our thoughts to the Lord, our hearts full of joy, with a prayer of thanksgiving for His mercy to us, which is manifested every day? We move and live only because of His merciful goodness. Is His kingdom not everywhere? He sees into the hearts of the wicked and sees also our good deeds. Of all the creatures created on earth according to His will, are we not the highest? We alone have the heavenly, precious gift of recognizing our Creator; these divine qualities, which indicate His image and likeness in us, prove to us also our own eternal, deathless existence in the future life.

A Short Biography of Archimandrite Panteleimon

The future Archimandrite Panteleimon was born Peter Adamovitch Nizhnik on January 16, 1895, in the village of Rechitsa, Grodno province, Russia. He was part of a large family, and his parents faced constant financial difficulties. Thus, when the young Peter reached 18 years of age, his parents sought to have him marry. He later recalled that "I very much did not want to marry and asked my parents to allow me to go to America, promising to send them material support from there." He remembered that his parents were simple people, illiterate, but faithful to God and His Church. They feared that if their son moved to America, he would soon grow rich in worldly wealth, but forget God. His mother wept inconsolably and through tears said, "Dear son, don't lose God." Father Panteleimon later confessed, "These words of my mother remained with me, in my heart and memory, for the rest of my life."

So it was that in 1913 he immigrated to America. He found work at a sugar processing factory near Chicago but soon began to wonder if it was possible in America "to live in a Christian manner like the people at home." However, the homeland he remembered was undergoing radical change as revolution followed war. This caused him to pray even more fervently to God for help and guidance. Seeking a way forward, at the age of 23, on April 18, 1918, he entered St Tikhon's Monastery in Pennsylvania. He was tonsured there as a monk in 1920 and ordained as a deacon. The following year he was ordained to the priesthood.

At St Tikhon's he became responsible for managing the agricultural economy and strove to fulfill this obedience to the best of his abilities. But a certain emptiness still prevailed in his soul and he yearned "to obtain a remote place in a forest, near a well, build a small chapel, pray there and live independently, far removed from all the vanity and bustle of the world." This dream began to come true after he met Ivan Andreevitch Kolos, a church choir director who was visiting St Tikhon's and was considering the monastic life.

With the blessing of his bishop, Metropolitan Platon, Father Panteleimon left the monastery and began to work as a laborer at the Sikorsky helicopter factory in Connecticut in order to earn money to purchase land. Ivan Kolos and James Mosheruk, who had also been a monk at St Tikhon's, soon joined him. Thus it was that in 1928 they were able to place a deposit on 300 acres of land near the town of Herkimer, New York. The balance was paid the following year, and in the spring of 1930, after Easter, Father Panteleimon was the first to move to the new property. He recalled, "I arrived alone on my land ⋯ everything here was primitive, silence all around, and not a soul in sight. Several times I climbed a hill in the forest, found joy in the prevailing peace, and looked at my farm." He soon purchased a cow and two horses and began farming. Soon Monk James left his job at Sikorsky and came to help.

Others, including Ivan Kolos, who secretly took monastic vows while continuing to work in the world, joined them. By 1934 they had a barn constructed with hay stalls for thirty cows, and, within the same building, living quarters with sixteen cells and a house church for fifty people. In 1935 Bishop Vitaly, the former head of the renowned Pochaev Lavra in Russia, arrived in America. The new brotherhood turned to him with an appeal to direct their undertakings and to consecrate their newly erected church in honor of the Holy Trinity. This took place on the day of Pentecost, June 17, 1935. From a human standpoint, it was a crowning moment, but God judged otherwise. At the end of the liturgy, fire was detected on the second floor and within three hours the newly built structure and much of its contents were lost. The brotherhood survived, but were penniless and out under an open sky. Rather than despair, they saw these events as an act of God's providence to purify them and test their resolve.

Miraculously, by the autumn of 1935 they had purchased a larger and better quality house and soon built a new barn for eighty head of cattle together with another 200 acres of farmland. A printing press was also acquired. As Father Panteleimon wrote, every time they were in need, "Suddenly a letter would arrive, and in it an unexpected contribution from a benefactor. And it was not just once that this happened."

In 1945 the decision was made to build a large stone monastery cathedral. By the autumn of 1946 the lower part of the cathedral was basically completed. Father Panteleimon remembered, "We were all exhausted under the burden of intense labor."

The monastery's publishing work was particularly important to Father Panteleimon. His aim was "with God's help to reprint books of exceptional spiritual content that had been destroyed by the satanic-atheistic authority in Russia." All the church service books and numerous volumes of spiritual content were printed in the Slavonic and Russian languages. In 1968 he began to print spiritual works in English with the first edition of *Eternal Mysteries Beyond the Grave*.

In 1970 he wrote exultantly of the addition of new printing facilities, the completion of a three-story extension to the main building to add living space, the construction of a new cemetery chapel (in memory of the Tsar Martyr Nicholas II, his family, and the new martyrs of Russia), and an additional large summer refectory for guests. He concluded, "Glory to God for everything."

In all these things he worked tirelessly with love for his Lord and Savior Jesus Christ and to preserve the Orthodox Christian faith. He fell asleep in the Lord in 1984 and was buried behind the cathedral church of the Holy Trinity Monastery, whose community still remember him with gratitude and prayer.

Largely extracted from *A Short History of the Holy Trinity Monastery* published in 1972.

SUBJECT INDEX

SCRIPTURE INDEX